CU00645935

CONTENTS

LIST OF ILLUSTRATIONS

ANCIENT LIGHTS

AND

CERTAIN NEW REFLECTIONS

BEING THE MEMORIES OF A YOUNG MAN

BY

FORD MADOX HUEFFER

AUTHOR OF "THE FIFTH QUEEN," "THE SOUL OF LONDON,"
"LADIES WHOSE BRIGHT EYES," ETC.

WITH NUMEROUS ILLUSTRATIONS

"A hundred years went by, and what was left of his haughty and
proud people full of free passions? They and all their generations
had passed away." PUSHKIN (*Sardanapalus*.)

LONDON
CHAPMAN AND HALL, LTD.

DEDICATION

TO CHRISTINA AND KATHARINE

MY DEAR KIDS,

Accept this book, the best Christmas present that I can give you. You will have received before this comes to be printed, or at any rate before—bound, numbered and presumably indexed—it will have come in book form into your hands—you will have received the amber necklaces, and the other things that are the outward and visible sign of the presence of Christmas. But certain other things underlie all the presents that a father makes to his children. Thus there is the spiritual gift of heredity.

It is with some such idea in my head—with the idea, that is to say, of analysing for your benefit what my heredity had to bestow upon you that I began this book. That of course would be no reason for making it a "book," which is a thing that should appeal to many thousands of people, if the appeal can only reach them. But, to tell you the strict truth, I made for myself the somewhat singular discovery that I can only be said to have grown up a very short time ago—perhaps three months, perhaps six. I discovered that I had grown up only when I discovered quite suddenly that I was forgetting my own childhood. My own childhood was a thing so vivid that it certainly influenced me, that it certainly rendered me timid, incapable of self-assertion, and as it were perpetually conscious of original sin until only just the other day. For you ought to consider that upon the one hand as a child I was very severely disciplined, and when I was not being severely disciplined I moved amongst somewhat distinguished people who all appeared to me to be morally and physically twenty-five feet high. The earliest thing that I can remember is this, and the odd thing is that, as I remember it, I seem to be looking at myself from outside. I see myself a very tiny child in a long blue pinafore looking into the breeding-box of some Barbary ring-doves that my grandmother kept in the window of the huge studio in Fitzroy Square. The window itself appears to me to be as high as a house and I myself to be as small as a doorstep, so that I stand on tiptoe, and just manage to get my eyes and nose over the edge of the box whilst my long curls fall forward and tickle my nose. And then I perceive greyish and almost shapeless objects with, upon them, little speckles, like the very short spines of hedgehogs, and I stand with the first surprise of my life and with the first wonder of my life. I ask myself: can these be doves?—these unrecognizable, panting morsels of flesh. And then, very soon, my grandmother comes in and is angry. She tells me that if the mother dove is disturbed she will eat her young. This I believe is quite incorrect. Nevertheless I know quite well that for many days afterwards I thought I had destroyed life and that

Dedication

I was exceedingly sinful. I never knew my grandmother to be angry again except once when she thought I had broken a comb which I had certainly not broken. I never knew her raise her voice, I hardly know how she can have expressed anger; she was by so far the most equable and gentle person I have ever known that she seemed to be almost not a personality but just a natural thing. Yet it was my misfortune to have from this gentle personality my first conviction—and this, my first conscious conviction was one of great sin, of a deep criminality. Similarly with my father, who was a man of great rectitude and with strong ideas of discipline. Yet for a man of his date he must have been quite mild in his treatment of his children. In his bringing-up, such was the attitude of parents towards children that it was the duty of himself and his brothers and sisters at the end of each meal to kneel down and kiss the hands of their father and mother as a token of thanks for the nourishment received. So that he was after his lights a mild and reasonable man to his children. Nevertheless, what I remember of him most was that he called me " the patient but extremely stupid donkey." And so I went through life until only just the other day with the conviction of extreme sinfulness and of extreme stupidity.

God knows that the lesson we learn from life is that our very existence in the nature of things is a perpetual harming of somebody—if only because every mouthful of food that we eat a mouthful taken from somebody else. This lesson you will have to learn in time. But if I write this book, and if I give it to the world, it is very much that you may be spared a great many of the quite unnecessary tortures that were mine until I " grew up." Knowing you as I do, I imagine that you very much resemble myself in temperament and so you may resemble myself in moral tortures ; and since I cannot flatter myself that either you or I are very exceptional, it is possible that this book may be useful, not only to you for whom I have written it, but to many other children in a world that is sometimes unnecessarily sad. It sums up the impressions that I have received in a quarter of a century. For the reason that I have given you—for the reason that I have now discovered myself to have " grown up," it seems to me that it marks the end of an epoch, the closing of a door.

As I have said, I find that my impressions of the early and rather noteworthy persons amongst whom my childhood was passed—that these impressions are beginning to grow a little dim. So I have tried to rescue them now before they go out of my mind altogether. And, whilst trying to rescue them, I have tried to compare them with my impressions of the world as it is at the present day. As you will see when you get to the last chapter of the book, I am perfectly contented with the world of to-day. It is not the world of twenty-five years ago, but it is a very good world. It is not so full of the lights of individualities, but it is not so full of shadow for the obscure. For you must remember that I always considered myself to be the most obscure of obscure persons—a very small, a very sinful, a very stupid child. And for such persons the world of twenty-five years ago was rather a dismal place. You see there were in those days a number of those terrible and forbidding things—the Victorian great figures. To me life was simply not worth living because of the existence of Carlyle, of Mr. Ruskin, of Mr. Holman Hunt, of Mr. Browning, or of the gentleman who built the Crystal Palace. These people were perpetually held up to me as standing upon unattainable heights, and at the same time I was perpetually being told that if I could not attain to these heights I might just as well not cumber the earth. What then was left for me? Nothing. Simply nothing.

Now, my dear children—and I speak not only to you but to all who have never grown up—never let yourselves be disheartened or saddened by such thoughts. Do not, that is to say, desire to be Ruskins or Carlyles. Do not desire to be Ancient Lights It will crush in you all ambition; it will render you timid, it will foil nearly all your efforts. Nowadays we have no great figures and I thank Heaven for it, because you and I can breathe freely. With the passing the other day of Tolstoy, with the death just a few weeks before of Mr. Holman Hunt, they all went away to Olympus where very fittingly they may dwell. And so you are freed from these burdens which so heavily and for so long hung upon the shoulders of one, and of how many others? For the heart of another is a dark forest, and I do not know how many thousands of other my fellow men and women have been so oppressed. Perhaps I was exceptionally morbid, perhaps my ideals were exceptionally high. For high ideals were always being held before me. My grandfather, as you will

read, was not only perpetually giving, he was perpetually enjoining upon all others the necessity of
giving never-endingly.   We were to give not only all
our goods, but all our thoughts, all our endeavours;
we were to stand aside always to give openings for
others.   I do not know that I would ask you to look
upon life otherwise, or to adopt another standard
of conduct, but still it is as well to know beforehand
that such a rule of life will expose you to innumerable miseries, to efforts almost superhuman and to
innumerable betrayals—or to transactions in which
you will consider yourself to have been betrayed.
I do not know that I would wish you to be spared
any of these unhappinesses.   The past generosities
of one's life are the only milestones of that road that
one can regret leaving behind.   Nothing else matters
very much since they alone are one's achievement.
And remember this, that when you are in any doubt,
tanding between what may appear right and what
may appear wrong, though you cannot tell which is
wrong and which is right and may well dread the
issue—act then upon the lines of your generous
emotions even though your generous emotions may
at the time appear likely to lead you to disaster.
So you may have a life full of regrets which are
fitting things for a man to have behind him, but so
you will have with you no causes for remorse.   Thus
at least lived your ancestors and their friends, and,
as I knew them, as they impressed themselves upon
me, I do not think that one needed or that one needs
to-day better men.   They had their passions, their
extravagancies, their imprudences, their follies.
They were sometimes unjust, violent, unthinking.

Dedication

But they were never cold, they were never mean,
they went to shipwreck with high spirits. I could
ask nothing better for you if I were inclined to
trouble Providence with petitions.

F. M. H.

P.S.—Just a word to make plain the actual nature
of this book. It consists of impressions. When some
parts of it appeared in serial form a distinguished
critic fell foul of one of the stories that I told. My
impression was and remains that I heard Thomas
Carlyle tell how at Weimar he borrowed an apron
from a waiter and served tea to Goethe and Schiller,
who were sitting in eighteenth-century court dress
beneath a tree. The distinguished critic of a distinguished paper commented upon this story, saying
that Carlyle never was in Weimar and that Schiller
died when Carlyle was aged five. I did not write
to this distinguished critic because I do not like
writing to the papers, but I did write to a third
party. I said that a few days before that date I
had been talking to a Hessian peasant, a veteran of
the war of 1870. He had fought at Sedan, at
Gravelotte, before Paris; and had been one of the
troops that marched in under the Arc de Triomphe.
In 1910 I asked this veteran of 1870 what the war
had been all about. He said that the Emperor of
Germany having heard that the Emperor Napoleon
had invaded England and had taken his mother-in-
law Queen Victoria prisoner—that the Emperor of
Germany had marched into France to rescue his distinguished connection. In my letter to my critic's
friend I said that if I had related this anecdote,

Dedication

I should not have considered it as a contribution to history, but as material illustrating the state of mind of a Hessian peasant. So with my anecdote about Carlyle. It was intended to show the state of mind of a child of seven brought into contact with a Victorian great figure. When I wrote the anecdote I was perfectly aware that Carlyle never was in Weimar whilst Schiller was alive, or that Schiller and Goethe would not be likely to drink tea and that they would not have worn eighteenth-century court dress at any time when Carlyle was alive. But as a boy I had that pretty and romantic impression, and so I presented it to the world—for what it was worth. So much I communicated to the distinguished critic in question. He was kind enough to reply to my friend, the third party, that whatever I might say he was right and I was wrong. Carlyle was only five when Schiller died; and so on. He proceeded to comment upon my anecdote of the Hessian peasant to this effect: At the time of the Franco-Prussian war there was no emperor of Germany; the Emperor Napoleon never invaded England; he never took Victoria prisoner, and so on. He omitted to mention that there never was and never will be a modern emperor of Germany.

I suppose that this gentleman was doing what is called "pulling my leg," for it is impossible to imagine that any one, even an English literary critic, or a German Philologist, or a mixture of the two could be so wanting in a sense of humour—or in any sense at all. But there the matter is, and this book is a book of impressions. My impression is that there have been six thousand four hundred and

Dedication

seventy-two books written to give the facts about the Pre-Raphaelite movement. My impression is that I myself have written more than 17,000,000 wearisome and dull words as to the facts about the Pre-Raphaelite movement. These you understand are my impressions ; probably there are not more than ninety books dealing with the subject ; and I have not myself really written more than 360,000 words on these matters. But what I am trying to get at is that, though there have been many things written about these facts, no one has whole-heartedly and thoroughly attempted to get the atmosphere of these twenty-five years. This book, in short, is full of inaccuracies as to facts, but its accuracy as to impressions is absolute. For the facts, when you have a little time to waste, I should suggest that you go through this book carefully, noting the errors. To the one of you who succeeds in finding the largest number I will cheerfully present a copy of the ninth edition of the Encyclopædia Britannica, so that you may still further perfect yourself in the hunting out of errors. But if one of you can discover in it any single impression that can be demonstrably proved not sincere on my part, I will draw you a cheque for whatever happens to be my balance at the bank for the next ten succeeding years. This is a handsome offer, but I can afford to make it, for you will not gain a single penny in the transaction. My business in life, in short, is to attempt to discover, and to try to let you see, where we stand. I don't really deal in facts, I have for facts a most profound contempt. I try to give you what I see to be the spirit of an age, of a town, of a movement. This can not be done with facts. Supposing that when I am walking beside a cornfield, I hear a great rustling, and a hare jumps out ; supposing now that I am the owner of that field and I go to my farm-bailiff. I should say " There are about a million hares in that field, I wish you would keep the damned beasts down." There would not have been a million hares in the field, and hares being soulless beasts cannot be damned, but I should have produced upon that bailiff the impression that I desired. So in this book. It is not always foggy in Bloomsbury; indeed I happen to be writing in Bloomsbury at this moment, and, though it is just before Christmas, the light of day is quite tolerable. Nevertheless, with an effrontery that will I am sure appal the critic of my Hessian peasant story, I say that the Pre-Raphaelite poets carried on their work amidst the glooms of Bloomsbury ; and this I think is a true impression. To say that on an average in the last 25 years there have been in Bloomsbury per 365 days, 10 of bright sunshine, 299 of rain, 42 of fog and the remainder compounded of all three would not seriously help the impression. This fact I think you will understand, though I doubt whether my friend the critic will.

F. M. H.

P.P.S. I find that I have written these words not in Bloomsbury but in the electoral district of East Saint Pancras. Perhaps it is gloomier in Bloomsbury. I will go and see.

P.P.P.S. It is.

THE LAST LIKENESS OF MADOX BROWN

ANCIENT LIGHTS

I

THE INNER CIRCLE

SAYS Thackeray :

" On his way to the City, Mr. Newcome rode to look at the new house, No. 120, Fitzroy Square, which his brother, the colonel, had taken in conjunction with that Indian friend of his, Mr. Binnie. . . . The house is vast but, it must be owned, melancholy. Not long since it was a ladies' school, in an unprosperous condition. The scar left by Madame Latour's brass plate may still be seen on the tall black door, cheerfully ornamented, in the style of the end of the last century, with a funeral urn in the centre of the entry, and garlands and the skulls of rams at each corner. . . . The kitchens were gloomy. The stables were gloomy. Great black passages; cracked conservatory; dilapidated bath-room, with melancholy waters moaning and fizzing from the cistern; the great large blank stone staircase—were all so many melancholy features in the general countenance of the house; but the Colonel thought it perfectly cheerful and pleasant, and furnished it in his rough-and-ready way."—*The Newcomes.*

And it was in this house of Colonel Newcome's that my eyes first opened, if not to the light of day, at least to any visual impression that has not since been effaced. I can remember vividly, as a very small boy, shuddering as I stood upon the door-step at the thought that the great stone urn, lichened, soot-stained, and decorated with a great ram's head by way of handle, elevated only by what looked like a square piece of stone of about the size and shape of a folio book, might fall upon me and crush me entirely out of existence. Such a possible happening, I remember, was a frequent subject of discussion among Madox Brown's friends.

Ford Madox Brown, the painter of the pictures called *Work* and *The Last of England*, and the first painter in England, if not in the world, to attempt to render light exactly as it appeared to him, was at that time at the height of his powers, of his reputation, and of such prosperity as he enjoyed. His income from his pictures was considerable, and since he was an excellent talker, an admirable host, extraordinarily and indeed unreasonably open-handed, the great, formal, and rather gloomy house had become a meeting-place for almost all the intellectually unconventional of that time. Between 1870 and 1880 the real Pre-Raphaelite Movement was long since at an end : the Æsthetic Movement, which also was nick-named Pre-Raphaelite, was, however, coming into prominence, and at the very heart of this movement was Madox Brown. As I remember him, with a square, white beard, with a ruddy complexion, and with thick white hair parted in the middle and falling to above the tops of his ears, Madox Brown exactly

2

resembled the king of hearts in a pack of cards. In passion and in emotions—more particularly during one of his fits of gout—he was a hard-swearing, old-fashioned Tory : his reasoning, however, and circumstances made him a revolutionary of the romantic type. I am not sure, even, that toward his later years he would not have called himself an anarchist, and have damned your eyes if you had faintly doubted this obviously extravagant assertion. But he loved the picturesque, as nearly all his friends loved it.

About the inner circle of those who fathered and sponsored the Æsthetic Movement there was absolutely nothing of the languishing. They were, to a man, rather burly, passionate creatures, extraordinarily enthusiastic, extraordinarily romantic, and most impressively quarrelsome. Neither about Rossetti nor about Burne-Jones, neither about William Morris nor P. P. Marshall—and these were the principal upholders of the firm of Morris & Company which gave æstheticism to the Western world—was there any inclination to live upon the smell of the lily. It was the outer ring, the disciples, who developed this laudable ambition for poetic pallor, for clinging garments, and for ascetic countenances. And it was, I believe, Mr. Oscar Wilde who first formulated this poetically vegetarian theory of life in Madox Brown's studio at Fitzroy Square. No, there was little of the smell of the lily about the leaders of this movement! Thus it was one of Madox Brown's most pleasing anecdotes—at any rate it was one that he related with the utmost gusto—how William Morris came out on to the

landing in the house of the " Firm " in Red Lion
Square and roared downstairs :

" Mary, those six eggs were bad.   I've eaten them,
but don't let it occur again."

Morris, also, was in the habit of lunching daily off
roast beef and plum pudding, no matter at what
season of the year, and he liked his puddings large.
So that, similarly, upon the landing one day he
shouted :

" Mary, do you call that a pudding ? "

He was holding upon the end of a fork a plum
pudding about the size of an ordinary breakfast cup,
and having added some appropriate objurgations,
he hurled the edible downstairs on to Red-Lion
Mary's forehead.   This anecdote should not be taken
to evidence settled brutality on the part of the poet-
craftsman.   Red-Lion Mary was one of the loyalest
supporters of the " Firm " to the end of her days.
No, it was just in the full-blooded note of the circle.
They liked to swear, and, what is more, they liked
to hear each other swear.   Thus, another of Madox
Brown's anecdotes went to show how he kept Morris
sitting monumentally still, under the pretence that
he was drawing his portrait, while Mr. Arthur
Hughes tied his long hair into knots for the purpose
of enjoying the explosion that was sure to come when
the released Topsy—Morris was always Topsy to his
friends—ran his hands through his hair.   This
anecdote always seemed to me to make considerable
calls upon one's faith.   Nevertheless, it was one that
Madox Brown used most frequently to relate, so
that no doubt something of the sort must have
occurred.

4

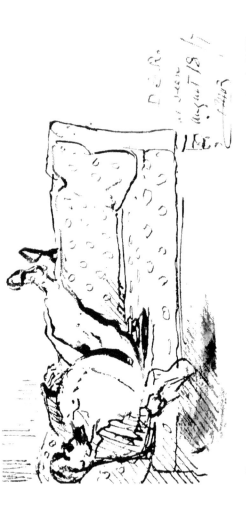

" NOT BECAUSE HE DESIRED TO PRESENT THE BEHOLDER WITH A BEAUTIFUL VISION.   HE LIKED
LYING ON SOFAS . . .   THEY DESIRED ROOM TO EXPAND . . ."

(D.G.R. from caricature by Madox Brown in Author's possession)

No, the note of these æsthetes was in no sense
ascetic. What they wanted in life was room to
expand and to be at ease. Thus I remember, in a
sort of golden vision, Rossetti lying upon a sofa in
the back studio with lighted candles at his feet and
lighted candles at his head, while two extremely
beautiful ladies dropped grapes into his mouth.
But Rossetti did this, not because he desired to
present the beholder with a beautiful vision, but
because he liked lying on sofas, he liked grapes, and
he particularly liked beautiful ladies. They desired,
in fact, all of them, room to expand. And when
they could not expand in any other directions they
expanded enormously into their letters. And—I
don't know why—they mostly addressed their letters
abusing each other to Madox Brown. There would
come one short, sharp note, and then answers
occupying reams of note-paper. Thus one great
painter would write :

"Dear Brown,—Tell Gabriel that if he takes my
model Fanny up the river on Sunday I will never
speak to him again."

Gabriel would take the model Fanny up the river
on Sunday, and a triangular duel of portentous
letters would ensue.

Or again, Swinburne would write :

"Dear Brown, if P—— says that I said that
Gabriel was in the habit of . . ., P—— lies."

The accusation against Rossetti being a Gargantuan impossibility which Swinburne, surely the most
loyal of friends, could impossibly have made, there
ensued a Gargantuan correspondence. Brown writes
to P—— how, when, and why the accusation was

made; he explains how he went round to Jones, who had nothing to do with the matter, and found that Jones had eaten practically nothing for the last fortnight, and how between them they had decided that the best thing that they could do would be to go and tell Rossetti all about it, and of how Rossetti had had a painful interview with Swinburne, and how unhappy everybody was. P—— replies to Brown that he had never uttered any such words upon any such occasion : that upon that occasion he was not present, having gone round to Ruskin, who had the toothache, and who read him the first hundred and twenty pages of *Stones of Venice*; that he could not possibly have said anything of the sort about Gabriel, since he knew nothing whatever of Gabriel's daily habits, having refused to speak to him for the last nine months because of Gabriel's intolerable habit of backbiting, which he was sure would lead them all to destruction, and so deemed it prudent not to go near him. Gabriel himself then enters the fray, saying that he has discovered that it is not P. at all who made the accusation, but Q., and that the accusation was made not against him, but about O. X., the Academician. If, however, he, P., accuses him, Gabriel, of backbiting, P. must be perfectly aware that this is not the case, he, Gabriel, having only said a few words against P.'s wife's mother, who is a damned old cat. And so the correspondence continues, Jones and Swinburne and Marshall and William Rossetti and Charles Augustus Howell and a great many more joining in the fray, until at last everybody withdraws all the charges, six months having passed, and Brown invites all the contestants

6

to dinner, Gabriel intending to bring old Plint, the picture-buyer, and to make him, when he has had plenty of wine, buy P.'s picture of the *Lost Shepherd* for two thousand pounds.

These tremendous quarrels, in fact, were all storms in teacups, and although the break-up of the " Firm " did cause a comparatively lasting estrangement between several of the partners, it has always pleased me to remember that at the last private view that Madox Brown held of one of his pictures, every one of the surviving Pre-Raphaelite brothers came to his studio, and every one of the surviving partners of the original firm of Morris & Company.

The arrival of Sir Edward Burne-Jones and his wife brought up a characteristic passion of Madox Brown's. Sir Edward had persuaded the president of the Royal Academy to accompany them in their visit. They were actuated by the kindly desire to give Madox Brown the idea that thus at the end of his life the Royal Academy wished to extend some sort of official recognition to a painter who had persistently refused for nearly half a century to recognize their existence. Unfortunately it was an autumn day and the twilight had set in very early. Thus not only were the distinguished visitors rather shadowy in the dusk, but the enormous picture itself was entirely indistinguishable. Lady Burne-Jones, with her peculiarly persuasive charm, whispered to me, unheard by Madox Brown, that I should light the studio gas, and I was striking a match, when I was appalled to hear Madox Brown shout, in tones of extreme violence and of apparent alarm :

7

" Damn and blast it all, Fordie !   Do you want us all blown into the next world ? "

And he proceeded to explain to Lady Burne-Jones that there was an escape of gas from a pipe. When she suggested candles or a paraffin lamp, Madox Brown declared with equal violence that he couldn't think how she could imagine that he could have such infernally dangerous things in the house. The interview thus concluded in a gloom of the most tenebrous, and shortly afterward we went downstairs, where, in the golden glow of a great many candles set against a golden and embossed wall-paper, tea was being served. The fact was that Madox Brown was determined that no " damned academician " should see his picture. Nevertheless, it is satisfactory to me to think that there was among these distinguished and kindly men still so great a feeling of solidarity. They had come, many of them from great distances, to do honour, or at least to be kind, to an old painter who at that time was more entirely forgotten than he has ever been before or since.

The " lily " tradition of the disciples of these men is, I should imagine, almost entirely extinguished. But the other day, at a particularly smart wedding, there turned up one staunch survivor in garments of prismatic hues—a mustard-coloured ulster, a green wide-awake, a blue shirt, a purple tie, and a suit of tweed. This gentleman moved distractedly among groups of correctly attired people. In one hand he bore an extremely minute painting by himself. It was, perhaps, of the size of a visiting-card set in an ocean of white mount. In the other he bore an enormous spray of Madonna lilies. That, I presume, was why he had failed to removed his green hat. He was approached by the hostess, and he told her that he wished to place the picture, his wedding gift, in the most appropriate position that could be found for it. And upon her suggesting that she would attend to the hanging after the ceremony was over, he brushed her aside. Finally he placed the picture upon the ground beneath a tall window, and perched the spray of lilies on top of the frame. He then stood back and, waving his emaciated hands and stroking his brown beard, surveyed the effect of his decoration. The painting, he said, symbolized the consolation that the arts would afford the young couple during their married life, and the lily stood for the purity of the bride. This is how in the 'seventies and the 'eighties the outer ring of the æsthetes really behaved. It was as much in their note as were the plum pudding and the roast beef in William Morris's. The reason for this is not very far to seek. The older men, the Pre-Raphaelites and the members of the " Firm," had too rough work to do to bother much about the trimmings.

It is a little difficult nowadays to imagine the acridity with which any new artistic movement was opposed when Victoria was Queen of England. Charles Dickens, as I have elsewhere pointed out, called loudly for the immediate imprisonment of Millais and the other Pre-Raphaelites, including my grandfather, who was not a Pre-Raphaelite. Blasphemy was the charge alleged against them, just as it was the charge alleged against the earliest upholders of Wagner's music in England. This may seem incredible, but I have in my possession three letters from three different members of the public addressed to my father, Dr. Francis Hueffer, a man of great erudition and force of character, who, from the early 'seventies until his death, was the musical critic of *The Times*. The writers stated that unless Doctor Hueffer abstained from upholding the blasphemous music of the future—and in each case the writer used the word blasphemous—he would be respectively stabbed, ducked in a horse-pond, and beaten to death by hired roughs. Yet to-day I never go to a place of popular entertainment where miscellaneous music is performed for the benefit of the poorest classes without hearing at least the overture to *Tannhäuser*. Nowadays it is difficult to discern any new movement in any of the arts. No doubt there is movement, no doubt we who write and our friends who paint and compose are producing the arts of the future. But we never have the luck to have the word " blasphemous " hurled at us. It would, indeed, be almost inconceivable that such a thing could happen, that the frame of mind should be reconstructed. But to the Pre-Raphaelites this word was blessed in the extreme. For human nature is such—perhaps on account of obstinacy or perhaps on account of feelings of justice—that to persecute an art, as to persecute a religion, is simply to render its practitioners the more stubborn and its advocates in their fewness the more united and the more effective in their union. It was the injustice of the attack upon the Pre-Raphaelites, it was the fury and outcry, that won for them the attention of Mr. Ruskin. And Mr. Ruskin's attention being aroused, he entered on that splendid and efficient

10

championing of their cause which at last established them in a position of perhaps more immediate importance than, as painters, they exactly merited. As pioneers and as sufferers they can never sufficiently be recommended. Mr. Ruskin, for some cause which my grandfather was used to declare was purely personal, was the only man intimately connected with these movements who had no connection at all with Madox Brown. I do not know why this was, but it is a fact that, although Madox Brown's pictures were in considerable evidence at all places where the pictures of the Pre-Raphaelites were exhibited, Mr. Ruskin in all his works never once mentioned his name. He never blamed him; he never praised him; he ignored him. And this was at a time when Ruskin must have known that a word from him was sufficient to make the fortune of any painter. It was sufficient, not so much because of Mr. Ruskin's weight with the general public, as because the small circle of buyers, wealthy and assiduous, who surrounded the painters of the Movement, hung upon Mr. Ruskin's lips and needed at least his printed sanction for all their purchases.

Madox Brown was the most benevolent of men, the most helpful and the kindest. His manifestations, however, were apt at times to be a little thorny. I remember an anecdote which Madox Brown's housemaid of that day was in the habit of relating to me when she used to put me to bed. Said she— and the exact words remain upon my mind :

" I was down in the kitchen waiting to carry up the meat, when a cabman comes down the area steps and says : ' I've got your master in my cab. He's very drunk.' I says to him—" and an immense intonation of pride would come into Charlotte's voice—" ' My master's a-sitting at the head of his table entertaining his guests. That's Mr. ——— Carry him upstairs and lay him in the bath.' "

Madox Brown, whose laudable desire it was at many stages of his career to redeem poets and others from dipsomania, was in the habit of providing several of them with labels upon which were inscribed his own name and address. Thus, when any of these geniuses were found incapable in the neighbourhood they would be brought by cabmen or others to Fitzroy Square. This, I think, was a stratagem more characteristic of Madox Brown's singular and quaint ingenuity than any that I can recall. The poet being thus recaptured would be carried upstairs by Charlotte and the cabman and laid in the bath—in Colonel Newcome's very bath-room, where, according to Thackeray, the water moaned and gurgled so mournfully in the cistern. For me, I can only remember that room as an apartment of warmth and lightness : it was a concomitant to all the pleasures that sleeping at my grandfather's meant for me. And indeed, to Madox Brown as to Colonel Newcome —they were very similar natures in their chivalrous, unbusinesslike, and naïve simplicity—the house in Fitzroy Square seemed perfectly pleasant and cheerful.

The poet having been put into the bath would be reduced to sobriety by cups of the strongest coffee that could be made (the bath was selected because he would not be able to roll out and to injure himself).

12

And having been thus reduced to sobriety, he would be lectured, and he would be kept in the house, being given nothing stronger than lemonade to drink, until he found the régime intolerable. Then he would disappear, the label sewn inside his coat collar, to reappear once more in the charge of a cabman.

Of Madox Brown's acerbity I witnessed myself no instances at all, unless it be the one that I have lately narrated. A possibly too stern father of the old school, he was as a grandfather extravagantly indulgent. I remember his once going through the catalogue of his grandchildren and deciding, after careful deliberation, that they were all geniuses with the exception of one, as to whom he could not be certain whether that one was a genius or mad. Thus I read with astonishment the words of a critic of distinction with regard to the exhibition of Madox Brown's works that I organized at the Grafton Gallery ten years ago. They were to the effect that Madox Brown's pictures were very crabbed and ugly—but what was to be expected of a man whose disposition was so harsh and distorted? This seemed to me to be an amazing statement. But upon discovering the critic's name I found that Madox Brown once kicked him downstairs. The gentleman in question had come to Madox Brown with the proposal from an eminent firm of picture-dealers that the painter should sell all his works to them for a given number of years at a very low price. In return they were to do what would be called nowadays " booming " him, and they would do their best to get him elected an Associate of the Royal

Academy. That Madox Brown should have received
with such violence a proposition that seemed to the
critic so eminently advantageous for all parties,
justified that gentleman in his own mind in declaring
that Madox Brown had a distorted temperament.
Perhaps he had.

But if he had a rough husk he had a sweet kernel,
and for this reason the gloomy house in Fitzroy
Square did not, I think, remain as a shape of gloom
in the minds of many people. It was very tall,
very large, very gray, and in front of it towered up
very high the mournful plane-trees of the square.
And over the porch was the funereal urn with the
ram's heads. This object, dangerous and threatening, has always seemed to me to be symbolical of this
circle of men, so practical in their work and so roman-
tically unpractical, as a whole, in their lives. They
knew exactly how, according to their lights, to paint
pictures, to write poems, to make tables, to decorate
pianos, rooms, or churches. But as to the conduct
of life they were a little sketchy, a little romantic,
perhaps a little careless. I should say that of them
all Madox Brown was the most practical. But his
way of being practical was always to be quaintly
ingenious. Thus we had the urn. Most of the Pre-
Raphaelites dreaded it : they all of them talked about
it as a possible danger, but never was any step taken
for its removal. It was never even really settled in
their minds whose would be the responsibility for
any accident. It is difficult to imagine the frame of
mind, but there it was and there to this day the urn
remains. The question could have been settled by
any lawyer, or Madox Brown might have had some

14

clause that provided for his indemnity inserted in his lease. And, just as the urn itself set the tone of the old immense Georgian mansion fallen from glory, so perhaps the fact that it remained for so long the topic of conversation set the note of the painters, the painter-poets, the poet-craftsmen, the painter-musicians, the filibuster verse-writers, and all that singular collection of men versed in the arts. They assembled and revelled comparatively modestly in the rooms where Colonel Newcome and his fellow directors of the Bundelcund Board had partaken of mulligatawny and spiced punch before the sideboard that displayed its knife-boxes with the green-handled knives in their serried phalanxes.

But, for the matter of that, Madox Brown's own sideboard also displayed its green-handled knives, which always seemed to me to place him as the man of the old school in which he was born and remained to the end of his days. If he was impracticable, he hadn't about him a touch of the Bohemian; if he was romantic, his romances took place along ordered lines. Every friend's son of his who went into the navy was destined in his eyes to become, not a pirate, but at least a port-admiral. Every young lawyer that he knew was certain, even if he were only a solicitor, to become Lord Chancellor, and every young poet who presented him with a copy of his first work was destined for the laureateship. And he really believed in these romantic prognostications, which came from him without end as without selection. So that if he was the first to give a helping hand to D. G. Rossetti, his patronage in one or two other instances was not so wisely bestowed.

He was, of course, the sworn foe of the Royal Academy. For him they were always, the members of that august body, " those *damned* academicians," with a particular note of acerbity upon the expletive. Yet I very well remember, upon the appearance of the first numbers of the *Daily Graphic*, that Madox Brown, being exceedingly struck by the line engravings of one of the artists whom that paper regularly employed to render social functions, exclaimed :

" By Jove ! if young Cleaver goes on as well as he has begun, those damned academicians, supposing they had any sense, would elect him president right away ! " Thus it will be seen that the business of romance was not to sweep away the Royal Academy, was not to found an opposing salon. It was to capture the established body by storm, leaping as it were on to the very quarter-deck, and setting to the old ship a new course. The characteristic, in fact, of all these men was their warm-heartedness, their enmity for the formal, for the frigid, for the ungenerous. It cannot be said that any of them despised money. I doubt whether it would even be said that any of them did not, at one time or another, seek for popularity, or try to paint, write, or decorate pot-boilers. But they were naïvely unable to do it. To the timid—and the public is always the timid— what was individual in their characters was always alarming. It was alarming even when they tried to paint the conventional dog-and-girl pictures of the Christmas supplement. The dogs were too like dogs and did not simper; the little girls were too like little girls. They would be probably rendered as just losing their first teeth.

16

The Inner Circle

In spite of the Italianism of Rossetti, who was never in Italy, and the mediævalism of Morris, who had never looked mediævalism, with its cruelties, its filth, its stenches, and its avarice, in the face—in spite of these tendencies that were forced upon them by those two contagious spirits, the whole note of this old, romantic circle was national, was astonishingly English, was Georgian even. They seemed to date from the Regency, and to have skipped altogether the baneful influences of early Victorianism and of the commerciality that the Prince Consort spread through England. They seem to me to resemble in their lives—and perhaps in their lives they were greater than their works—to resemble nothing so much as a group of old-fashioned ships' captains. Madox Brown, indeed, was nominated for a midshipman in the year 1827. His father had fought on the famous *Arethusa* in the classic fight with the *Belle Poule*. And but for the fact that his father quarrelled with Commodore Coffin, and so lost all hope of influence at the Admiralty, it is probable that Madox Brown would never have painted a picture or have lived in Colonel Newcome's house. Indeed, on the last occasion when I saw William Morris I happened to meet him in Portland Place. He was going to the house of a peer that his firm was engaged in decorating, and he took me with him to look at the work. He was then a comparatively old man, and his work had grown very flamboyant, so that the decoration of the dining-room consisted, as far as I can remember, of one huge acanthus-leaf design. Morris looked at this absent-mindedly, and said that he had just been talking to some members

c   17

of a ship's crew whom he had met in Fenchurch
Street. They had remained for some time under
the impression that he was a ship's captain. This
had pleased him very much, for it was his ambition
to be taken for such a man. I have heard, indeed,
that this happened to him on several occasions, on
each of which he expressed an equal satisfaction.
With a gray beard like the foam of the sea, with
gray hair through which he continually ran his hands
erect and curly on his forehead, with a hooked nose,
a florid complexion, and clean, clear eyes, dressed in
a blue serge coat, and carrying, as a rule, a satchel, to
meet him was always, as it were, to meet a sailor
ashore. And that in essence was the note of them
all. When they were at work they desired that
everything they did should be shipshape; when they
set their work down they became like Jack ashore.
And perhaps that is why there is, as a rule, such a
scarcity of artists in England. Perhaps to what is
artistic in the nation the sea has always called
too strongly.

II

THE OUTER RING

" 7TH NOVEMBER.—Dined with William Rossetti
and afterwards to Browning's where there was a
woman with a large nose. Hope I may never meet
her again. Browning's conversational powers very
great. He told some good stories, one about the
bygone days of Drury Lane—about the advice of a
very experienced stage carpenter of fifty years'
standing at the theatre, given to a young man who
wished for an engagement there, but had not, it
was objected, voice enough—the advice was to get
a pot of XXXX (ale) and put it on the stage beside
him, and having the boards all to himself he was
first to drink and then to holloa with all his might,
then to drink again, and so on—which the aspirant
literally did—remaining of course a muff as he had
begun. However I spoil that one ! Browning said
that one evening he was at Carlyle's. That sage
teacher, after abusing Mozart, Beethoven, and
modern music generally, let Mrs. Carlyle play to show
Browning what was the right sort of music, which
was some Scotch tune on an old piano with such
bass as pleased Providence—or rather, said Browning,
as did *not* please Providence. An Italian sinner
who belonged to the highest degree of criminality
which requires some very exalted dignitary of the

Church before absolution can be obtained for atrocities too heinous for the powers of the ordinary priest, Browning likened to a spider who, having fallen into a bottle of ink, gets out and crawls and sprawls and blots right over the whole of God's table of laws.

" 8th.—Painted at William Rossetti from eight till twelve. Gabriel came in. William, wishing to go early, Gabriel proposed that he should wait five minutes and they would go together, when, William being got to sleep on the sofa, Gabriel commenced telling me how he intended to get married at once to Guggums [Miss Siddall] and off to Algeria ! and so poor William's five minutes lasted till half-past two a.m. . . . I went to a meeting of the sub-committee about the testimonial of Ruskin's, he having noticed my absence from the previous one with regret. Ruskin was playful and childish and the tea-table overcharged with cakes and sweets as for a juvenile party. Then about an hour later cake and wine was again produced of which Ruskin again partook largely, reaching out with his thin paw and swiftly absorbing three or four large lumps of cake in succession. At home he looks young and rompish. At the meeting at Hunt's he looked old and ungainly, but his power and eloquence as a speaker were homeric. But I said at the time that but for his speaking he was in appearance like a cross between a fiend and a tallow-chandler . . . At night to the Working Men's College with Gabriel and then a public meeting to hear Professor Maurice spouting and Ruskin jawing. Ruskin was as eloquent as ever and is wildly popular with the men. He

flattered Rossetti in his presence hugely and spoke of Munroe in conjunction with Baron Marochetti as the two noble sculptors whom all the aristocracy patronized—and never one word about Woolner whose bust he had just before gone into ecstasies about and invited to dinner. This at a moment when Woolner's pupils of the college were all present. Rossetti says Ruskin is a sneak and loves him, Rossetti, because he is one, too, and Hunt he half likes because he is half a sneak but he hates Woolner because he is manly and straightforward and me because I am ditto. He adored Millais because Millais was the prince of sneaks, but Millais was too much so, for he sneaked away his wife and so he is obliged to hate him for too much of his favourite quality. Rossetti, in fact, was in such a rage about Ruskin and Woolner that he bullied Munroe all the way home, wishing to take every cab he encountered.

" 27th January.—To Jones's [Sir Edward Burne-Jones] yesterday evening with an outfit that Emma had purchased at his request for a poor miserable girl of seventeen he had met in the streets at 2 a.m. The coldest night this winter—scarcely any clothes and starving after five weeks of London life. Jones gave her money and told her to call next morning, which she did, telling her story and that she had parents willing to receive her back again in the country. Jones got me to ask Emma to buy her this outfit and has sent her home this morning. Jones brought Miss Macdonald and I didn't ask any questions. [Miss Macdonald is now Lady Burne-Jones.] This little girl seems to threaten to turn out another genius. She is coming here to paint to-morrow. Her designs in pen-and-ink show real intellect. Jones is going to cut Topsy [William Morris]. He says his overbearing temper is becoming quite insupportable as well as his conceit. At Manchester, to give one recording line to it, all that I remember is that an old English picture with Richard II in it was the only beautiful work of the old masters, and Hunt and Millais's the only fine among the new. Hunt, in fact, made the exhibition. The music was jolly and the waiters tried very hard to cheat."

Such were the daily preoccupations of this small circle as recorded—with a spelling whose barbarity I have not attempted to reproduce—in Madox Brown's diary If the bickerings seem unreasonably ferocious let it be remembered that in spite of them the unions were very close. Rossetti, who called Ruskin and himself sneaks, put up with Ruskin's eccentricities, and Ruskin put up with Rossetti's incredible and trying peculiarities for many years; and Burne-Jones, who was going to cut Topsy for good, retained for this friend of his to the end of their lives a friendship which is amongst the most touching of modern times. And the secret of it is, no doubt, to be found in the spirit of the last passage that I have quoted. These men might say that so-and-so was a sneak or that some one else was the prince of sneaks, but they said also that so-and-so " made " an exhibition with his pictures and that the other man's were the finest of modern works. It was the strong personalities that made them bicker constantly, but it was the strong personalities that gave them their devotion to their art, and it was the devotion to their art that held them all together. It is for this reason that these painters and these poets, distinguished by singular merits and by demerits as singular, made upon the English-speaking world a mark such as perhaps no body of men has made upon intellectual Anglo-Saxondom since the days of Shakespeare. For it is one of the saddening things in Anglo-Saxon life that any sort of union for an æsthetic or for an intellectual purpose seems to be almost an impossibility. Anglo-Saxon writers as a rule sit in the British Islands each on his little hill surrounded each by his satellites, moodily jealous of the fame of each of his rivals, incapable of realizing that the strength of several men together is very much stronger than the combined strengths of the same number of men acting apart. But it was the union of these men in matters of art that gave them their driving force against a world which very much did not want them. They pushed their way amongst buyers, they pushed their way into exhibitions, and it was an absolutely certain thing that as soon as one of them had got a foothold he never rested until he had helped in as many of his friends as the walls would hold. With just the same frenzy as in private and amongst themselves these men proclaimed each other sneaks, muffs, and even thieves—with exactly the same frenzy did they declare each other to picture buyers to be great and incomparable geniuses. And, as may be observed by the fore-going quotations, for any one of them to leave the other of them out of his praises was to commit the unpardonable sin. So, bickering like swashbucklers or like schoolboys, about wine, women and song, they pushed onwards to prosperity and to fame.

In those days there was in England a class of rich merchant which retained still the mediæval idea that to patronize the arts had about it a sort of super-virtue. Such patronage had for them something glamorous, something luxurious, something splendid. They were mostly in the north and in the midlands. Thus there was Peter Millar of Liverpool, George Rae of Birkenhead, Leathart of Gateshead and Plint of Birmingham. And whilst the artists strove amongst themselves so did these patrons, each with his own eccentricities, contend for their works. They were as a rule almost as bluff as the artists; and they had also almost as keen a belief that the fine arts could save a man's soul. Here is a portrait of one of these buyers—Mr. Peter Millar, a ship-owner of Liverpool who supported out of his own pocket several artists of merit sufficient to let them starve. His name should have its little niche amongst the monuments devoted to good Samaritans and to merchant princes :

" I may notice that Mr. Millar's hospitality is somewhat peculiar in its kind. His dinner which is at six is of one joint and vegetable *without* pudding. Bottled beer for only drink—I never saw any wine. His wife dines at another table with his daughters. After dinner he instantly hurries you off to tea and then back again to smoke. He calls it a meat tea and boasts that few people who have ever dined with him have come back again. All day long I was going here and there with him, dodging back to his office

24

to smoke and then off again after something fresh. The chief things I saw were chain cables forged and Hilton's ' Crucifixion,' which is jolly fine. . . . This Millar is a jolly kind old man with streaming white hair, fine features and a beautiful keen eye, like Mulready and something like John Cross, too. A rich brogue, a pipe of Cavendish and a smart rejoinder, with a pleasant word for every man, woman or child he meets in the streets, are characteristic of him. His house is full of pictures even to the kitchen, which is covered with them. Many he has at all his friends' houses in Liverpool, and his house in Bute is filled with his inferior ones. Many splendid Linnells, fine Constables and good Turners, and works by a Frenchman, Dellefant, are among the most marked of his collection plus a host of good pictures by Liverpool artists, Davis, Tonge and Windus chiefly."

These extracts from Madox Brown's diary belong to a period somewhat earlier than that of which I wrote in the preceding chapter. They show the movement getting ready, as it were, to move faster but moving already, and they reveal the principal figures very much as they were. And gradually these principal actors attracted to themselves each a host of satellites, of parasites, of dependents, of disciples. Some of these achieved fame and died: some of them spunged all their lives and died in the King's Bench prison: some achieved fame and disgrace: some, like Mr. William de Morgan, still live and have honourable renown: some, like Meredith and like Whistler became early detached from the great swarm, to shine solitary planets in the sky. But there are very few of the older or of the lately deceased men of prominence in the arts who were not in one way or other connected with this Old Circle. Thus, Swinburne, young, golden-haired, golden-tongued and splendid, was the constant companion of Rossetti and his wife, the almost legendary Miss Siddall, and later a very frequent inmate of the house in Fitzroy Square. And indeed the bonds between this poet and this painter were closer than any such statements can imply. Meredith's connection with the movement was, as to its facts, somewhat more mysterious but is none the less readily comprehensible. What has been called the famous " ham-and-egg story " seems to put Mr. Meredith in the somewhat ridiculous position of being unable to face the spectacle of ham and eggs upon Rossetti's breakfast table; but this was very unlike Mr. Meredith, who, delicate and austere poet as he was, had as a novelist a proper appreciation for the virtues of such things as beef and ale. The position of Mr. Meredith in the household at Cheyne Walk—a large mansion that in Tudor days had been the dower-house of the Queens of England, and in which at one time D. G. Rossetti, William Rossetti, Swinburne and Meredith attempted a not very successful communal household—the position of Mr. Meredith in this settlement remains a little mysterious. The ham-and-egg story made it appear that Mr. Meredith did not stop for more than one minute in the establishment, but fled at the sight of the substantial foods upon the table. In a letter to the *English Review* of last year Mr. Meredith altogether denied the ham-and-egg story, pointing out that his version of the affair would be that, during a stay of an indefinite period in the household at Cheyne Walk he had observed with alarm Rossetti's habit of consuming large quantities of meat and neglecting altogether to take exercise. Mr. Edward Clodd, on the other hand, informed me the other day that Meredith had assured him that he had never lived with Rossetti at all. I have, however, in my possession letters which, by their date prove that Mr. Meredith lived for at least one month in the household at Cheyne Walk. Madox Brown's own version of the episode—and he was so constantly at Cheyne Walk that his story, if picturesque, has in it the possibility of truth—Madox Brown's story was as follows:

The Pre-Raphaelite painters and writers were attracted earlier than any other men by the merits and charms of Mr. Meredith's poems. From this connection sprang an acquaintanceship between Rossetti and Meredith, and the acquaintanceship led to the suggestion by Rossetti that Meredith should make a fourth in the household. This suggestion Meredith accepted. The arrangement was that each of the four men should contribute his share of the rent and of household bills; but Mr. Meredith was at that time in circumstances of an extreme poverty, and, whilst paying his rent he was unable, or unwilling, to join in the household expenses. Thus he never appeared at table. This may have been because he disliked the food, but the Pre-Raphaelites imagined that he was starving himself for the sake of pride. They attempted, therefore, by sending up small breakfast dishes to

his room and by similar attentions to provide him
with some measure of comfort. It is possible that
these dishes disgusted him, but it is still more possible
that they disturbed his pride, which was considerable.
According to Madox Brown, the end came one day
when the benevolent poets substituted for the
cracked boots which he put outside his door to be
cleaned a new pair of exactly the same size and
make. He put on the boots, went out, and having
forwarded a cheque for the quarter's rent, never
returned.

But supposing this story to be a mere delusion of
Madox Brown's—though I can well believe it to be
true enough—there is no reason why something of the
sort should not have happened, and why Meredith
should not equally truthfully represent that Rossetti's methods of housekeeping were trying to his
refined sensibilities. For in person and in habits Mr.
Meredith, with his mordant humour, his clean, quick
intelligence and his impatience of anything approaching the slovenly, was exactly the man to suffer the
keenest anguish in any household that was conducted
by the poet-artist. It is true that at that time
Rossetti was not sole ruler of the house, but he was
certainly the dominant spirit ; and his was a spirit, in
matters of the world, easy-going, disorderly and large
in the extreme. You have to consider the Cheyne
Walk house as a largish, rather gloomy, Queen Anne
mansion, with portions of a still older architecture.
The furnishings were in no sense æsthetic. It is true
there were rather garish sofas designed for and executed by Morris & Company, but most of the things
had been picked up by Rossetti without any particular

regard for coherence of æsthetic scheme. Gilded sun-fishes hung from the ceilings along with drop lustres of the most excruciatingly Victorian type, and gilded lamps from the palace of George IV at Brighton. There were all sorts of chinoiseries, cabinets, screens, blue china and peacocks' feathers. The dustbins were full of priceless plates off which Rossetti dined and which the servants broke in the kitchen. Rossetti, in fact, surrounded himself with anything that he could find that was quaint and bizarre whether of the dead or the live world. So that the image of his house, dominated as it was by his wonderful personality was that of a singular warren of oddities. Speaking impressionistically we may say that supposing an earthquake had shaken the house down, or still more, supposing that some gigantic hand could have taken it up and shaken its contents out as from a box, there would have issued out a most extraordinary collection—racoons, armadillos, wombats, a Zebu bull, peacocks, models, mistresses, and an army of queer male and female "bad hats" who might be as engagingly criminal as they liked as long as they were engaging, as long as they were quaint, as long as they were interesting. They cadged on Rossetti, they stole from him, they blackmailed him, they succeeded indeed in driving him mad, but I think they all worshipped him. He had, in fact, a most extraordinary gift of inspiring enthusiasm, this singular Italianate man, who had all an Italian's powers of extracting money from clients, who worried people to death with his eccentricities, who drove them crazy with his jealousies, who charmed them into ecstasies with his tongue and with his eyes.

" Why is he not some great king," wrote one Pre-Raphaelite poet, who was stopping with him, to another, " that we might lay down our lives for him ? " And curiously enough one of the watchers at Whistler's bedside during that painter's last hours has informed me that, something to the discredit of Rossetti having been uttered in conversation, Whistler opened his eyes and said : " You must not say anything against Rossetti. Rossetti was a king."

This may have been said partly to tease his listeners whose styles of painting were anything rather than Rossettian, but Whistler certainly received nothing but kindness at the hands of the Pre-Raphaelite group. Looking through some old papers the other day I came upon a circular that Madox Brown had had printed, drawing the attention of all his own patrons to the merits of Whistler's etchings and begging them in the most urgent terms to make purchases because Whistler was " a great genius."

Now upon one occasion Madox Brown, going to a tea party at the Whistlers' in Chelsea, was met in the hall by Mrs. Whistler, who begged him to go to the poulterer's and purchase a pound of butter. The bread was cut but there was nothing to put upon it. There was no money in the house, the poulterer had cut off his credit, and Mrs. Whistler said she dare not send her husband for he would certainly punch that tradesman's head.

So that not nearly all the men whom this circle encouraged, helped, taught or filled with the contagion of enthusiasm, were by any means ignoble. Indeed, every one of them had some quality or other.

Thus there was a painter whom we will call P. whose indigence was remarkable but whose talents are now considerably recognized. This painter had a chance of a commission to make illustrations for a guide-book dealing with Wales. The commission, however, depended upon the drawings meeting with approval and Mr. P. being without the necessary means of paying for his travels applied to Madox Brown for a loan. Madox Brown produced the money and then, remembering that he had intended to take a holiday himself, decided to accompany his friend. They arrived upon a given morning towards two o'clock in some Welsh watering-place, having walked through the day and a greater part of the night with their knapsacks on their backs. They were unable to rouse anybody at the inn, there was not a soul in the streets, there was nothing but a long esplanade with houses whose windows gave on to the ground.

"Well, I'm going to have a sleep," P. said. "But that is impossible," Madox Brown answered. "Not at all," P. rejoined with a happy confidence, and pulling his knapsack round his body he produced his palette-knife. With this in his hand, to the horror of Madox Brown he approached the drawing-room window of one of the lodging-houses. He slipped the knife through the crack, pushed back the catch, opened the window and got in, followed eventually by his more timid companion. Having locked the door from the inside to prevent intrusion they lay down upon the sofa and on chairs, and proceeded to sleep till the morning when they got out of the window once more, closed it and went on their way. I have always wondered what the housemaid thought when she came down and found the drawing-room door locked from the inside.

On the next night they appeared to be in an almost similar danger of bedlessness. They arrived at a small village which contained only one inn and that was filled with a large concourse of Welsh-speaking people. The landlord, in broken English, told them that they could not have a room or a bed. There was a room with two beds in it but they could not have it. This enraged Mr. P. beyond description. He vowed that not only would he have the law of the landlord but he would immediately break his head, and Mr. P. being a redoubtable boxer, his threat was no mean one. So that having consulted with his Welsh friends, the host made signs to them that they could have the room in an hour, which he indicated by pointing at the clock. In an hour, accordingly, they were ushered into a room which contained a large and comfortable double bed. Mr. P. undressed and retired. Madox Brown similarly undressed and was about to step into bed when he placed his bare foot upon something of an exceedingly ghastly coldness. He gave a cry which roused Mr. P. Mr. P. sprang from the bed and bending down caught hold of a man's hand. He proceeded to drag out a body which displayed a throat cut from ear to ear. "Oh, is that all?" Mr. P. said, and having shoved the corpse under the bed he retired upon it and slept tranquilly. Madox Brown passed the night in the coffee room.

Upon this walking tour Mr. P. picked up a gipsy girl who afterwards served as a model to many famous

Academicians. He carried her off with him to London where he installed her in his studio. There was nothing singular about this, but what amazed Mr. P.'s friends was the fact that Mr. P., the most bellicose of mortals, from that moment did not go outside his house. The obvious reason for this was a gipsy of huge proportion and forbidding manner who had taken up his quarters at a public-house at the corner of the street. P.'s friends gibed at him for his want of courage, but P. continued sedulously and taciturnly to paint. At last he volunteered the information that he could not afford to damage his hands before he had finished his Academy picture. The picture finished, he sallied forth at once, knocked all the gipsy's teeth down his throat and incidentally broke both his knuckles. The gipsy girl was credited with a retort that was once famous in London. When P., who had been given a box at the Opera proposed to take her with him she refused obdurately to accompany him, and for a long time would give no reason. Being pressed she finally blurted out: "Ye don't put a toad in your waistcoat pocket." In this saying she under-rated the charm of one, who, till quite a short time ago, was a popular and beloved hostess in London, for she married one of P.'s wealthiest patrons, whilst poor P. remained under a necessity of borrowing small loans to the end of his life.

III

IT has always seemed at first sight a mystery to me how in the 'seventies and 'eighties such an inordinate number of poets managed to live in the gloom of central London. Nowadays, English poets live as far as I know—and I have reasons for knowing the addresses of an infinite number of them—English poets live—they cannot by any stretch of the imagination be said to flourish, unless they have what is called private means—they live in Bedford Park, a few in Chelsea and a great many in the country. Bedford Park is a sort of rash of villas crowded not so very close together or so very far out of town; Chelsea has the river to give it air. At any rate the poets of to-day crowd towards the light.

But in those old days they seemed filled with a passion for gloom. For I cannot imagine anything much more Cimmerian than Bloomsbury and the west central districts of the capital of England. Yet here—I am speaking only impressionistically—all the Pre-Raphaelite poets seemed to crowd together, full of enthusiasms, pouring forth endless songs about the loves of Launcelot and Guinevere, about music and moonlight. You have to think of it as a region of soot-blackened brick houses, with

34

here and there black squares whose grimy trees reach up into a brownish atmosphere. What there is not black is brownish. Yet here all these dead poets seemed to live. Fitzroy Square, of which I have written, is such a square; the Rossettis always circled round Bloomsbury. Though D. G. Rossetti travelled as far afield as Chelsea, William Rossetti until very lately lived in Euston Square which, to celebrate a murder, changed its name to Endsleigh Gardens; and Christina, who for me is the most satisfactory of all the poets of the nineteenth century, died in times of fog in Woburn Square.

I suppose they sang of Launcelot and Guinevere to take their own minds off their surroundings, having been driven into their surroundings by the combined desire for cheap rents and respectable addresses. Some of them were conscious of the gloom, some no doubt were not. Mr. Joaquin Miller, coming from Nicaragua and Arizona to stay for a time in Gower Street—surely the longest, the grayest and the most cruel of all London streets—this author of " Songs of the Sierras " was greeted rapturously by the Pre-Raphaelite poets and wrote of life in London as a rush, a whirl, a glow—all the motion of the world. He wrote ecstatically and at the same time with humility, pouring out his verses as one privileged to be at table with all the great ones of the earth. In the mornings he rode in the Row amongst the " swells," wearing a red shirt, cowboy boots and a sombrero; in the evenings he attended in the same costume at the dinners of the great Intellectuals where " brilliantly " he was a " feature." Had he not been with Walker the

Filibuster in Nicaragua ? I can dimly remember the face of Mark Twain—or was it Bret Harte ?—standing between open folding doors at a party, gazing in an odd, puzzled manner at this brilliant phenomenon. I fancy the great writer, whichever it was, was not too pleased that this original should represent the manners and customs of the United States in the eyes of the poets. Mr. Miller did them good, if it were an injustice to Boston. He represented for the poets Romance.

But if Mr. Miller saw in London life, light and the hope of fame, and if some others of the poets saw it in similar terms, there were others who saw the city in terms realistic enough. Thus poor James Thomson, writing as B.V., sang of the City of Dreadful Night and, we are told, drank himself to death. That was the grisly side of it. If you were a poet you lived in deep atmospheric gloom and to relieve yourself, to see colour, you must sing of Launcelot and Guinevere. If the visions would not come you must get stimulants to give you them. I remember as a child being present in the drawing-room of a relative just before a dinner at which Tennyson and Browning had been asked to meet a rising poet to whom it was desired to give a friendly lift. It was the longest and worst quarter-of-an-hour possible. The celebrities fidgeted, did not talk, looked in olympian manners at their watches. At last they went into dinner without the young poet. I was too little and too nervous to tell them that half-an-hour before I had seen the poor fellow lying hopelessly drunk across a whelk-stall in the Euston Road.

One of the grimmest stories that I have heard

even of that time and neighbourhood was told me by the late Mr. William Sharp. Mr. Sharp was himself a poet of the Pre-Raphaelites, though later he wrote as Fiona Macleod and thus joined the Celtic School of poetry that still flourishes in the person of Mr. W. B. Yeats. Mr. Sharp had gone to call on Philip Marston, the blind author of " Songtide" and of many other poems that in their day were considered to be a certain passport to immortality. Going up the gloomy stairs of a really horrible house near Gower Street Station he heard proceeding from the blind poet's rooms a loud sound of growling, punctuated with muffled cries for help. He found the poor blind man in the clutches of the poet I have just omitted to name—crushed beneath him and, I think, severely bitten. This poet had had an attack of delirium tremens and imagined himself a Bengal tiger. Leaving Marston he sprang on all fours towards Sharp, but he burst a blood vessel and collapsed on the floor. Sharp lifted him on to the sofa, took Marston into another room and then rushed hatless through the streets to the hospital that was round the corner. The surgeon in charge, himself drunk and seeing Sharp covered with blood, insisted on giving him in charge for murder; Sharp always a delicate man, fainted. The poet was dead of hæmorrhage before assistance reached him.

But in gloom and amidst horror they sang on bravely of Launcelot and Guinevere, Merlin and Vivien, ballads of staffs and scrips, of music and moonlight. They did not, that is to say, much look at the life that was around them; in amidst the glooms they built immaterial pleasure houses. They were not brave enough—that, I suppose, is why they are very few of them remembered and few of them great.

I have, however, very little sense of proportion in this particular matter. There were Philip Bourke Marston, Arthur O'Shaughnessy, "B. V.," Theo Marzials, Gordon Hake, Christina Rossetti, Mr. Edmund Gosse, Mr. Hall Caine, Oliver Madox Brown, Mr. Watts-Dunton, Mr. Swinburne, D. G. Rossetti, Robert Browning ! . . . All these names have been exceedingly familiar to my mouth and ears ever since I could speak or hear. In their own day each of them was a great and serious fact. For there was a time—yes, really there was a time !—when the publication of a volume of poems was still an event —an event making great names and fortunes not merely mediocre. I do not mean to say that in the 'seventies and 'eighties carriages still blocked Albemarle Street, but if Mr. O'Shaughnessy was understood to be putting the finishing touches to the proof-sheets of his next volume there arose an immense excitement amongst all the other poets, amongst all the Pre-Raphaelite Circle and all the outsiders connected with the Circle and all the connections of all the outsiders. What the book was going to be like was discussed eagerly. So-and-so was understood to have seen the proof-sheets, and what the *Athenæum* would say, or what the *Athenæum* did say, excited all the circumjacent authors quite as much as would nowadays the winning of the Derby by a horse belonging to His Majesty the King. All these things are most extraordinarily changed. Small volumes of poems

descend upon one's head in an unceasing shower. They come so quickly that one cannot even imagine the authors have time themselves to read the proof-sheets. How much less, then, their friends ! But as for fame or fortune ! . . .

I am acquainted with an author—I am much too well acquainted with an author who one day had what in the language of the 'nineties was called " a boom." At the height of this agreeable period he published a volume of poems. It cannot be said that the press did not welcome him rapturously : he received a column and a half of praise in the *Daily Telegraph*, something more than a column in the *Daily Chronicle*, just over two columns in *The Times* itself, and three lines of contempt in the *Spectator*, which alone in the 'eighties would have sufficed to make the fortune of any poet. Of this volume of poems, heralded and boomed as it was, and published in the year 1908, the public demanded seventeen copies. Exactly seventeen ! I remember being informed by a person in authority that the sale of the last volume of poems that Swinburne published was exactly six hundred copies, of which four hundred and eighty were bought in Germany, leaving one hundred and twenty enthusiasts for the British Isles and the rest of the Continent. And this seems to me to be a record of indifference heroic in itself. I do not know that it is a record particularly interesting, however, to anybody who is not interested in poets. But faced with these facts both of the outside and inside I may well be excused if I say that I have not any sense of proportion, or any but the remotest idea as to the relative value of the Pre-Raphaelite or Semi-Pre-Raphaelite poets.

My childhood was in many respects a singular one. The names of these distinguished persons were as much in daily use in my grandfather's house when I was a child, and many of the distinguished persons were nearly as often in the house itself, as are in England such ordinary household things as Black's Mustard, Dash's Worcestershire Sauce; or as, in the case of the United States, that beverage which lately I saw everywhere advertised in enormous letters that seemed to flame from New York to Philadelphia conveying the command, "Drink Boxie. You will not like it at first." I could not think that D. G. Rossetti was a person any more remarkable than the gentleman with gold braid round his hat who opened for me the locked gates of Fitzroy Square, nor when I shook hands with a clergyman called Franz Liszt was it any more of an event than when, as I was enjoined to do, I performed the same ceremony with the cook's husband. Dimly, but with vivid patches, I remember being taken for a walk by my father along what appeared to me to be a grey stone quay. I presume it was the Chelsea Embankment. There we met a very old, long-bearded man. He frightened me quite as much as any of the other great Victorian figures who, to the eye of a child, appeared monumental, loud-voiced and distressing. This particular gentleman, at the instance of my grandfather, related to me how he had once been at Weimar. In a garden restaurant beneath a may-tree in bloom he had seen Schiller and Goethe drinking coffee together. He

40

had given a waiter a thaler to be allowed to put on
a white apron and to wait upon these two world-
shaking men, who, in court dress with wigs and
swords, sat at a damask-covered table. He had
waited upon them. Later, I remember that whilst
I was standing with my father beside the doorstep
in Tite Street of the house that he was entering, I
fell down and he bent over to assist me to rise. His
name was Thomas Carlyle, but he is almost confounded in my mind with a gentleman called Pepper.
Pepper very much resembled Carlyle except that
he was exceedingly dirty. He used to sell penny
dreadfuls which I was forbidden to purchase, and
I think the happiest times of my childhood were
spent in a large coal-cellar. Into this I used to lock
myself to read of the exploits of Harkaway Dick,
who lived in a hollow tree, possessed a tame, black
panther and a pair of Winchester repeating rifles,
with which at one sitting he shot no less than forty-
five pirates through a loophole in the bark of the
tree. I think I have never since so fully tasted of
the joys of life, not even when Captain Hook . . .
But what was even Peter Pan to compare with
Harkaway Dick !

There were all these things jumbled up in
my poor little mind together. I presume I should
not remember half so vividly the story of Carlyle
and the author of *Wilhelm Meister* if my father
had not afterwards frequently jogged my memory
upon the point. My father was a man of an encyclopædic knowledge and had a great respect for the
attainments of the distinguished. He used, I
remember, habitually to call me " the patient

but exceedingly stupid donkey." This phrase occurred in Mavor's spelling book, which he read as
a boy in the city of Münster in Westphalia where
he was born. He had a memory that was positively
extraordinary and a gift of languages no less great.
Thus whilst his native language was German he
was for a long course of years musical critic to
The Times, London correspondent to the *Frank-
furter Zeitung*, London musical correspondent to *Le
Menestrel* of Paris and the *Tribuna* of Rome. He
was also, I believe, in his day the greatest authority
upon the troubadours and the romance languages,
and wrote original poems in modern Provençal;
he was a favourite pupil of Schopenhauer and
the bad boy of his family. He was a doctor of
philosophy of Göttingen University, at that time
premier university of Germany, though he had
made his studies at the inferior institution in
Berlin. From Berlin he was expelled because of
his remarkable memory. The circumstances were
as follow:

My father occupied a room in an hotel which had
a balcony overlooking the Spree. In the same
hotel, but in the next room, there dwelt the rector
of the university, and it happened that one of the
Prussian princes was to be present at the ceremony
of conferring degrees. Thus one evening my father
was sitting upon his balcony whilst next door the
worthy rector read the address that he was afterwards to deliver to the prince. Apparently the
younger members of the institution addressed the
prince before the dons. At any rate, my father
having heard it only once, delivered word for word

the rector's speech to His Royal Highness. The result was that the poor man, who spoke only with difficulty, had not a single word to say and my father was forthwith expelled without his degree. Being, though freakish, a person of spirit, that same day he took the express to Göttingen and as a result in the evening he telegraphed to his mother : " Have passed for doctor with honours at Göttingen " to the consternation of his parents, who had not yet heard of his expulsion from Berlin. The exploit pleased nobody. Berlin did not desire that he should be a doctor at all : Göttingen was disgusted that a student from an inferior university should have passed out on top of their particular tree, and I believe that in consequence, in Germany of to-day, a student can only take his " doctor " at his own particular university.

Possibly at the suggestion of Schopenhauer or possibly because his own lively disposition made parts of Germany too hot to hold him, Dr. Hueffer came to England. He had letters of introduction to various men of letters in England, for, for time out of mind, in the city of Münster the Hueffer family have belonged to the class that battens upon authors. They have been, that is to say, printers and publishers. Following his intention of spreading the light of Schopenhauer in England, that country for which Schopenhauer had so immense a respect, Dr. Hueffer founded a periodical called the *New Quarterly Review*, which caused him to lose a great deal of money and to make cordial enemies amongst the poets and literary men to whom he gave friendly lifts. I fancy that the only traces of the *New Quarterly Review* are contained in the limerick by Rossetti which runs as follows :

" There was a young German called Huffer,
A hypochondriacal buffer;
To shout Schopenhauer
From the top of a tower
Was the highest enjoyment of Huffer."

In London Dr. Hueffer lived first in Chelsea, half-way between Rossetti and Carlyle, who were both, I believe, very much attached to him for various reasons. Indeed, one of the first things that I can remember, or seem to remember, for the memory is probably inaccurate, is that I lay in my cradle amongst proof-sheets of Rossetti's poems which my father was amiably occupied in reading for the press.

In their day Rossetti's limericks were celebrated. I do not know whether they have ever been collected. I certainly seem to remember having heard that some one was, or is, engaged in collecting them. In that case I may here make him a present of one more which was written on the fly-leaf of a volume of " Lear's Nonsense Verses " presented by the poet to Oliver Madox Brown :

" There was a young rascal called Nolly,
Whose habits though dirty were jolly,
And when this book comes
To be marked with his thumbs,
You may know that its owner is Nolly."

This engaging trait may perhaps be capped by an anecdote related of another poet, a descendant of many Pre-Raphaelites, of whom it was related that whilst reading his friend's valuable books at that friend's breakfast table he was in the habit of marking his place with a slice of bacon.

44

Gloom and the Poets

This excellent and touching anecdote I know to
be untrue, but it is to this day being related of one
living poet by the wife of a living painter of distinction, she herself being to some extent of Pre-
Raphaelite connection.   Such as it is, it goes to show
that the habit of anecdote, incisive however wanting
in veracity, is still remaining to the surviving connections of this Old Circle.   For whatever may have
been the value of the poetic gifts of these poets there
cannot be any doubt that in their private conversations they had singular powers of picturesque nar-
ration.   And certainly picturesque things were in the
habit of happening to them—odd, irresponsible, and
partaking perhaps a little of nightmares.   I remember
as a boy being set somewhat inconsiderately the
task of convoying home a very distinguished artist,
practising, however, an art other than that of
poetry.   We had been at a musical evening in the
neighbourhood of Swiss Cottage and arrived at the
Underground Station just before the last train came
in.   My enormously distinguished temporary ward
was in the habit of filling one of his trouser pockets
with chocolate creams and the other with large,
unset diamonds.   With the chocolate creams he
was accustomed to solace his sense of taste whilst
he sat in the artistes' room waiting for his turn to
play.   With the diamonds on similar occasions he
solaced his sense of touch, plunging his hand amongst
them and moving them about luxuriously.   He
would have sometimes as many as twenty or thirty
large and valuable stones.   On this occasion M.—,
always an excitable person, was in a state of extreme
rage.   For at the party where he had played

M. Saint-Saens the composer had also been invited to play the piano. As far as I can remember Saint-Saens was not a very good pianist; he had the extremely hard touch of the organist, and M. considered that to have invited him to sit down on the same piano-stool was an insult almost beyond bearing.

The platform of the Underground Railway was more than usually gloomy, since, the last down train having gone, the lamps upon the other platform had been extinguished. M.—volleyed and thundered, and at last, just as the train came in, he thrust both his hands into his trouser pockets and then waved them wildly above his head in execration of my insufficient responsiveness. There flew from the one pocket a shower of chocolate creams, from the other a shower of large diamonds. M. gave a final scream upon a very high note and plunged into a railway carriage. I was left divided as to whether my duty were towards the maestro or his jewels. I suppose it was undue materialism in myself, but I stayed to look after the diamonds. It was a long and agonizing search. The station-master, who imagined that I was as mad as the vanished musician, insisted that there were no diamonds and extinguished the station lamps. A friendly porter, however, assisted me with a hand-lantern and eventually we recovered about five diamonds, each perhaps as large as my little finger-nail. Whether any more remained upon the platform I never knew, for M. also never knew how many jewels he possessed or carried about with him. It was a night certainly of nightmare, for being so young a boy I had not sufficient money to take a cab and the last train into Town had gone. I had, therefore, to walk to Claridge's Hotel, a distance of perhaps four miles, and arriving there I could not discover that the porter had seen anything of M. I therefore thought it wise to arouse his wife. Mme.—— was accustomed to being awakened at all hours of the night. Her distinguished husband, was in the habit of dragging her impetuously out of bed to listen to his latest rendering of a passage of Chopin ; and indeed upon this account, she subsequently divorced the master, such actions being held by the French courts to constitute incompatibility of temperament. She did not, however, take my arousing her with any the greater equanimity, and when I produced the diamonds she upbraided me violently for having lost the master. There ensued a more agonizing period of driving about in cabs before we discovered M. detained at the police station nearest Baker Street. He had in his vocabulary no English at all except some very startling specimens of profanity. Upon arriving at Baker Street Station he had spent a considerable amount of time and energy in attempting to explain to the ticket collector in French that he had lost a sacred charge, a weakly little boy incapable of taking care of himself; and as he did not even know the name of his hotel the police had taken charge of him and were attempting kindly to keep him soothed by singing popular songs to him in the charge-room where we found him quite contented and happy, beating time with his feet to the melody of "Two Lovely Black Eyes." I think this was upon the whole the unhappiest night I ever spent.

The mention of chocolate creams reminds me of another musician who was also a Pre-Raphaelite poet—Mr. Theo Marzials. Mr. Marzials was in his young days the handsomest, the wittiest, the most brilliant and the most charming of poets. He had a career tragic in the extreme and, as I believe, is now dead. But he shared with M. the habit of keeping chocolate creams loose in his pocket, and on the last occasion when I happened to catch sight of him looking into a case of stuffed birds at South Kensington Museum, he had eaten five large chocolates in the space of two minutes. As a musician he wrote some very charming songs of which I suppose the best known are "Twickenham Ferry" and the canon, "My True Love Hath my Heart." He wrote, I believe, only one volume of poems called "A Gallery of Pigeons" but that contains verse of a lyrical and polished sort that, as far as my predilections serve, seems to me to be by far the most exquisite that were produced by any of the lesser Pre-Raphaelite poets. As the volume must probably be very rare, and is perhaps quite unknown nowadays, I venture to reproduce a couple of his miniature poems called "Tragedies." They have lingered in my memory ever since I was a young child.

I.

"She was only a woman, famish'd for loving,
   Mad for devotion, and such slight things ;
And he was a very great musician,
   And used to finger his fiddle-strings.

Her heart's sweet gamut is cracking and breaking
   For a look, for a touch,—for such slight things ;
But he's such a very great musician,
   Grimacing and fing'ring his fiddle-strings."

48

Gloom and the Poets

"In the warm wax-light one lounged at the spinet,
  And high in the window came peeping the moon ;
At his side was a bowl of blue china, and in it
  Were large blush-roses, and cream and maroon.

They crowded, and strain'd, and swoon'd to the music,
  And some to the gilt board languor'd and lay ;
They open'd and breathed, and trembled with pleasure,
  And all the sweet while they were fading away."

And here is a third little poem by Marzials which I quote because it is headed simply " Chelsea " :

"And life is like a pipe,
  And love is the fusee ;
The pipe draws well, but bar the light,
  And what's the use to me ?

So light it up, and puff away
  An empty morning through,
And when it's out—why love is out,
  And life's as well out too ! "

But I do not know whether this was suggested by Rossetti or Carlyle.

Another of these forgotten or not quite forgotten geniuses was Oliver Madox Brown, who, though he died at the age of eighteen, had proved himself at once a painter, a novelist and a poet. Before his death he had exhibited several pictures at the Royal Academy and had published with considerable success one novel, leaving two others to be produced after his death. He must, indeed, have been a very remarkable boy if we are to believe at all in the sincerity of the tributes to his memory left by the distinguished men of the Pre-Raphaelite group and Madox Brown remained passionately devoted to his memory until his dying day. Just before his death Oliver complained that his father smelt of tobacco, whereupon Madox Brown said : " Very well, my dear, I will never smoke again until you are better." And he never again did smoke although before that time he had been a very heavy smoker. He had, indeed, one singular accomplishment that I have never noticed in any other man. With the palette fixed upon his left hand he was able to charge and roll a cigarette with his right, rubbing the paper against his trousers and doing it with quite extraordinary rapidity, so that the feat resembled a conjurer's trick. Oliver Madox Brown died of blood poisoning in 1875 and it was not till many years after his death that it was discovered that beneath his study, which was at the bottom of the old house in Fitzroy Square, there was a subterranean stable whose open door was in the mews behind the house and which had neither drains nor ventilation of any kind. So that there cannot be any doubt that the emanations from this ancient place of horrors were responsible for Oliver's death—so frail a thing is genius and so tenuous its hold upon existence.

As a boy I had a similar study at the back and bottom of another old house of Madox Brown's. And one of the other most unpleasant memories of mine were the incursions made upon me by a Pre-Raphaelite poetess, Miss Mathilde Blind. Miss Blind was descended from a distinguished family of revolutionaries. Indeed, one of the brothers attempted to assassinate Bismarck, and disappeared, without any trace of him ever again being heard of, in the dungeons of a Prussian fortress. She

was, moreover, a favourite pupil of Mazzini the liberator of Italy, and a person, in her earlier years, of extreme beauty and fire. Upon the death of their son and the marriage of their two daughters, the late Mrs. William Rossetti and Mrs. Francis Hueffer, the Madox Browns adopted Mathilde Blind who from thenceforward spent most of her time with them. As a boy—I wrote my first book when I was sixteen and its success alas! was more tremendous than any that I can ever again know—I would be sitting in my little study intent either upon my writing or my school tasks, when ominous sounds would be heard at the door. Miss Blind, with her magnificent aquiline features and fine grey hair, would enter, alarming slip proofs dangling from both her hands. "Fordie," she would say, "I want a synonym for 'dun.'" On page 152 of her then volume of poems she would have written of dun cows standing in green streams. She was then correcting the proofs of page 154 to find that she had spoken of the dun cows returning homewards over the leas. Some other adjective would have to be found for this useful quadruped. Then my bad quarter-of-an-hour would commence. I would suggest "strawberry-coloured" and she would say that that would not fit the metre. I would try "roan" but she would say that that would spoil the phonetic syzygy. I did not know what that was but I would next suggest "heifers," whereupon she would say that heifers did not give milk and that, anyhow, the accentuation was wrong. I would be reduced to a miserable muteness; Miss Blind frightened me out of my life. *And rising* up and gathering her proof-sheets together, the poetess, with her Medusa head, would regard me with indignant and piercing brown eyes. "Fordie," she would say with an awful scrutiny, "your grandfather says you are a genius, but I have never been able to discover in you any signs but those of your being as stupid as a donkey." I never *could* escape from being likened to that other useful quadruped.

They took themselves with such extreme seriousness—these Pre-Raphaelite poets—and nevertheless I have always fancied that they are responsible for the death of English poetry. My father once wrote of Rossetti that he put down the thoughts of Dante in the language of Shakespeare, and the words seem to me to be extremely true and extremely damning. For what is wanted of a poet is that he should express his own thoughts in the language of his own time. This, with perhaps the solitary exception of Christina Rossetti, the Pre-Raphaelite poets never thought of.

I remember once hearing Stephen Crane—the author of *The Red Badge of Courage* and of *The Open Boat*, which is the finest volume of true short stories in the English language,—I remember hearing him, with his wonderful eyes flashing and his extreme vigour and intonation, comment upon a sentence of Robert Louis Stevenson that he was reading. The sentence was: "With interjected finger he delayed the motion of the timepiece." "By God, poor dear!" Crane exclaimed. "That man put back the clock of English fiction fifty years." I do not know that this is exactly what Stevenson did do. I should say myself that the art of writing in English received the numbing blow of a sandbag when Rossetti wrote, at the age of eighteen, *The Blessed Damozel*. From that time forward and until to-day—and for how many years to come !— the idea has been inherent in the mind of the English writer that writing was a matter of digging for obsolete words with which to express ideas for ever dead and gone. Stevenson did this, of course, as carefully as any Pre-Raphaelite, though instead of going to mediæval books he ransacked the seventeenth century. But this tendency is unfortunately not limited to authors misusing our very excellent tongue. The other day I was listening to an excellent Italian *conférencier* who assured an impressed audience that Signor D'Annuncio is the greatest Italian stylist there has ever been, since in his last book he has used over 2,017 obsolete words which cannot be understood by a modern Italian without the help of a mediæval glossary.

IV

CHRISTINA ROSSETTI AND PRE-RAPHAELITE LOVE

IT always appears to me that whereas D. G. Rossetti belongs to a comparatively early period of nineteenth-century literature Christina's was a much more modern figure. Dates, perhaps, do not bear me out in this. Rossetti was born in the 'twenties, printed his first poem when he was perhaps ten, and wrote *The Blessed Damozel* when he was eighteen. On the other hand his first published volume of original poetry did not appear until the late 'seventies. Yet he died in the 'eighties. Christina Rossetti's *Goblin Market* volume was published in the late 'sixties, but she lived well on into the 'nineties; and she wrote poems until practically the day of her death. I am perhaps eccentric when I say that I consider Christina Rossetti to be the greatest master of words—at least of English words—that the nineteenth century gave us. Her verse at its best is as clean in texture and as perfect in the choice of epithet as any of Maupassant's short stories. And although the range of her subjects was limited—although it was limited very strictly within the bounds of her personal emotions, yet within those limits she expressed herself consummately. And it was in this rather more than by her dates of publication that she proved herself a poet more modern than her brother who in his day bulked so much more largely in the public eye. It was perhaps for this reason, too, that Mr. Ruskin—and in this alone he would have earned for himself my lasting dislike—that Mr. Ruskin pooh-poohed and discouraged Christina Rossetti's efforts at poetry. For there is extant at least one letter from the voluminous critic in which he declares that the *Goblin Market* volume was too slight and too frivolous a fascicule to publish, and to the end of his days Mr. Ruskin considered that Christina damaged her brother. It was not good for Gabriel's fame or market, he considered, that there should be another Rossetti in the field. And I must confess that when I consider these utterances and this attitude I am filled with as hot and as uncontrollable an anger as I am when faced by some more than usually imbecile argument against the cause of women's franchise. Yesterday I was arguing upon this latter subject with a distinguished ornament of the London stipendiary bench. Said the police magistrate : No woman ever administered financial interests, ever reigned or ever fought. I mentioned with a quite feigned humility and with apologies for the antiquated nature of my illustrations the prioresses and mothers superior who with never-questioned financial abilities had administered, and do administer, the innumerable convents, schools, almshouses, hospitals and penitentiaries of Catholic Christendom. His Worship mentioned with a snigger Sœur C— of Paris who obtained fraudulent credit from jewellers in order to support almshouses. Thus with one sneer and the

mention of a lady who was not a nun at all,
Mr. —— considered himself to have demolished the
claims to consideration of all Catholic womanhood.
I said that his argument reminded me of a Park
orator who claimed to demolish the whole historical and social record of the Church of England
by citing the name of one Herring, a sham clergyman, who had extorted contributions from the
charitable in favour of a fraudulent almshouse, and
I mentioned Joan of Arc. The legal luminary
remarked that he never *had* liked her, and when I
produced Queen Elizabeth and Queen Victoria as
arguments in favour of the fact that a country might
enormously extend its bounds, and enormously
flourish, whilst a queen reigned, my superior inter-
locutor remarked that Victoria was a horrid old
woman and that Elizabeth ought to have been a
man.

I do not say that my friend's methods of argument
made me angry, since they gave me the chance of
roasting him alive before an able and distinguished
assembly, but I could not help being reminded by him
of Mr. Ruskin's attitude towards Christina Rossetti.
It was the same fine superiority as made the police
magistrate embrace St. Catharine of Sienna, Joan
of Arc and Queen Elizabeth in one common sneer.
But after all, Queen Elizabeth and the other two
could look after themselves. Did not one St.
Catharine confute forty thousand doctors, amongst
whom were nine hundred and sixty police magistrates? And did she not in Heaven decide the
ticklish case as to whether penguins, when they had
been baptized, must be considered to possess souls?

Christina Rossetti and Pre-Raphaelite Love

But Christina Rossetti's was a figure so tragic, so sympathetic and, let me emphasize it, so modern, that I could wish for any one who put obstacles in her way—and there were several—that fate which was adjudged the most terrible of all, that a mill-stone should be set about his neck and that he should be cast into the deep sea. And, indeed, it would seem that Mr. Ruskin has fallen into a deep, a very deep, a bottomless sea of oblivion with, around his neck, all his heavy volumes for a millstone. (I am at this moment corrected in this exaggerated statement, for I am informed that you will always find *Sesame and Lilies* in every library catalogue !) And indeed, I am no doubt unduly hard upon Mr. Ruskin, little though his eloquent ghost may mind it. For the fact is that Ruskin and the Pre-Raphaelites whom he heralded so splendidly and so picturesquely survived—that these men marked the close of an era. Ruskin was engaged in setting the seal on a pot. Christina Rossetti was, if not a genie in the form of a cloud of smoke, at least a subtle essence that was bound not only to escape his embalming but to survive him.

Ruskin pooh-poohed her because she was not important. And I fancy he disliked her intuitively because importance was the last thing in this world that she would have desired. I remember informing her shortly after the death of Lord Tennyson that there was a very strong movement, or at any rate a very strong feeling abroad, that the laureateship should be conferred upon her. She shuddered. And I think that she gave evidence then to as strong an emotion as I ever knew in her. The idea of such a

position of eminence filled her with real horror. She
wanted to be obscure and to be an obscure hand-
maiden of the Lord as fervently as she desired to be
exactly correct in her language. Exaggerations
really pained her. I remember that when I told
her that I had met hundreds of people who thought
the appointment would be most appropriate she
pinned me down until she had extracted from me
the confession that not more than nine persons had
spoken to me on the subject. And a letter of hers
which I possess, acknowledging the receipt of my first
book begins : " My dear young relation (if you will
permit me to style you so, though I am aware that I
should write more justly ' connection.' Yet you are
now too old for me to call you ' Fordie '). . . ."

And there we have one symptom of the gulf that
separated Christina Rossetti as a Modernist from
Ruskin and the old Pre-Raphaelite Circle. The very
last thing that these, the last of the Romanticists,
desired was precision. On one page of one of Mr.
Ruskin's book I have counted the epithet " golden "
six times. There are " golden days," " golden-
mouthed," " distant golden spire," " golden peaks "
and " golden sunset," all of them describing one
picture by Turner in which the nearest approach to
gold discernible by a precise eye is a mixture of
orange red and madder brown. His was another
method; it was the last kick of Romanticism—of
that romanticism that is now so very dead.

Pre-Raphaelism in itself was born of Realism.
Ruskin gave it one white wing of moral purpose.
The Æstheticists presented it with another, dyed all
the colours of the rainbow, from the hues of mediæval

tapestries to that of romantic love. Thus it flew rather unevenly and came to the ground. The first Pre-Raphaelites said that you must paint your model exactly as you see it, hair for hair or leaf-spore for leaf-spore. Mr. Ruskin gave them the added canon that the subject they painted must be one of moral distinction. You must, in fact, paint life as you see it and yet in such a way as to prove that life is an ennobling thing. How one was to do this one got no particular directions. Perhaps one might have obtained it by living only in the drawing-room of Brantwood House, Coniston, when Mr. Ruskin was in residence.

I do not know that in her drawing-room in the gloomy London square Christina Rossetti found life in any way ennobling or inspiring. She must have found it, if not exceedingly tragic, at least so full of pain as to be almost beyond supporting. Her poetry is very full of a desire, of a passionate yearning for the country, yet there in box-like rooms she lived, her windows brushed by the leaves, her rooms rendered dark by the shade of those black-trunked London trees that are like a grim mockery of their green-boled sisters of the open country. I do not know why she should have resided in a London square. There were no material circumstances that forced it on her, but rather the psychological cravings of her inner life. And again her poetry is very full of a love, of a desire, of a passionate yearning for love. Yet there in her cloistral seclusion she lived alone in pain, practising acts of charity and piety, and seeking almost as remorselessly as did Flaubert himself, and just as solitarily, for correct expression

—for that, that is to say, which was her duty in life. As I have pointed out elsewhere, this black-robed figure with eyes rendered large by one of the most painful of diseases, and suffering always from the knife-stabs of yet two other most painful diseases— this black-robed figure with the clear-cut and olive-coloured features, the dark hair, the restrained and formal gestures, the hands always folded in the lap, the head always judicially a little on one side and with the precise enunciation, this tranquil Religious was undergoing within herself always a fierce struggle between the pagan desire for life, the light of the sun and love, and an asceticism that, in its almost more than Calvinistic restraint, reached also to a point of frenzy. She put love from her with both hands and yearned for it unceasingly, she let life pass by and wrote of glowing tapestries, of wine and pomegranates; she was thinking always of heaths, the wide sands of the sea-shore, of south walls on which the apricots glow, and she lived always of her own free will in the gloom of a London square. So that if Christianity have its saints and martyrs I am not certain that she was not one of the most distinguished of them. For there have been ascetics, but there can have been few who could have better enjoyed a higher life of the senses. She was at the very opposite end of the hagæological scale from St. Louis Gonzaga of whom it is recorded that he was so chaste that he had never raised his eyes to look upon a woman, not even upon his mother. Her last harrowing thoughts upon her racked death-bed were that she had not sufficiently denied herself, that she had not worked sufficiently in the olive-garden of the Saviour, that she had merited, and without the right of complaint she had ensued, an eternal damnation. It was a terrible thought to go down to Death with, and it has always seemed to me to be a condemnation of Christianity that it should have let such a fate harass such a woman, just as perhaps it is one of the greatest testimonies to the powers of discipline of Christianity, that it should have trained up such a woman to such a life of abnegation, of splendid literary expression, and of meticulous attention to duty. The trouble was, of course, that whereas by blood and by nature Christina Rossetti was a Catholic, by upbringing and by all the influences that were around her she was forced into the Protestant Communion. Under the influence of a wise confessor the morbidities of her self-abnegation would have been checked, her doubts would have been stilled with an authoritative " yes " or " no "; and though such sins as she may have sinned might have led her to consider that she had earned a more or less long period of torture in Purgatory, she would have felt the comfort of the thought that all the thousands whom by her work she had sustained in religion and comforted in the night—that the prayers and conversions of all those thousands would have earned for her a remission of her penalties and great bliss and comfort in an ultimate Heaven. There are, of course, Protestant natures as there are Catholic, just as there are those by nature agnostic and those by nature believing in every fibre ; and Heaven is, without doubt, wide enough for us all. But Christina Rossetti's nature was mediæval in the sense that it cared for little things and for arbitrary arrangements. In the same sense it was so very modern. For the life of to-day is more and more becoming a life of little things. We are losing more and more the sense of a whole, the feeling of a grand design, of the co-ordination of all Nature in one great architectonic scheme. We have no longer any time to look out for the ultimate design. We have to face such an infinite number of little things that we cannot stay to arrange them in our minds, or to consider them as anything but as accidents, happenings, the mere events of the day. And if in outside things we can perceive no design but only the fortuitous materialism of a bewildering world, we are thrown more and more in upon ourselves for comprehension of that which is not understandable and for analysis of things of the spirit. In this way we seem again to be returning to the empiricism of the middle ages and in that way, too, Christina herself, although she resembled the figure of a mediæval nun, seems also a figure very modern amongst all the romantic generalizers who surrounded her, who overwhelmed her, who despised and outshouted her.

For in the nineteenth century men still generalized. Empirical religion appeared to be dead and all the functions of life could be treated as manifestations of a Whole, ordered according to one school of thought or another. Thus, love, according to the Pre-Raphaelite canon, was a great but rather sloppy passion. Its manifestations would be Paolo and Francesca, or Launcelot and Guinevere. It was a thing that you swooned about on broad, general lines, your eyes closed, your arms outstretched. It excused all sins, it sanctified all purposes and, if you went to hell over it, you still drifted about amongst snow-flakes of fire with your eyes closed and in the arms of the object of your passion. For it is impossible to suppose that when Rossetti painted his picture of Paolo and Francesca in hell, he, or any of his admirers, thought that these two lovers were really suffering. They were not. They were suffering perhaps with the malaise of love which is always an uneasiness, but an uneasiness how sweet! And the flakes of flames were descending all over the rest of the picture, but they did not fall upon Paolo and Francesca. No, the lovers were protected by a generalized, swooning passion that formed, as it were, a moral and very efficient macintosh all over them. And no doubt what D. G. Rossetti and his school thought was that, although guilty lovers have to go to hell for the sake of the story, they will find hell pleasant enough because the aroma of their passion, the wings of the great god of love and the swooning intensity of it all will render them insensible to the inconveniences of their lodgings. As much as to say that you do not mind the bad cooking of the Brighton hotel if you are having otherwise a good time of it.

But with its glamour, its swooning, its ecstasies and its all-embracing justification the Pre-Raphaelite view of mediæval love was a very different thing from real mediævalism. That was a state of things much more like our own. Mediæval people, took their own individual cases on their own individual merits, and guilty love exacted some kind of retribution very frequently painful, as often as not grotesque. Or sometimes there was not any retribution at all—a successful intrigue "came off" and became material for a joyous *conte*. It was a matter of individual idiosyncrasies then as it is to-day. You got roasted in hell or an injured husband stuck a dagger into you, or you were soundly cudgelled, drenched with water or thrown on to noxious dung-heaps, just as nowadays you get horsewhipped, escape or do not escape the divorce courts and do or do not get requested to resign from your club. There was not then, as there is not now, any protective glamour about it. The things happened, hard, direct and without the chance of ignoring them. Dante's lovers in hell felt bitter cold, stinging flame, shame, horror, despair and possibly even all the eternity of woe that was before them. All the hard, direct, ferocious and unrelenting spirit of the poet went into the picture as into all his other pictures of mediæval after-life. So it was with the Rossetti who dwelt for so long in the same house as Dante Gabriel, writing her poems on the corner of the washhand-stand in her bed-room and making no mark at all in the household, whilst all the other great figures spouted and generalized about love and the musical glasses in every other room of the gloomy and surely glamorous houses that in Bloomsbury the Rossettis successively inhabited. They talked and generalized about life and love and they pursued their romantic images along the lines of least resistance. They got into scrapes or they did not, they squabbled or they made it up, but they always worked out a moral theory good enough to justify themselves and to impress the rest of the world.

And that in essence was the note of the Victorian Great. It did not matter what they did, whether it was George Eliot living in what we should call to-day "open sin"; or Schopenhauer trying to have all noises suppressed by law because they interrupted his cogitations. No matter what their personal eccentricities or peccadilloes might be, they were always along the lines of the higher morality. I am not saying that such figures are not to be found to-day. If you will read the works of Mr. —— you will find the attitude of the Victorian Great Man exactly reproduced. For whatever this gentleman may desire to do in a moment of impulse or of irritation, or in the search for copy or in the quest for health, at once he will write a great big book to prove that this, his eccentricity, ought, according to the higher morals, to be the rule of life for the British middle classes. And there are ten or twenty of such gentlemen now-adays occupied in so directing our lives, and waxing moderately fat upon the profits of their spiritual dictatorships, but they have not anything like the ascendancy of their predecessors. We have not any longer our Ruskins, Carlyles, George Eliots and the rest. We have in consequence very much to work out our special cases for ourselves and we are probably a great deal more honest in consequence. We either do our duties and have very bad times, with good consciences, or we do not do our duties and enjoy ourselves with occasional pauses for unpleasant reflections. But we look, upon the whole, in our little unimportantly individual ways, honestly at our special cases. The influence of Jean Jacques Rousseau, in fact, is on the wane, and the gentleman to-day who left his illegitimate children on the steps of a foundling hospital would think himself rather a dirty dog and try to forget the incident.

And this, as much as her closed bed-room door, separated Christina Rossetti from the other artists and poets and critics and social reformers that frequented her father's house. She was not influenced by Rousseauism at all. She took her life and her love unflinchingly in hand, and how very painfully she proceeded along the straight path of duty !

> " 'Does the road wind up-hill all the way ? '
>   'Yea, to the very end.'
>   'Will the day's journey last the whole long day ? '
>   'From dawn to night, my friend.' "

So writing in her early youth she forecasted her life. The record is an insensate one; still, from the point of view of the man who said that to make a good job of a given task is the highest thing in life, then surely Christina Rossetti achieved the very highest of high things. There is no anchorite who so denied himself and no Simeon upon his pillar. Of course, if we speak about the uselessness of sacrifice. . . .

In the beginning, even from that point of view, the poetess was somewhat badly used. She bestowed her affections and became engaged to a poor specimen of humanity, one of the seven Pre-Raphaelite brethren and like herself a member of the Church of England. Shortly after the engagement this gentleman's spiritual vicissitudes forced him to become a Roman Catholic. Christina put up with the change though it grieved her. She consented to remain engaged to him, for was not her father at least nominally Catholic

and her mother Protestant ?   But no sooner had she
adjusted herself to the changed conditions than her
lover once more reverted to Anglicanism.   I am not
certain how many religions he essayed.   But certainly
there came a point when the poetess, whose religion
was the main point of her life, cried that it was enough.
The breaking-off of her engagement was a very severe
blow and tinged her life and work with melancholy.
Later, she became engaged to a very charming
man of a mild humour, great gifts, a touching absence
of mind and much gentleness of spirit.   This was
Cayley, the translator of Homer and the brother of
the great mathematician.   But Cayley himself offered
one very serious obstacle.   He was an agnostic, and
in spite of Christina's arguments and remonstrances
he remained an agnostic.   She found it therefore to
be her duty not to marry him and they remained
apart to the end of their lives.   And I think that the
correspondence of this essentially good and gentle
man and this nun-like and saintly woman is one of
the most touching products that we have of human
love and abstention.   As love letters theirs are all
the more touching in that no note at all of passion
is sounded.   The lover presents the poetess with the
sea-mouse, a spiny creature like an iridescent slug,
and the poetess writes a poem to her mouse and
chronicles its fate and fortunes; and they write about
the weather and their households and all such
things—little, quaint, humorous and not at all
pathetic letters, such as might have passed between
Abelard and Heloise if those earlier Christians had
been gifted with senses of humour, decency and
renunciation.   So that the figure of Christina

Rossetti remains mediæval or modern, but always nun-like. And, since she suffered nearly always from intense physical pain and much isolation, there was little wonder that her poems were almost altogether introspective—just indeed as all modern poetry is almost altogether introspective. I remember being intensely shocked at reading in the Dictionary of National Biography that Dr. Garnett, himself one of the quaintest, most picturesque and most lovable of the later figures of English literary life—that Dr. Garnett considered Christina Rossetti's poetry to be uniformly morbid. I was so distressed by this discovery that—though I suppose it was no affair of mine—I hurried to the Principal Librarian's book-hidden study in the British Museum and I remonstrated even with some agitation against the epithet that he had selected. Dr. Garnett, however, was exceedingly impenitent. With his amiable and obstinate smile and his odd, caressing gestures of the hand he insisted that the word "morbid" as applied to literature signified that which was written by a person suffering from diseases. I insisted that it meant such writing as was calculated to disease the mind of the reader, but we got no further than the statement of our respective opinions several times repeated. Dr. Garnett, surely the most erudite man as far as books were concerned, in the world of his day was also a gentleman of strong and unshakable opinions, apparently of the Tory and High Church, but at any rate of the official, type. I remember being present at an impressive argument between this scholar and another member of my family. It concerned the retention by Great Britain of Egypt and it ran like this :—

Said Mr. R—— : " My dear Garnett, the retention by Great Britain of the Egyptian Territory is a sin and a shame, and the sooner we evacuate it the sooner our disgrace will come to an end."

Said Dr. Garnett : "My dear R—, but if we evacuated Egypt we should lose the Empire of India."

Said Mr. R—— : " My dear Garnett, the retention by Great Britain of the Egyptian Territory is a sin and a shame, and the sooner we evacuate it the sooner our disgrace will come to an end."

Said Dr. Garnett : " My dear R—, but if we evacuated Egypt we should lose the Empire of India."

Said Mr. R—— : " My dear Garnett, the retention by Great Britain . . ."

So this instructive discussion continued for I cannot say how long. It reminded me of the problem : " What would happen if an irresistible force came against an immovable post ? " The words of both gentlemen were uttered without any raising of the voice or without engendering the least heat. But at last one of my cousins ended the discussion by letting loose in the room a tame owl and the conversation passed into other channels.

V

MUSIC AND MASTERS

WHEN I was a very small boy indeed I was taken to a concert. In those days, as a token of my Pre-Raphaelite origin, I wore very long golden hair, a suit of greenish-yellow corduroy velveteen with gold buttons, and two stockings of which the one was red and the other green. These garments were the curse of my young existence and the joy of every street-boy who saw me. I was taken to this concert by my father's assistant on *The Times* newspaper. Mr. Rudall was the most kindly, the most charming, the most gifted, the most unfortunate—and also the most absent-minded—of men. Thus, when we had arrived in our stalls—and in those days the representative of *The Times* always had the two middle front seats—Mr. Rudall discovered that he had omitted to put on his neck-tie that day. He at once went out to purchase one, and, having become engrossed in the selection, he forgot all about the concert, went away to the Thatched House Club, and passed there the remainder of the evening. I was left, in the middle of the front row, all alone and feeling very tiny and deserted, the sole representative of the august organ that in those days was known as the Thunderer.

Music and Masters

Immediately in front of me, standing in the vacant space before the platform, which was all draped in red, there were three gilt arm-chairs and a gilt table. In the hall there was a great and continuing rustle of excitement. Then, suddenly, this became an enormous sound of applause. It volleyed and rolled round and round the immense space; I had never heard such a sound and I have never again heard such another. Then I perceived that from beneath the shadow of the passage that led into the artistes' room —in the deep shadow—there had appeared a silver head, a dark brown face, hook-nosed, smiling the enigmatic, Jesuit's smile, the long locks falling backwards so that the whole shape of the apparition was that of the Sphynx head. Behind this figure came two others that excited no proportionate attention, but, small as I then was, I recognized in them the late King and the present Queen Mother.

They came closer and closer to me; they stood in front of the three gilt arm-chairs; the deafening applause continued. The old man with the terrible enigmatic face made gestures of modesty. He refused, smiling all the time, to sit in one of the gilt arm-chairs. And suddenly he bowed down upon me. He stretched out his hands; he lifted me out of my seat, he sat down in it himself and left me standing, the very small lonely child with the long golden curls, underneath all those eyes and stupefied by the immense sounds of applause.

The King sent an equerry to entreat the Master to come to his seat; the Master sat firmly planted there smiling obstinately. Then the Queen came and took him by the hand. She pulled him—I don't know how much strength she needed—right out of his seat and—to prevent his returning to it she sat down there. After all it was *my* seat. And then, as if she realized my littleness and my loneliness, she drew me to her and set me on her knee. It was a gracious act.

There is a passage in Pepys's Diary in which he records that he was present at some excavations in Westminster Abbey when they came upon the skull of Jane Seymour, and he kissed the skull on the place where once the lips had been. And in his Diary he records: " It was on such and such a day of such and such a year that I did kiss a Queen," and then, his feelings overcoming him, he repeats: " It was on such and such a day of such and such a year that I did kiss a Queen "—I have forgotten what was the date when I sat in a Queen's lap. But I remember very well that when I came out into Piccadilly the cabmen, with their three-tiered coats, were climbing up the lamp-posts and shouting out: " Three cheers for the Habby Liszt ! " And indeed the magnetic personality of the Abbé Liszt was incredible in its powers of awakening enthusiasm.

A few days later my father took me to call at the house where Liszt was staying—it was at the Lytteltons', I suppose. There were a number of people in the drawing-room and they were all asking Liszt to play. Liszt steadfastly refused. A few days before he had had a slight accident that had hurt one of his hands. Suddenly he turned his eyes upon me, and then, bending down, he said in my ear:

" Little boy, I will play for you, so that you will

be able to tell your children's children that you have heard Liszt play."

And he played the first movement of the *Moonlight Sonata.* I do not remember much of his playing, but I remember very well that I was looking, whilst Liszt played, at a stalwart, florid Englishman who is now an earl. And suddenly I perceived that tears were rolling down his cheeks. And soon all the room was in tears. It struck me as odd that people should cry because Liszt was playing the *Moonlight Sonata.*

Ah! that wonderful personality; there was no end to the enthusiasms it aroused. I had a distant connection—oddly enough an English one—who became by marriage a lady-in-waiting at the Court of Saxe-Weimar. I met her a few years ago, and she struck me as a typically English and unemotional personage. But she had always about her a disagreeable odour that persisted to the day of her death. When they came to lay her out, they discovered that round her neck she wore a sachet, and in that sachet there was the half of a cigar that had been smoked by Liszt. Liszt had lunched with her and her husband thirty years before.

And ah! the records of musical enthusiasms! How dead they are and how mournful is the reading of them! How splendid it is to read how the students of Trinity College, Dublin, took the horses out of Malibran's carriage, and, having amidst torchlight drawn her round and round the city, they upset the carriage in the quadrangle and burnt it to show their joy. They also broke six hundred and eighty windows. The passage in the life of Malibran always reminds me of a touching sentence in Carlyle's Diary :

" To-day on going out I observed that the men at the corner were more than usually drunk. And then I remembered that it was the birthday of their Redeemer."

But what becomes of all the once-glorious ones ? When I was a boy at Malvern my grandfather went about in a bath-chair because he was suffering from a bad attack of gout. Sometimes beside his chair another would be pulled along. It contained a little old lady with a faint and piping voice. That was Jenny Lind.

I wonder how many young persons of twenty-five to-day have even heard the name of Jenny Lind ? And this oblivion has always seemed to me unjust. But perhaps Providence is not so unjust after all. Sometimes, when I am thinking of this subject, I have a vision. I see, golden and far away, an island of the Hesperides—somewhere that side of Heaven. And in this island there is such an opera-house as never was. And in this opera-house music is for ever sounding forth, and all these singers are all singing together—Malibran and Jenny Lind and Scalchi and even Carolina Bauer. And Mario stands in the wings smoking his immense cigar and waiting for his time to go on. And beside him stands Campanini. And every two minutes the conductor stops the orchestra so that twenty bouquets, each as large as a mountain, may be handed over the foot-lights to each of the performers.

The manifestation of the most virtuous triumph that was ever vouchsafed me to witness occurred when I was quite a child. A *prima donna* was calling upon my father. She had been lately touring round America as one of the trainloads of *prime donne* that Colonel Mapleson was accustomed to take about with him. Mme. B—— was a dark and fiery lady, and she related her triumphant story somewhat as follows:

"My best part it is Dinorah—my equal in the 'Shadow Song' there is not. Now what does Colonel Mapleson do but give this part of Dinorah to Mme. C——. Is it not a shame? Is it not a disgrace? She cannot sing, she cannot sing for nuts, and she was announced to appear in *Dinorah* for the whole of the tour. The first time she was to sing it was in Chicago, and I say to myself: ' Ah! only wait, you viper, that has stolen the part for which the good God created me!' Mme. C—— she is a viper! I tell you so! I, Eularia B——! But I say she shall not sing in *Dinorah*. You know the parrots of Mme. C——. Ugly green beasts, they are the whole world for her. If one of them is indisposed she cannot sing—not one note. Now the grace of God comes in. On the very night when she was to sing in *Dinorah* in Chicago, I passed the open door of her room in the hotel; and God sent at the same moment a waiter who was carrying a platter of ham upon which were many sprigs of parsley. So by the intercession of the blessed saints it comes into my head that parsley is death to parrots. I seize the platter from the waiter"—and Mme. B——'s voice and manner became those of an august and avenging deity—"I seize the platter, I tear from it the parsley, I rush into the room of Mme. C——. By the grace of God Mme. C—— is absent, and I throw the parsley to the ugly green fowls. They devour it with voracity, and they die; they all die. Mme. C— has fits for a fortnight, and I—I sing *Dinorah*. I sing it like a miracle; I sing it like an angel, and Mme. C——- has never the face to put her nose on the stage in that part again. Never!"

This was perhaps the mildest of the stories of the epic jealousies of musicians with which my father's house re-echoed, but it is the one which remains most vividly in my mind, I suppose because of the poor parrots.

It was the dread of these acridities that eventually drove from my mind all hope of a career as a composer. There was something so harsh in some of the manifestations that met me, I being at the time an innocent and gentle boy, that I am filled with wonder when I consider that any composer ever has the strength of mind to continue in his avocation or that any executant ever struggles through as far as the concert platform. At the last public school which I attended—for my attendances at schools were varied and singular, according as my father ruined himself with starting new periodicals or happened to be flush of money on account of new legacies—at my last public school I was permitted to withdraw myself every afternoon to go to concerts. This brought down upon me the jeers of one particular German master who kept order in the afternoons, and upon one occasion he set for translation the sentence:

" Whilst I was idling away my time at a concert,

the rest of my classmates were diligently engaged in study of the German language."

Proceeding mechanically with the translation—for I paid no particular attention to Mr. P——, because my father, in his reasonable tones, had always taught me that schoolmasters were men of inferior intelligence to whom personally we should pay little attention, though the rules for which they stood must be exactly observed—I had got as far as *Indem ich faulenzte* . . . when it suddenly occurred to me that Mr. P—— in setting this sentence to the class was aiming a direct insult not only at myself, but at Beethoven, Bach, Mozart, Wagner and Robert Franz. An extraordinary and now inexplicable fury overcame me. At all my schools I was always the good boy of my respective classes, but on this occasion I rose in my seat propelled by an irresistible force, and I addressed Mr. P—— with words the most insulting and the most contemptuous. I pointed out that music was the most divine of all arts, that German was a language fit only for horses; that German literature contained nothing that any sensible person could want to read except the works of Schopenhauer, who was an anglomaniac, and in any case was much better read in an English translation; I pointed out that Victor Hugo has said that to utter the lowest type of inanities, " il faut être stupide comme un maître d'école qui n'est bon à rien que pour planter des choux." I can still feel the extraordinary indignation that filled me, though I have to make an effort of the imagination to understand why I was so excited; I can still feel the way the breath

poured through my distended nostrils. With, I
suppose, some idea of respect for discipline I had
carefully spoken in German which none of my classmates understood. My harangue was suddenly
ended by Mr. P——'s throwing his large inkpot at
me ; it struck me upon the shoulder and ruined my
second-best coat and waistcoat.

I thought really no more of the incident. Mr.
P—— was an excellent man, with a red face, a
bald head, golden side-whiskers and an apoplectic
build of body. Endowed by nature with a temper
more than volcanic it was not unusual for him to
throw an inkpot at a boy who made an exasperating
mistranslation, but he had never before hit anybody;
so that meeting him afterwards in the corridors I
apologized profusely to him. He apologized almost
more profusely to me, and we walked home together,
our routes from school being exactly similar. I had
the greatest difficulty in preventing his buying me a
new suit of clothes, whilst with a gentle reproachful-
ness he reproved me for having uttered blasphemies
against the language of Goethe, Schiller, Lessing
and Jean Paul Richter. It was then towards
the end of the term, and shortly afterwards the
headmaster sent for me and informed me that I
had better not return to the school. He said—and
it was certainly the case—that it was one of the
founder's rules that no boy engaged in business
could be permitted to remain. This rule was intended
to guard against gambling and petty huckstering
amongst the boys. But Mr. K——said that he understood I had lately published a book and had received
for it not only publicity but payment, the payment

being against the rules of the school and the publicity calculated to detract from a strict spirit of discipline. Mr. K——was exceedingly nice and sympathetic, and he remarked that in his day my uncle Oliver Madox Brown had had the reputation of being the laziest boy at that establishment, whilst I had amply carried on that splendid tradition.

That was the last of my school-days, but nearly fifteen years later I met in the Strand a man who was an officer in the Burmese Civil Service. At school he had been my particular chum. And he told me that he had been so shocked by Mr. P——'s throwing the inkpot at me that, without telling anybody about it, he had gone straight to the headmaster and had reported the whole matter. The headmaster had taken Mr. P—— to task to such effect that the poor man resigned from the school and shortly afterwards died in Alsace-Lorraine. Apparently the offence of my having written a book was only a pretext for getting rid of me from the school. Mr. P——, it appears, had reported that my powers of invective were so considerable that I must gravely menace the authority of any master. And yet, from that day to this and never before, can I remember having addressed a cutting speech to any living soul except once to a German waiter in the refreshment-room of Frankfort Hauptbahnhof.

Thus music or the enthusiasm for music put an end to my lay education in these islands, and I entered upon a course more distinctly musical. Having received instruction from more or less sound musicians, and a certain amount of encouragement from musicians more or less eminent, I attempted the

entrance examination of one of the British royal
institutions for education in music. I acquitted
myself reasonably well or even exceedingly well
as far as the theory of music was concerned, but
this institution has, or perhaps it was only that
it had, a rule that seemed to me inscrutable in its
stupidity. Every pupil must take what is called
a second study—the study of some instrument or
other. I had a nodding acquaintance with practically
every instrument of the orchestra except the drums,
which I could never begin to tackle. The principal
of the institution in question set it down to my dismay that my second study must be the piano. Now
I could not play the piano; I dislike the piano, which
seems to me to be the most soulless of the instruments,
and, in any case, to acquire mastery of the piano, or
indeed of any other instrument, requires many hours
of practising a day which would interfere, as it seemed
to me, rather seriously with the deep study that I
hoped to make of the theory of music. I accordingly
asked to be allowed to interview the principal—an
awful being who kept himself splendidly remote.
Having succeeded with a great deal of difficulty
in penetrating into his room, I discovered a silent
gentleman who listened to my remarks without any
appearance of paying attention to them. But when
I had finished and was waiting in nervous silence,
he suddenly overwhelmed me with a torrent of
excited language. What it amounted to was that,
during his lifetime my father had domineered over
that institution and that, if I thought I was going to
keep up the tradition I was exceedingly mistaken.
On the contrary, the professors were determined

80

to give me a hot time of it, or—as Sir C— D—
put it—to treat me with the utmost rigour of the
rules.

This gave me food for several days of reflection.
I had to consider that Sir C— D— was in private
life an unemotional English gentleman—frigid and
rather meticulous in the matter of good form.
Musical emotion had worked such a person up to
a pitch of passion as egregious as was manifested
in all his features; musical passion had worked
me up to such a pitch of emotion as to let me
insult in the most outrageous manner a harmless
person like Mr. P——, whom I really liked. There
must then be something so unbalancing in a
musical career as to leave me very little opening, I
being, at any rate in my own conception, a person
singularly shy and wanting in the faculty which is
called "push." I had to remember, too, that my
best friends—the young men and women with
whom personally I got on in the extreme of geniality
—became invariably frigid and monosyllabic as soon
as I mentioned my musical ambitions. There was
about these people on such occasions an air of reserve, an air almost of deafness; whereas when they
spoke of their own ambitions they became animated,
gay, enthusiastic. This might be evidence that all
musicians were hopelessly self-centred, or it might
be evidence that my music was no good at all. I
dare say both were true. Whether it were both or
either it seemed to me that here was no career for
a person craving the sympathy of enthusiasm and
the contagious encouragement of applause. Possibly
had I lived in Germany it would have been different,

for in Germany there is musical life, a musical atmosphere. In the German establishments for musical education there is none of this deafness, there is none of this reserve, there is none of this self-centred abstraction. There is a busy, there is a contagious life, and student keeps watch on student with an extreme anxiety which may be evidence of no more than a determination to know what the other fellow is doing and to go one better.

In England, at any rate in the musical world, as in the world of all the other arts, a general change seems gradually to have come over the atmosphere in the last quarter of a century. Jealousies amongst executants, amongst composers, have diminished; and along with them have diminished the enthusiasm and the partisanships of the public. In the 'fifties and 'sixties there was an extraordinary outcry against the Pre-Raphaelite movement, in the 'seventies and 'eighties there was an outcry almost more extraordinary against what was called the Music of the Future. As I have said elsewhere, Charles Dickens attempted to get the authorities to imprison the Pre-Raphaelite painters because he considered that their works were blasphemous. And he was backed by a whole, great body of public opinion. In the 'seventies and 'eighties there were cries for the imprisonment alike of the critics who upheld and the artistes who performed the Music of the Future. The compositions of Wagner were denounced as being atheistic, sexually immoral, and tending to further socialism and the throwing of bombs. Wagnerites were threatened with assassination, and assaults between critics of the rival schools were things not

"AT THE HOUSE OF THE FEROCIOUS CRITIC OF THE CHIEF
NEWSPAPER OF ENGLAND"
(Mrs. Francis Hueffer, from pastel by Madox Brown.

unknown in the foyer of the opera. I really believe that my father, as the chief exponent of Wagner in these islands, did go in some personal danger. Extraordinary pressures were brought to bear upon the more prominent critics of the day, the pressure coming, as a rule, from the exponents of the school of Italian opera. Thus, at the openings of the opera seasons packing-cases of large dimensions and considerable in number would arrive at the house of the ferocious critic of the chief newspaper of England. They would contain singular assortments of comestibles and of objects of art. Thus I remember half-a-dozen hams, the special product of some north Italian town, six cases of Rhine wine, which were no doubt intended to propitiate the malignant Teuton; a reproduction of the Medici Venus in marble, painted with phosphoric paint so that it gleamed blue and ghostly in the twilight; a case of Bohemian glass and several strings of Italian sausages. And these packing cases, containing no outward sign of their senders, would have to be unpacked and then once more repacked, leaving the servants with fingers damaged by nails and passages littered with straw. Inside would be found the cards of Italian *prime donne*, tenors or basses, newly arrived in London, and sending servile homage to the illustrious critic of the " Giornale Times." On one occasion a letter containing bank-notes for £50 arrived from a *prima donna* with a pathetic note begging the critic to absent himself from her first night. Praise from a Wagnerite she considered to be impossible, but she was ready to pay for silence. I do not know whether this letter inspired my father with the idea of writing to the next suppliant that he was ready to accept her present—it was the case of Bohemian glass—but that in that case he would never write a word about her singing. He meant the letter, of course, as a somewhat clumsy joke, but the lady—she was not, however, an Italian—possessing a sense of humour, at once accepted the offer. This put my father rather in a quandary, for Mme. H——was one of the greatest exponents of emotional tragic music that there had ever been, and the occasion on which she was to appear was the first performance in England of one of the great operas of the world. I do not exactly know whether my father went through any conscientious troubles—I presume he did, for he was a man of a singular moral niceness. At any rate he wrote an enthusiastic notice of the opera and an enthusiastic and deserved notice of the impersona- trix of Carmen. And since the Bohemian glass— or the poor remains of the breakages of a quarter of a century—still decorate my sideboard, I presume that he accepted the present. I do not really see what else he could have done.

Pressure of other sorts was also not unknown. Thus, there was an opera produced by a foreign baron who was a distinguished figure in the diplo- matic service, and who was very well looked on at Court. In the middle of the performance my father received a command to go into the royal box, where a royal personage informed him that in his august opinion the work was one of genius. My father replied that he was sorry to differ from so distinguished a connoisseur—but that in his opinion the music was absolute rubbish—*Lauter Klatsch.*

The reply was undiplomatic and upon the whole regrettable, but my father had been irritated by the fact that a good deal of Court pressure had already been brought to bear upon him. I believe that there were diplomatic reasons for desiring to flatter the composer of the opera, who was attached to a foreign embassy—the embassy of the nation with whom for the moment the diplomatic relations of Great Britain were somewhat strained. So that without doubt His Royal Highness was as patriotically in the right as my father was in a musical sense. Eventually, the notice of the opera was written by another hand. The performance of this particular opera remains in my mind because during one of its scenes, which represented the frozen circle of Hell, the cotton wool, which figured as snow on the stage, caught fire and began to burn. An incipient panic took place among the audience, but the orchestra, under a firm composer whose name I have unfortunately forgotten, continued to play, and the flames were extinguished by one of the singers using his cloak. But I still remember being in the back of the box and seeing in the foreground, silhouetted against the lights of the stage, the figures of my father and of some one else—I think it was William Rossetti —standing up and shouting down into the stalls : " Sit down, brutes !   Sit down, cowards ! "

On the other hand, it is not to be imagined that acts of kindness and good-fellowship were rare under this seething mass of passions and of jealousies. Thus at one of the Three Choir Festivals, my father, having had the misfortune to sprain his ankle, was unable to be present in the cathedral.   His notice was written for him by the critic of the paper which was most violently opposed to views at all Wagnerian—a gentleman whom till that moment my father regarded as his bitterest personal enemy. This critic happened to be staying in the same hotel, and having heard of the accident volunteered to write the notice out of sheer good feeling. This gentleman, an extreme *bon vivant* and a man of an excellent and versatile talent, has since told me that he gave himself particular trouble to imitate my father's slightly cumbrous Germanic English and his extreme modernist views. This service was afterwards repaid by my father in the following circumstances. It was again one of the Three Choir Festivals—at Worcester, I think, and we were stopping at Malvern—my father and Mr. S—— going in every day to the cathedral city. Mr. S—— was either staying with us or in an adjoining house, and on one Wednesday evening, his appetite being sharpened by an unduly protracted performance of "The Messiah," Mr. S——partook so freely of the pleasures of the table that he omitted altogether to write his notice. This fact he remembered just before the closing of the small local telegraph office, and although Mr. S——was by no means in a condition to write his notice, he was yet sufficiently mellow with wine to be lachrymose and overwhelmed at the idea of losing his post. We rushed off at once to the telegraph office and did what we could to induce the officials to keep the wires open whilst the notice was being written. But all inducements failed. My father hit upon a stratagem at the last moment. At that date it was a rule of the Post

Office that if the beginning of a long message were
handed in before eight o'clock the office must be
kept open until its conclusion as long as there was
no break in the handing in of slips. My father
therefore commanded me to telegraph anything
that I liked to the newspaper office as long as
I kept it up whilst he was writing the notice of
" The Messiah." And the only thing that came
into my head at the moment was the Church Service.
The newspaper was therefore astonished to receive
a long telegram beginning : *When the wicked man
turneth away from the sin that he has committed*
and continuing through the *Te Deum* and the *Nunc
Dimittis*, till suddenly it arrived at " The Three Choirs
Festival. Worcester, Wednesday, July 27th, 1887."

Nowadays the acts of kindliness no doubt remain
a feature of the musical world, but I think the
enthusiasms as well as the ferocities have diminished
altogether. Composers like Strauss and Debussy
steal upon us as it were in the night. Both
Strauss and Debussy must be nearly as incom-
prehensible to good Wagnerites as were the works
of Wagner to enthusiastic followers of Rossini and
the early Verdi. Yet there are no outcries; there
is no clamouring for the instant imprisonment of
Strauss or the critic of the ——. Nor is this want
of enthusiasm limited to England. A little time
ago I was present at the first performance in Paris
of Strauss's *Also sprach Zarathustra*. The hall
was filled with " All Paris "—all Paris polite, indifferent, *blagueur*, anxious to be present at anything
that was new, foreign and exotic. There was a
respectable amount of applause, there was some

yawning decently concealed. In the middle of it
the old gentleman who had taken me to the performance got up suddenly and made for the door.
He had, as I heard, some altercation with the atten-
dants, for there was a rule that the doors could not
be opened whilst the music played. I followed him
to the door and found my friend—the late General
du T——, one of the veterans of the war of 1870—
explaining to the attendant that he felt himself
gravely indisposed and that he must positively be
allowed to go away. We were at last permitted to
go out. Outside, the general said that Strauss's
music really had made him positively ill. And it
had made him still more ill to have it received with
applause. He wanted to know what had happened
to France—what had happened to Paris, to that
Paris which in the 'seventies had resisted by force
of arms the production of *Tannhäuser* at the
Opéra. The music appeared to him horrible, un-
bearable, and yet no one had protested.

I could not help asking him why he had been
present at all, and he said with an air of fine reason :

" Well, we move in modern times. I still think
it was wrong to produce Wagner at the Opera so
soon after the war. It was unpatriotic, it was to
take revenge in the wrong direction. But I have had
time enough, my friend, to become reconciled to
the music of Wagner as music. And I thought to
myself, 'Now here is a new German composer; I will
not again make the mistake of violently abusing
his music, before I have heard a note of it.' For the
music of Wagner I abused violently before I had
heard a note of it."

Music and Masters

The general went on to say that this new music was worse than nonsense, it was an outrage. The high discordant notes gripped the entrails and gave one colic.

"Nevertheless," he said, "you will see that no critic says a word against this music. They are all afraid. They all fear to make themselves appear as foolish as did the critics who opposed the school of Wagner."

And upon the whole, I am inclined to think that the general was right. The other day I attended a concert consisting mainly of the Song Cycles of Debussy, setting the words of Verlaine. They were sung by an Armenian lady who had escaped from a Turkish harem and had had no musical training. She was a barbaric creature who uttered loud howls, and the effect was to me disagreeable in the extreme; all the same, the audience was large and enthusiastic and the most enlightened organ of musical opinion of to-day spoke of the performance with a chastened enthusiasm. I happened to meet the writer of the notice in the course of the following afternoon, and I asked him what he really got for himself out of that singular collocation of sounds. He said airily : " Well, you see, one gets emotions ! "

I said : " Good God ! what sort of emotions ? "

He answered : " Well, you see, if one shuts one's eyes one can imagine that one is eating strawberry jam and oysters in a house of ill-fame, and a cat is rushing violently up and down the keyboard of the piano with a cracker tied to its tail."

I said : " Then why in the world didn't you say so in your notice ? "

He smiled blandly :

" Well, you see, an ignorant public might take such a description for abuse, and we cannot afford to abuse anything now."

I said : " You mean that you're still frightened of Wagner ? "

" Oh, we're all most frightened of Wagner," he answered, " and it's not only that. The business managers of our newspapers won't let us abuse anything, or the papers would never get any more concert advertisements."

I fancy that this last statement was in the way of pulling my leg, for as a matter of fact there is only one newspaper in London that has any concert advertisements worth speaking of, and this was not the paper that my friend represented. The remark would, however, have been true enough of the reviewers of books, for owing to the dread of losing publishers' advertisements there is practically no paper—or there is practically only one paper in London that will insert an unfriendly review. Personally, being a writer of exclusive tastes or of a jealous temperament, I am never permitted to review a book at all. Going, however, the other day into the house of a friend who reviews books for one of our leading organs, I perceived upon a table the book of a much-boomed author who appeared to me to be exceedingly nauseous. I said :

" Do, for goodness' sake, let me save you the trouble of noticing that work."

And it was placed in my hand. I wrote a column of fairly moderate criticism ; I extinguished the book, I murdered the author with little stilettoes. The notice was never printed, though my friend the reviewer duly received her cheque for one column —£1 17s. 6d., which I presume was the price of silence.

And there in a nutshell the whole matter is. The ferocity of the critics for one reason or another has come to an end. The eccentricities of the artists are curbed, the enthusiasms of the public are dead. I do not know where we should have to go nowadays to find the cosy musical enthusiasms that subsisted into the 'eighties and 'nineties. Where now shall we find the performers of the old Monday "Pops"? Where now shall we find the old, little family party that the audience was? We used to pay a shilling and we used to go in through passages that resembled rats' holes, in the back of the old St. James's Hall. We used to sit in the semicircle of hard wooden seats that held the orchestra on symphony days. But these were quartette concerts. There was Joachim, with the leonine, earnest head; there was Piatti with a grey, grizzled, shaggy hair and beard, so that his features seemed exactly to reproduce the lines of the head of his violoncello; there was Ries with broad, honest, blonde Teutonic features; there was Strauss with the head of a little bald, old mole with golden spectacles and a myopic air. Joachim would take a glance round the hall, having his violin resting already upon a handkerchief upon his chest beneath his chin. He would make a little flourish with his bow like the conductor at an orchestra, the other three sitting silent, intent, caught up away from the world. Joachim would lay his bow upon the strings; the sounds of the opening notes of the quartette would steal into the air and, engrossed all round the orchestra, we would follow the music in the little miniature scores with the tiny notes—first subject, second subject, working out, free phantasia, recapitulation. We should be almost as intent as the performers, and we should know each other—all of the audience—almost as well. You could not doubt the excellence of the music or the fellowship; there would never be a wrong note, just as there would never be a moment's lapse in our attention.

When these concerts were over it was sometimes my privilege to walk home along with Joachim and to carry his almost too precious violin. Almost too precious, since it made the privilege so very nervous an honour. And I remember that on one occasion somewhere in a by-street we came upon an old blind fiddler playing a violin whose body was formed of a corned-meat tin. Joachim stood for some minutes regarding the old man, then suddenly he took the violin into his own hands and, having dusted it, asked me to produce his own bow from his own case. He stood for some little time playing a passage from the Trillo del Diabolo of Tartini, looking as intent, as earnest and as abstracted there in the empty street as he was accustomed to do upon the public platform. After a time he restored the instrument to the old fiddler along with a shilling and we pursued our way. Any executant of a personality more florid would have conducted the old blind fiddler into a main road, would have passed round the hat himself, would have crumpled into it several bank notes, and would without doubt have had the affair reported in the newspapers. I saw indeed only yesterday such a feat reported of a celebrated advertising 'cellist. Joachim, however, merely wanted to know how an instrument with a metal belly would sound if it were properly played, and having the information, since it seemed to him to be worth one shilling, he paid a shilling for it. I do not know where we could go nowadays to recapture that spirit of earnestness. On the other hand, I do not know where I should go to find a *prima donna* who would boast of having administered parsley to another's parrot. And of one thing I am fairly confident—if practically none of us any more get very excited about rival schools of music, very few of us at social functions talk quite so loudly as used to be the case in the days of Cimabue Brown, and the *Punch* of Mr. du Maurier. We talk, of course, and we talk all the time, but we talk in much lower voices. We find that music agreeably accompanies conversation as long as we do not try to outshout the instruments. We find indeed that music is so stimulating to our ideas that, whereas small talk may come exceedingly difficult to us at any other time, there is nothing that so makes irresistibly interesting topics bubble up in the mind as a pianissimo movement in the strings. Waiting impatiently, therefore, for a passage in louder tones we commence avidly our furtive and whispered conversation which continues till the last note of the selection. And this last note leaves us conveniently high and dry with a feeling of nakedness and of abashment. Thus indeed music has come into its own. If it be less of an art it has a greater utility. It has helped the Englishman to talk. A few years ago one might drearily have imagined that that was impossible.

The other day I was at a wedding reception—there was a very large crowd. In one corner an excellent quintette discussed selections from the *Contes d'Hofmann*. We were all talking twenty to the dozen. My *vis-à-vis* was telling me something that did not interest me, when the voice of a man behind me said : " So they left him there in prison with a broken bottle of poison in his pocket. ' And then the music stopped suddenly and I never heard who the man was, or what he had done to get into prison, or why he had broken the bottle of poison.

VI

PRE-RAPHAELITES AND PRISONS

WHEN I was a little boy, there still attached
something of the priestly to all the functionaries
of the Fine Arts or the humaner Letters. To be a
poet like Mr. Swinburne, or like Mr. Rossetti, or
even like Mr. Arthur O'Shaughnessy, had about it
something tremendous, something rather awful. If
Mr. Swinburne was in the house we children knew
of it up in the nursery. A hush communicated
itself to the entire establishment. The scullery-
maid, whose name, I remember, was Nelly; the
cook, whose name was Sophy; the housemaid, who
was probably Louie or it may have been Lizzie;
and the nurse, who was certainly Mrs. Atter-
bury—she had seen more murders and more gory
occurrences than any person I have ever since met;
even the tremendous governess who was known as
Miss Hall, though that was not her name—and who
had attached to her some strange romance such as
that she was wooed too persistently by a foreign
count with a name like Pozzo di Borgo, though
that was not the name,--we all of us, all the inhabitants of the back nooks and crannies of a large stucco
house fell to talking in whispers. I used to be
perfectly convinced that the ceiling would fall in if

I raised my voice in the very slightest. This excitement, this agitation, these tremulous undertones would become exaggerated if the visitor was the editor of the *Times*, Richard Wagner or Robert Franz, a composer whom we were all taught especially to honour, even Richard Wagner considering him the greatest song-writer in the world. And indeed he was the mildest and sweetest of creatures, with a face like that of an etherealized German pastor, and smelling more than any other man I ever knew of cigars. Certain other poets—though it was more marked in the case of poetesses—made their arrival known to the kitchen, the back, and the upper parts of the house by the most tremendous thunders. The thunders would reverberate, die away, roll out once more and once more die away for periods that seemed very long to the childish mind. And these reverberations would be caused, not by Apollo, the god of song, nor by any of the Nine Muses, nor yet by the clouds that surrounded, as I was then convinced, the poetic brow. They were caused by dissatisfied cabmen.

And this was very symptomatic of the day. The poet—and still more the poetess—of the 'seventies and 'eighties, though an awful, was a frail creature who had to be carried about from place to place, and generally in a four-wheeled cab. Indeed, if my recollection of these poetesses in my very earliest days was accompanied always by thunders and expostulations, my images of them in slightly later years, when I was not so strictly confined to the nursery—my images of them were always those of somewhat elderly ladies, forbidding in aspect, with

grey hair, hooked noses, flashing eyes and continued trances of indignation against reviewers.
They emerged ungracefully—for no one ever yet
managed to emerge gracefully from the door of a
four-wheeler—sometimes backwards from one of
those creaking and dismal tabernacles and pulling
behind them odd-shaped parcels. Holding the door
open, with his whip in one hand would stand the
cabman. He wore an infinite number of little
capes on his overcoat; a grey worsted muffler would
be coiled many times round his throat and the lower
part of his face, and his top hat would be of some
unglossy material that I have never been able to
identify. After a short interval his hand would
become extended, the flat palm displaying such coins
as the poetess had laid in it. And, when the poetess
with her odd bundles was three-quarters of the way
up the doorsteps, the cabman, a man of the slowest
and most deliberate, would be pulling the muffler
down from about his mouth and exclaiming:

" Wot's this ? "

The poetess without answering, but with looks of
enormous disdain, would scuffle into the house and
the front door would close. Then upon the knocker
the cabman would commence his thunderous
symphony.

Somewhat later more four-wheelers would arrive
with more poetesses. Then still more four-wheelers
with elderly poets; untidy-looking young gentlemen
with long hair and wide-awake hats, in attitudes of
dejection and fatigue would ascend the steps; a
hansom or two would drive up containing rather
smarter, stout elderly gentlemen wearing, as a rule,

black coats with velvet collars and most usually
black gloves. These were reviewers, editors of the
Athenæum and of other journals. Then there
would come quite smart gentlemen with an air of
prosperity in their clothes, and with deference
somewhat resembling that of undertakers in their
manners. These would be publishers.

You are to understand that what was about to
proceed was the reading to this select gathering of
the latest volume of poems by Mrs. Clara Fletcher—
that is not the name—the authoress of what was
said to be a finer sequence of sonnets than those
of Shakespeare. And before a large semicircle of
chairs occupied by the audience that I have described,
and, with Mr. Clara Fletcher standing obsequiously
behind her to hand her, from the odd-shaped
bundles of manuscripts, the pages that she required,
Mrs. Clara Fletcher, with her regal head regally
poised, having quelled the assembly with a single
glance, would commence to read.

Mournfully then, up and down the stone staircases
there would flow two hollow sounds. For in those
days it was the habit of all poets and poetesses to
read aloud upon every possible occasion, and whenever they read aloud to employ an imitation of the
voice invented by the late Lord Tennyson, and known
in those days as the *ore rotundo*—" with the round
mouth mouthing out their hollow o's and a's."

The effect of this voice heard from outside a door
was to a young child particularly awful. It went
on and on, suggesting the muffled baying of a large
hound that is permanently dissatisfied with the
world. And this awful rhythm would be broken

in upon from time to time by the thunders of the cabman. How the housemaid—the housemaid was certainly Charlotte Kirby—dealt with this man of wrath I never could rightly discover. Apparently the cabman would thunder upon the door; Charlotte, keeping it on the chain, would open it for about a foot. The cabman would exclaim, " Wot's this ? " and Charlotte would shut the door in his face. The cabman would remain inactive for four minutes in order to recover his breath. Then once more his stiff arm would approach the knocker and again the thunders would resound. The cabman would exclaim : " A bob and a tanner from the Elephant and Castle to Tottenham Court Road ! " and Charlotte would again close the door in his face. This would continue for perhaps half-an-hour. Then the cabman would drive away to meditate. Later he would return and the same scenes would be gone through. He would retire once more for more meditation and return in the company of a policeman. Then Charlotte would open the front door wide and by doing no more than ejaculate " My good man ! " she would appear to sweep out of existence policeman, cab, cabhorse, cabman and whip. A settled peace would descend upon the house, lulled into silence by the reverberation of the hollow o's and a's. In about five minutes' time the policeman would return and converse amiably with Charlotte for three-quarters of an hour, through the area railings. I suppose that was really why cabmen were always worsted and poetesses protected from these importunities in the dwelling over whose destinies Charlotte presided for forty years.

The function that was proceeding behind the closed doors would now seem incredible. For the poetess would read on from two to three and a half hours. At the end of this time—such was the fortitude of the artistic when Victoria was still the Widow at Windsor—an enormous high babble of applause would go up. The forty or fifty poetesses, young poets, old poets, painter poets, reviewers, editors of *Athenæums* and the like would divide themselves into solid bodies, each body of ten or twelve surrounding one of the three or four publishers, and forcing this unfortunate man to bid against his unfortunate rivals for the privilege of publishing this immortal masterpiece. My grandfather would run from body to body, ejaculating "Marvellous genius!" "First woman poet of the age!" "Lord Tennyson himself said he was damned if he wasn't envious of the sonnet to Mehemet Ali!"

Mr. Clara Fletcher would be trotting about on tiptoe fetching for the lady from whom he took his name—now exhausted and recumbent in a deep arm-chair—smelling bottles, sponges full of aromatic vinegar to press upon her brow, glasses of sherry, thin biscuits, and raw eggs in tumblers. As a boy, I used to think vaguely that these comestibles were really nectar and ambrosia.

In the early days I was only once permitted to be present at these august ceremonies. I say I was permitted to be present, but actually I was caught and forced very much against my will to attend the rendition by my aunt, Lucy Rossetti, who, with persistence that to me at the time appeared fiendish, insisted upon attempting to turn me into a genius

100

too. Alas, hearing Mr. Arthur O'Shaughnessy read
Music and Moonlight did not turn poor little me into
a genius. It sent me to sleep, and I was carried
from the room by Charlotte, disgraced, and destined
from that time forward only to hear those hollow
sounds from the other side of the door. Afterwards
I should see the publishers, one proudly descending
the stairs, putting his cheque-book back into his
overcoat pocket, and the others trying vainly to
keep their heads erect under the glances of scorn
that the rest of the departing company poured upon
them. And Mr. Clara Fletcher would be carefully
folding the cheque into his waistcoat pocket whilst
his wife from a large reticule produced one more
eighteenpence wrapped up in tissue paper.

This would to-day seem funny—the figure of Mrs.
Clara Fletcher would be grotesque, if it were not for
the fact that, to a writer, the change that has taken
place is so exceedingly tragic. For who nowadays
would think of reading poetry aloud, or what publisher would come to listen ? As for a cheque . . . !
Yet this glorious scene that I have described, these
eyes of mine once beheld.

And then there was that terrible word "genius."
I think my grandfather with his romantic mind first
obtruded it on my infant notice. But I am quite
certain that it was my aunt, Mrs. William Rossetti,
who filled me with a horror of its sound that persists
to this day. In school-time the children of my
family were separated from their cousins, but in the
holidays, which we spent as a rule during our young
years in lodging-houses side by side, in places like
Bournemouth or Hythe, we were delivered over to

the full educational fury of our aunt. For this, no
doubt, my benevolent but misguided father was
responsible. He had no respect for schoolmasters,
but he had the greatest possible respect for his
sister-in-law. In consequence our mornings would
be taken up in listening to readings from the poets
or in improving our knowledge of foreign tongues.
My cousins, the Rossettis, were horrible monsters of
precocity. Let me set down here with what malig-
nity I viewed their proficiency in Latin and Greek at
ages incredibly small. Thus, I believe, my cousin
Olive wrote a Greek play at the age of something like
five. And, they were perpetually being held up to
us—or perhaps to myself alone, for my brother was
always very much the sharper of the two—as marvels
of genius whom I ought to thank God for merely
having the opportunity to emulate. For my cousin
Olive's infernal Greek play which had to do with
Theseus and the Minotaur, draped in robes of the
most flimsy butter muslin, I was drilled, a lanky boy
of twelve or so, to wander round and round the back
drawing-room of Endsleigh Gardens, imbecilely flap-
ping my naked arms before an audience singularly
distinguished who were seated in the front room.
The scenery which had been designed and painted
by my aunt was, I believe, extremely beautiful; and
the chinoiseries, the fine furniture and the fine
pictures were such that had I had been allowed to
sit peaceably amongst the audience, I might really
have enjoyed the piece. But it was my unhappy
fate to wander round in the garb of a captive before
an audience that consisted of Pre-Raphaelite poets,
ambassadors of foreign powers, editors, poets

laureate, and Heaven knows what. Such formidable beings at least did they appear to my childish imagination. From time to time the rather high voice of my father would exclaim from the gloomy depths of the auditorium, " Speak up, Fordie ! " Alas, my aptitude for that sort of sport being limited, the only words that were allotted to me were the Greek lamentation, " Theu ! Theu ! Theu ! " and in the meanwhile my cousin Arthur Rossetti, who appeared only to come up to my knee, was the hero Theseus, strode about with a large sword, slew dragons and addressed perorations in the Tennysonian " o " and " a " style, to the candle-lit heavens, with their distant view of Athens. Thank God, having been an adventurous youth whose sole idea of true joy was to emulate the doings of the hero of a work called *Peck's Bad Boy and His Pa*, or at least to attain to the lesser glories of Dick Harkaway, who had a repeating rifle and a tame black jaguar and who bathed in gore almost nightly—thank God, I say, that we succeeded in leading our unsuspecting cousins into dangerous situations from which they only emerged by breaking limbs. I seem to remember the young Rossettis as perpetually going about with fractured bones. I distinctly remember the fact that I bagged my cousin Arthur with one collarbone, broken on a boat slide in my company, whilst my younger sister brought down her cousin Mary with a broken elbow fractured in a stone hall. Olive Rossetti, I also remember with gratification, cut her head open at a party given by Miss Mary Robinson because she wanted to follow me down some dangerous steps and fell on to a flower-pot.

Thus, if we were immolated in butter-muslin fetters and in Greek plays, we kept our own end up a little and we never got hurt.   Why, I remember pushing my brother out of a second-floor window so that he fell into the area, and he didn't have even a bruise to show ; whilst my cousins in the full glory of their genius were never really all of them together quite out of the bone-setter's hands.

My aunt gave us our bad hours with her excellent lessons, but I think we gave her hers so let the score be called balanced. Why, I remember pouring a pot of ink from the first-story banisters on to the head of Ariadne Petrici when she was arrayed in the robes of her namesake whose part she supported.   For let it not be imagined that my aunt Rossetti foisted my cousin Arthur into the position of hero of the play through any kind of maternal jealousy.   Not at all.   She was just as anxious to turn me into a genius or to turn *anybody* into a genius.   It was only that she had such much better material in her own children.

Ah, that searching for genius, that reading aloud of poems, that splendid keeping alive of the tradition that a poet was a seer and a priest by the sheer virtue of his craft and mystery ! Nowadays, alas, for a writer to meet with any consideration at all in the world, he or she must be at least a social reformer. That began, for the æsthetic set at least, with William Morris.   He first turned all poets and poetesses into long-necked creatures with red ties, or into round-shouldered maidens dressed in blue curtain serge.   For indeed when æstheticism merged itself in social propaganda, the last poor little fortress

of the arts in England was divested of its gallant garrison. It might be comic that my aunt Lucy should turn her residence into a sort of hot-house and forcing school for geniuses; it might be comic that my grandfather should proclaim that Mrs. Clara Fletcher's sonnets were finer than those of Shakespeare; it might be comic even that all the Pre-Raphaelite poets should back each other up, and all the Pre-Raphaelite painters spend hours every day in jobbing each other's masterpieces into municipal galleries. But behind it, there was a feeling that the profession of the arts or the humaner letters was a priestcraft and of itself consecrated its earnest votary. Nowadays . . .

Last week upon three memorable days I had for me three memorable conversations. On the Saturday I was sitting in Kensington Gardens with a young French student of letters, and after we had conversed for sufficiently long for the timid young man to allow himself a familiarity, he said :

" Now tell me why it is that all your English novelists so desperately desire to be politicians ? "

This seemed to him to be an astonishing, an unreasonable and even a slightly indecent state of affairs, so that he mentioned it under his breath.

On the next day, being Sunday, I had the privilege of being admitted into the drawing-room of a very old lady of distinction. She happened, after talking of persons as long dead as D'Orsay, to mention that the wife of a cabinet minister had come into her drawing-room on an afternoon shortly before, and had said that she had been present at the first night of a play. This had so enormously moved her that she had fainted and had been removed from the theatre by another cabinet minister, a friend of her husband's. This play dealt with prison life; the scene which so moved the lady showed you a silent stage—a convict seated in his cell. From a distance there came the sound of violently shaken metal. It was repeated nearer, it was echoed still nearer and nearer. And then the convict, an enormous agitation reaching him with all these contagious sounds, flew desperately at his cell door and shook it to the accompaniment of an intolerable jangle of iron. This scene of this poor wretch, with his agonized nerves shaken by long solitary confinement, so worked upon the sympathetic nerves of the cabinet minister's wife that she declared herself determined to leave no stone unturned until the prison laws of the United Kingdom were altered infinitely for the more humane.

We have thus one more instance of a work of literature which destroys whole methods of thought and sweeps away whole existent systems. And this play must take its rank along with *Uncle Tom's Cabin*, which destroyed slavery in the United States; along with *Oliver Twist*, which destroyed the Poor Law system in England; with *Don Quixote*, which destroyed chivalry; or with Beaumarchais' *Figaro*, which led in the French Revolution. But as an epilogue I should like to add my third conversation, which took place on a Monday. On that occasion I was afforded the privilege of talking for a long time with a convict—a gentleman on the face of him, one of the most degenerate Irish Cockneys that our

modern civilization could bless us with. In his
queer uniform of mustard-colour and blue this odd,
monstrous little chap with a six days' beard and a
face like that of a wizard monkey, trotted beside me
and uttered words of wisdom. He told me many
interesting things. Thus, being a criminal of the
lowest type, he was a Roman Catholic, and he
enlarged upon the hardships that prisoners of his
religion had to put up with in gaol. Thus, for
instance, one of the two meat courses which prisoners
are allowed during the week falls upon Friday and
the poor papists do not eat meat upon Fridays. Or
again, Roman Catholic prisoners are not allowed the
enormous luxury of a daily religious service. And
readers of Mr. Cunningham Grahame's prison ex-
periences will realize how enormous this deprivation
is. With its hours, giving possibilities of conversation, of joining in the hoarsely roared Psalms and
of meeting, under the shadow of God Almighty, even
the warder's eyes on some sort of equality, there are
few occasions of joy more absolute in the life of a
convict or of any man. Yet these deprivations my
friend Hennessy cheerfully suffered, and talking of a
prisoner called Flaherty, who had written himself
down a Protestant in order to earn these extra
privileges, Mr. Hennessy said in tones of the deepest
reprobation : " I call that a poor sort of conjuring
trick ! " and, spitting out a piece of oakum that
he had been chewing, he repeated in abstracted
tones, " a b—— poor kind of conjuring trick ! "

Mr. Hennessy, you will observe, was the worst
type of criminal, the greater part of his life having
been spent on " the Scrubbs," as the prisoners call

it when they are talking amongst themselves, or " in the cruel place," as they say when they are being interviewed by gentle philanthropists. Mr. Hennessy pulled another small piece of oakum from the lining of his waistcoat, which boasted a broad arrow upon either chest; and proceeded to soliloquize :

" Cor ! " he said, " it *do* do you blooming good to be in this blooming hotel. It soaks the beer out of you. Reg'lar *soaks* the beer out of you. When you've bin in 'ere free days, you feels another man. *Soaks* the beer out of you, that's what it does."

He proceeded upon the old line, harking back upon his thoughts :

" A poor sort of conjuring trick, that's what it is. And I guess God A'mighty looks after us. He sends the b—— sparrows."

For the sparrows, recognizing the chapel-time of the Protestants, are accustomed to fly in at the cell windows whilst chapel is on and to search the cell for crumbs. And if by chance they find a Catholic there, they do not seem to mind him very much. My friend Hennessy indeed had a " b—— sparrow " that would come and perch upon his forefinger, and this appeared to afford him as much gratification as if he had earned all the profits of his poor sort of conjuring trick. It afforded him much solace, too, since it appeared to him a visible sign from the Almighty that He who disregardeth not the fall of a sparrow could by means of that little bird find means and leisure to solace him whilst he suffered from sectarian injustice. For this sectarian inequality would pursue my friend Hennessy even when he left the gaol gates, the Protestant chaplain being provided with a sum of money wherewith to pay the fares home of departed prisoners, to furnish them with boots, and even to set them up in coster's stalls. "Flaherty," Mr. Hennessy said, "he'll get his blooming half-crown or free-and-six, but our blooming priest, he's as poor as meself." And Mr. Hennessy once more spat reflectively, and added, "But I call it a poor sort of conjuring trick."

Considering the opportunity an excellent one for getting information, I proceeded to describe as vividly as I could the scene from the play that I have mentioned—the scene which had made the cabinet minister's wife faint, the scene which had so drastically altered the prison laws of the United Kingdom. Mr. Hennessy listened to me with an air somewhat resembling philosophic disgust.

"Cor !" he said. He crooked his two forefingers one into the other and drew my attention to them.

"D'ye know what that means, sor?" he asked.

I said I didn't, and he continued: "It means Flanagan's trick. When we make that sign to each other at exercise it means that every man jack in gaol will shake his door after lights out. If you all make the row together, the b—— bloaters can't spot any one of you, and they can't have the whole b—— prison up before Dot and Dash in the morning. It's the fun of yer life to hear the bloaters curse."

The "bloaters" are, of course, the warders, and Dot and Dash was the nickname for the governor of this particular gaol, since one of his legs was slightly shorter than the other and he walked unequally.

109

Thus " the fun of your life," invented by the immortal Flanagan, whoever he was, and celebrated by my excellent friend Mr. Hennessy, becomes the epoch-making scene of a drama which changes the law of an empire. I have no particular comment to make, being a simple writer, recording things that have come under my own observation, but I should like to put on record, as linking up the *constatation* of what may otherwise appear an extremely loose dissertation, my reply to my young friend the Frenchman, who, with his eyes veiled, as if he were asking a rather obscene question, had put it to me : " Is it true, then, that all you English novelists desire to be politicians ? "

I answered that it was entirely true, and the reason was that in England a writer, not being regarded as a gentleman, except in the speech of the cabinet minister who may happen to reply to the toast of Literature at a Royal Academy banquet, or if he happens to sit upon a jury when he becomes *ipso facto* one of the " gentlemen " to whom learned counsel yearningly addresses himself—in England all writers being well aware that they are not regarded as gentlemen, and indeed aware that they are hardly regarded as men, since we must consider the practitioners of all the arts as at least effeminate if not a decent kind of eunuch—all writers in England desire to be something else as well. Sometimes, anxious to assert their manhood, they cultivate small holdings, sail the seas, hire out fishing boats, travel in caravans, engage in county cricket or become justices of the peace. I related to my young French friend how, one day, it being my great privilege to

110

lunch with the gentleman whom I consider to be the finest writer of English in the world, the man possessing the most limpid, the most pure, the most beautiful of English styles, I happened modestly and bashfully to express my opinion of his works to the great man. He turned upon me with an extra-ordinary aquiline fury and exclaimed :

"Stylist ! Me a stylist ! Stevenson was a stylist, Pater was a stylist, I have no time for that twiddling nonsense. I'm a coleopterist."

And there, as I explained to my young French friend, you have the whole thing in a nutshell. This great writer had the strongest possible objection to being classed with a tuberculous creature like Stevenson, or with an Oxford Don like Pater. He wanted to be remembered as one who had chased dangerous reptiles—if coleoptera *are* dangerous reptiles !—through the frozen forests of Labrador to the icy recesses of the Pole itself. He wanted to be remembered as a Man, a sort of creature once removed from an orang-outang, who smote a hairy breast and roared defiance to the rough places of the earth. So that some of us plough the seas, some of us dig up potatoes, some of us jump the blind baggage on transcontinental trains in the United States of America. Some of us are miners and some of us open rifle ranges, some of us keep goats, others indulge in apiculture—but by far the most of us desire to be influences.

"And I assure you, my dear young friend," I said to the Frenchman, " this is a very great tempta-tion. *L'autre jour j'étais assis dans un club littéraire—* I was seated in a literary club, conversing with some

111

of *Messieurs mes confrères*, when there entered a young man like yourself—very much like yourself, but not so modest. We were drinking tea. Yes, my young friend, in England all the literary men drink, not absinthe, nor orgeat, nor bocks, nor even *chassis*, but tea—and this young man who entered, being young, with great confidence, contradicted every single word that was uttered by my distinguished confrères, but, more particularly, every single word that was uttered by myself. He contradicted me indeed before I could get my words out at all, and I felt very refreshed and happy, for it is very pleasant when the extremely young treat one still as an equal. But it happened that one of my distinguished confrères, possessed of a loud and distinct organ, pronounced my name so that it could not escape the ears of this young man, who until that moment did not know who I was. He was lifting a cup of tea to his mouth, and—it struck me as an extraordinary fact—the cup of tea remained suspended between mouth and saucer for an immensely long period of time. The young man's eyes became enormous; his jaws fell open and he remained silent. The conversation drifted on. He succeeded in drinking his tea eventually, but still—he remained silent. My honoured confrères, one by one, went away on their errands to make, each one, the world a little better. I remained alone with our silent young friend, and at last, making my decent excuses, I rose to go. Suddenly this young man sprang up, and formally addressing me by name he brought out in rather trembling tones :

" ' I want to thank you for all you've done for me.' "

112

" ' My God ! ' I ejaculated. ' What is all this ? What have I done for you ? '

" ' You have,' he answered, ' by your writings influenced my whole life.'

" I was so overwhelmed, I was so appalled, I was so extraordinarily confused, that I bolted out of the room. I did not, my young French friend, know in the least what to do with this singular present. And I am bound to say that in about five minutes I felt extraordinarily pleased.

" I had never been so pleased before in my life. One kind writer once said that I wrote as preciously —though I was not of course half as important—as the late Robert Louis Stevenson ! Another kindly editor once told me to my face that he considered me to be the finest novelist in England. He added that there was only one person who was my equal, and that the latest literary knight ! That, my young French friend, was a present whose flavour you will hardly appreciate.

" But *kurz und gut*, I have had my triumphs. Yet never—no, never till that moment had I been called an influence. Oh yes, the pleasure was extraordinary. I walked through the streets as if I were dancing on air. Never had the world looked so good. I imagined that my words must be heard deferentially in the War Office which I was then passing, and I proceeded to walk down Downing Street to look at the several ministries where obviously my words must have immense weight. Very nearly I sent in my card to the foreign minister with the view of giving him my opinions on the relations between England and Germany.

" In the Green Park, continuing my walk home, I said to myself: I am an influence! By God, I am an influence like A and B and C and D and E and F and G and H and like all of them—all of them influences.

" I felt as important as the Pope must have done when he penned the encyclical *Pascendi Greges*. I was astounded that no one turned round in awe to observe my passing by. The sweetest moment in my life! . . .

" Of course reaction came. It could not have been otherwise, since I was brought up in the back rooms and nurseries of Pre-Raphaelism, which for better or for worse held that to be an artist was to be the most august thing in life. And nowadays I seldom think of that sweet moment. Only when I am very drunk indeed, deep, deep drunk in tea, do I remember that once for five minutes I looked upon myself as an influence.

" Being a man of enormous moral integrity (my young French friend, you come of a nation inferior and unacquainted with the sterner virtues)—being a man of an enormous moral integrity—or being a low-spirited sort of a person—I have resolutely put from me this temptation. Or, if you will, I have never had the courage again to aspire to these dizzy heights.

" But now I can well understand why it is that my distinguished confrères A, B, C, D, and all the rest of the letters of the alphabet, aspire to the giddy heights of power. For figure to yourself, my dear young French friend, how I, the mere writer, despisedly walk the streets. But should I just once take up the cause, let us say, of my oppressed friend Hennessy, at once all sorts of doors and all sorts of columns would be open to me. *The Times* would print my letters; I should be admitted into the private room of whatever cabinet minister it was that had Hennessy in his charge. I would—yes, by Heavens, I would—make that cabinet minister's wife not only faint, but go into three separate fits of hysterics by my gruesome accounts of Hennessy's wrongs. I should dine with archbishops. I should receive a letter of thanks from the Pope. I should eventually triumphantly contest the Scotland division of Liverpool, and, becoming arbitrator of the destinies of the empire, I should be styled before the Speaker of the mother of parliaments not only a gentleman, but, by Heavens, an honourable gentleman ! . . ."

At this point of my rhapsody we were approached by an official, and on his refusal to believe that we had already paid for our chairs we were summarily ejected.

Now do not let me be suspected of preaching a campaign to the effect that the writer should stick to his pen. I am merely anxious to emphasize the lights and shadows of Pre-Raphaelite days by contrasting them with the very changed conditions that to-day prevail. You might say on the one hand our poets are now influences, and that on the other they no longer get cheques. And you might continue the pros and cons to the end of the chapter. Nor do I wish to say that the author ought to steel his heart against the wrongs of suffering humanity or of the brute creation. By all means if he shall observe individual examples of the oppressed and of the

suffering—poor devils like my friend Hennessy, or
the miserable horses that we export to Belgium, let
him do his best to alleviate their unhappy lots.   But
these, the old-fashioned Pre-Raphaelite would have
said, are the functions of the artist as private citizen.
His art is something more mysterious and something
more sacred.   As I have elsewhere pointed out, my
grandfather, a romantic old gentleman, of the Tory
persuasion by predisposition, was accustomed to
express himself as being advanced in the extreme in
his ideas.   Such was his pleasant fancy that I am
quite certain he would have sported a red tie had it
not clashed with the blue linen shirts that he habitually wore.   And similarly my aunt Rossetti, to
whom my infant thoughts were so frequently
entrusted—this energetic and romantic lady was of
such advanced ideas that I have heard her regret that
she was not born early enough to be able to wet her
handkerchief in the blood of the aristocrats during
the French Reign of Terror.   Nay more, during
that splendid youth of the world in the 'eighties
and 'nineties the words " the Social Revolution "
were for ever on our lips.   We spoke of it as if it
were always just round the corner, like the three-
horse omnibus which used to run from Portland
Place to Charing Cross Station—a bulky conveyance
which we used to regard with longing eyes as being
eminently fitted, if it were upset, to form the very
breastwork of a barricade.   In these young, splendid
and stern days, my cousins the Rossettis, aided, if
not pushed to it, by my energetic romantic aunt,
founded that celebrated anarchist organ known as
the *Torch*.   But though my grandfather hankered

116

after wearing a red tie, said that all lords were
damned flunkeys, that all Her Majesty's judges were
venial scoundrels, all police magistrates worse than
Judas Iscariot, and all policemen worse even than
Royal Academicians—it would never, no, it would
never have entered his head to turn one of his frescoes
in the Town Hall, Manchester, into a medium for
the propaganda of the Social Revolution. He hated
the bourgeoisie with a proper hatred, but it was
the traditional hatred of the French artist. The
bourgeoisie returned his hatred to more purpose,
for, just before his death, the town council of Manchester with the Lord Mayor at its head, sitting
in private, put forward a resolution that his frescoes
in the Town Hall should be whitewashed out and
their places taken by advertisements of the wares of
the aldermen and the councillors. Thus perished
Ford Madox Brown—for this resolution, which was
forwarded to him, gave him his fatal attack of
apoplexy. The bourgeoisie had triumphed.

Or again, Madox Brown, in his picturesque desire
to champion the oppressed, once took up the cause of
a Royal Academician. This poor gentleman, having
grown extremely old and being entirely colour
blind, so that he painted pictures containing green
heads and blue hands, was no longer permitted by
his brothers of the immortal Forty to occupy with
his work the one hundred and forty feet on the line
that are allotted to every Academician at Burlington
House. Madox Brown entered into the fray for
redressing the wrongs of this injured and colour-
blind person. He wrote articles about Mr. D—— in
the late Mr. Quilter's *Universal Review*. He deluged

The Times with letters in which he said that "though dog does not eat dog the academic vulture was ready to feed on its own carrion." He trundled off in four-wheelers to interview the art critic of almost every daily paper in London. Indeed I never remember such a row in that picturesque household as was caused by the sorrows of this unfortunate Academician. But it never, no it never entered Madox Brown's head to paint a gigantic picture representing all the forty Academicians gorging enormously on turkeys, walnuts and port, whilst outside the walls of Burlington House, on a winter night with the snow four feet thick, the unfortunate D—— with placards bearing the words "Colour Blind" on his chest, and his bony shoulders sticking through his ragged clothes, drew in chalks upon the pavement exquisite classical pictures whose heads were green and whose hands were blue. This, however, was what William Morris, breaking away from his dyes and his tapestries, taught the young artist to do.

VII

ANARCHISTS AND GREY FRIEZE

THE art with which William Morris and such disciples of his as Commendatore Walter Crane propagandized on behalf of that splendid thing, " The Social Revolution " was, upon the whole, still within the canons which would have been allowed by the Æsthetes who called themselves Pre-Raphaelites. In his *News from Nowhere* Morris tried to show us young things what a beautiful world we should make of it if, sedulously, we attended the Sunday evening lectures at Kelmscott House, the Mall, Hammersmith. At Kelmscott House, I believe, the first electric telegraph was constructed; and it was in the shed where the first cable was made that we used to meet to hasten on the Social Revolution and to reconstruct a lovely world. As far as I remember those young dreams, it was to be all a matter of huge-limbed and splendid women, striding along dressed in loose curtain-serge garments, and bearing upon the one arm such sheaves of wheat as never were, and upon the other such babies as every proud mother imagines her first baby to be. And on Sunday afternoons, in a pleasant lamplight, to a number perhaps of a hundred and fifty, there we used to gather in that shed.

William Morris would stride up and down between the aisles, pushing his hands with a perpetual irate movement through his splendid hair. And we, the young men with long necks, long fair hair, protruding blue eyes and red ties, or the young maidens in our blue curtain-serge with our round shoulders, our necks made as long as possible to resemble Rossetti drawings, uttered with rapt expression, long sentences about the Social Revolution that was just round the corner. We thought we were beautiful; we thought we were very beautiful, but Pre-Raphaelism is dead, Æstheticism is dead. Poor William Morris is dead too, and the age when poetry was marketable is most dead of all. It is dead, all dead, and that beautiful vision, the Social Revolution, has vanished along with the 'bus that used to run from the Langham Hotel, beloved of American visitors, to Charing Cross—the 'bus with its three horses abreast, its great length, and its great umbrella permanently fixed above the driver's head. Alas, that 'bus will serve to build up no barricade when the ultimate revolution comes, and when it comes the ultimate revolution will not be our beloved Social one of the large women, curtain-serge, wheat-sheaves, and the dream babies. No, it will be different. And I suppose, the fine flower that those days produced is none other than Mr. Bernard Shaw.

But in those days we had no thought of Fabianism. Nevertheless, we managed to get up some pretty tidy rows amongst ourselves. I must, personally, have had three separate sets of political opinions. To irritate my relatives, who advocated advanced thought, I dimly remember that I professed myself a Tory. Amongst the bourgeoisie whom it was my inherited duty to *épater* I passed for a dangerous anarchist. In general speech, manner and appearance, I must have resembled a socialist of the Morris group. I don't know what I was : I don't know what I am. It doesn't, I suppose, matter in the least, but I fancy I must have been a very typical young man of the sort who formed the glorious meetings that filled the world in the 'eighties and early 'nineties. There used to be terrific rows between Socialists and Anarchists in those days. I think I must have been on the side of the anarchists, because the socialists were unreasonably aggressive. They were always holding meetings at which the subject for debate would be, " The Foolishness of Anarchism." This would naturally annoy the harmless and gentle anarchists who only wanted to be let alone, to loaf in Goodge Street, and to victimize any one who came into the offices of the *Torch* and had half-a-crown to spend on beer.

In the *Torch* office, which, upon the death of my aunt Rossetti, left the house of William Rossetti, you would generally find some dirty, eloquent scoundrel called Ravachol or Vaillant. For the price of a pint of beer, he would pour forth so enormous a flood of invective and of self-glorification that you would not believe him capable of hurting a rabbit. Then, a little afterwards, you would hear of a bomb thrown in Barcelona or Madrid, and Ravachol or Vaillant, still eloquent and still attitudinizing, would go to his

death under the guillotine or in the garrotte. I
don't know where the masses came from that
supported us as anarchists, but I have seldom seen
a crowd so great as that which attended the funeral
of the poor idiot who blew himself to pieces in the
attempt on Greenwich Observatory. This was, of
course, an attempt fomented by the police agents
of a foreign state with a view to forcing the hand
of the British Government. The unfortunate idiot
was talked by these *agents provocateurs* into taking
a bomb to Greenwich Park, where the bomb exploded
in his pocket and blew him into many small fragments. The idea of the government in question was
that this would force the hand of the British Government, so that they would arrest wholesale every
anarchist in Great Britain. Of course the British
Government did nothing of the sort, and the crowd
in Tottenham Court Road which attended the funeral
of the small remains of the victim was, as I have
said, one of the largest that I have ever seen. Who
were they all ? Where did they all come from ?
Whither have they all disappeared ? I am sure I
don't know, just as I am pretty certain that in all
those thousands who filled Tottenham Court Road
there was not one who was more capable than myself
of beginning to think of throwing a bomb. I suppose
it was the spirit of romance !—of youth, perhaps
of sheer tomfoolery, perhaps of the spirit of adventure, which is no longer very easy for men to find
in our world of grey and teeming cities. I couldn't
be Dick Harkaway with a Winchester rifle, so I
took it out in monstrous solemn fun, of the philosophic anarchist kind, and I was probably one of

twenty thousand. My companion upon this occasion
was Comrade P—— who until quite lately might be
observed in the neighbourhood of the British Museum,
a man with an immensely long beard, with immensely
long hair, bare-headed, bare-legged, in short running-
drawers and a boatman's jersey, that left bare his
arms and chest. Comrade P——, was a medical man
of great skill, an eminently philosophic anarchist.
He was so advanced in his ideas that he dispensed
with animal food, dispensed with alcohol, and intensely desired to dispense with all clothing. This
brought him many times into collision with the
police, and as many times he was sent to prison for
causing a crowd to assemble in Hyde Park, where
he would appear to all intents and purposes in a
state of nature. He lived, however, entirely upon
crushed nuts. Prison diet, which appeared to
him sinfully luxurious, inevitably upset his digestion.
They would place him in the infirmary and would
feed him on boiled chicken, jellies, beef-tea, and
caviare, and all the while he would cry out for nuts,
and grow worse and worse, the prison doctors
regularly informing him that nuts were poison.
At last Comrade P—— would be upon the point of
death, and then they would give him nuts. P——
would immediately recover, usually about the time
that his sentence had expired. Then upon the
Sunday he would once more appear like a Greek
athlete running through Hyde Park. A most
learned and gentle person, most entertaining and
the best of company, this was still the passion of
his life. The books in the British Museum were
almost a necessity of his existence, yet he would

walk into the reading room attired only in a blanket, which he would hand to the cloak-room attendant, asking for a check in return. Eventually his reader's ticket was withdrawn, though with reluctance, on the part of the authorities, for he was a fine scholar and they were very humane men. Some time after this, Comrade P—— proposed to me that I should accompany him on the top of a 'bus. His idea was, that he would be attired in a long ulster; this he would take off and hand to me, whereupon I was to get down and leave him in this secure position. My courage was insufficient—the united courages of all Comrade P——'s friends were insufficient to let them aid him in giving thus early a demonstration of what nowadays we call the Simple Life, and Comrade P—— had to sacrifice his overcoat. He threw it, that is to say, from the top of the 'bus, and with his hair and beard streaming over his uncovered frame defied alike the elements and the police. The driver took the 'bus, Comrade P—— and all into an empty stable, where they locked him up until the police arrived with a stretcher from Bow Street. At last the magistrate before whom Comrade P—— habitually appeared grew tired of sentencing him. Comrade P——was moreover so evidently an educated and high-minded man that the stipendiary perhaps was touched by his steadfastness. At all events, he invited P——to dinner—I don't know what clothes P—— wore upon this occasion. Over this friendly meal he extracted from P—— a promise that he would wear the costume of running-drawers, an oarsman's jersey, and sandals which I have already described and which the magistrate himself designed. Nothing

124

would have persuaded P—— to give this promise had
not the magistrate promised in return to get
for P—— the reader's ticket at the British Museum
which he had forfeited. And so for many years
in this statutory attire, P——, growing greyer and
greyer, might be seen walking about the streets of
Bloomsbury. Some years afterwards when I occupied
a cottage in the country, P—— wrote and asked to
be permitted to live in my garden in a state of
nature. But dreading the opinions of my country
neighbours, I refused, and that was the last I heard
of him.

What with poets, arts and craftsmen, anarchists,
dock strikes, unemployed riots and demonstrations
in Trafalgar Square, those years were very lively
and stirring for the young. We continued to be
cranks in a high-spirited and tentative manner.
Nowadays, what remains of that movement seems
to have become much more cut and dried; to have
become much more theoretic; to know much more
and to get much less fun out of it. You have on
the one hand the Fabian Society, and on the other
the Garden Cities, where any number of Comrade
P——s can be accommodated. The movement has
probably spread numerically, but it has passed, as
a factor, out of the life of the day. I don't know
what killed it.

As far as I am personally concerned, my interest
seemed to wane at about the time when there was a
tremendous row in one of the socialist clubs, because
some enthusiastic gentleman in a red tie publicly
drank wine out of a female convert's shoe. Why
there should have been a row, whether it was wrong

to drink wine, or to drink it out of a shoe, or what it was all about, I never could quite make out. But the life appeared to die out of things about then. Perhaps it was about that time that the first Fabian Tract was published. I remember being present, later, at a Fabian debate as to the attributes of the Deity. I forget what it was all about, but it lasted a very considerable time. Towards the end of the meeting an energetic lady arose— it was, I think, her first attendance at a Fabian meeting—and remarked :

" All this talk is very fine, but what I want to know is, whether the Fabian Society does, or does not, believe in God ? "

A timid gentleman rose and replied :

" If Mrs. Y—— will read Fabian Tract 312, she will discover what she ought to think upon this matter."

They had codified everything by then. But in the earliest days we all wobbled gloriously. Thus upon his first coming to London Mr. Bernard Shaw wrote a pamphlet called *Why I am an Anarchist*. This was, I think, printed at the *Torch* Press. At any rate, the young proprietors of that organ came into possession of a large number of copies of the pamphlet. I have twice seen Mr. Shaw unmanned—three times, if I include an occasion upon a railway platform when a locomotive out-voiced him. One of the other occasions was when Mr. Shaw, having advanced a stage further towards his intellectual salvation, was addressing in the Park a Socialist gathering on the tiresome text of " The Foolishness of Anarchism." The young proprietors of the *Torch* walked round and round in the outskirts of the crowd offering copies of Mr. Shaw's earlier pamphlet for sale, and exclaiming at the top of their voices, " *Why I am an Anarchist !* By the Lecturer ! "

But even in those days Mr. Shaw had us for his enthusiastic supporters. I suppose we did not put much money into his pockets, for I well remember his relating a sad anecdote whose date must have fallen among the 'eighties. As Mr. Shaw put it, like every poor young man when he first comes to London he possessed no presentable garments at all save a suit of dress clothes. In this state he received an invitation to a soirée from some gentleman high in the political world—I think it was Mr. Haldane. This gentleman was careful to add a postscript in the kindness of his heart, begging Mr. Shaw not to dress, since every one would be in their morning clothes. Mr. Shaw was accordingly put into an extraordinary state of perturbation. He pawned or sold all the articles of clothing in his possession, including his evening suit, and with the proceeds purchased a decent suit of black, resembling, as he put it, that of a Wesleyan minister. Upon his going up the staircase of the house to which he was invited, the first person he perceived was Mr. Balfour, in evening dress; the second was Mr. Wyndham in evening dress; and immediately he was introduced into a dazzling hall that was one sea of white shirt fronts relieved by black swallow-tails. He was the only undressed person in the room. Then his kind host presented himself, his face beaming with philanthropy and with the thought of kindly encouragement that he had given to

struggling genius ! I think Mr. Shaw does not "dress"
at all nowadays, and, in the dress affected, at all
events by his disciples, the grey homespuns, the
soft hats, the comfortable bagginesses about the
knees, and the air that the pockets have of always
being full of apples, the last faint trickle of Pre-
Raphaelite influence is to be perceived. Madox
Brown always wore a black morning coat edged with
black braid during the day, but Rossetti, at any rate
when he was at work, was much addicted to grey
frieze. He wore habitually a curious coat of pepper-
and-salt material, in shape resembling a clergyman's
ordinary dress but split down the lateral seams so
that the whole front of the coat formed on each side
one large pocket. When he went out—which, as
Mr. Meredith has informed us, was much too seldom
for his health—he wore a grey frieze inverness cape
of a thickness so extraordinary that it was as stiff
as millboard. This greyness and roughness very
much influenced his disciples and spread to the
disciples of William Morris, with the results that we
see at present. I know this to be the fact from the
following circumstances. Upon Rossetti's death,
his inverness, to which I have alluded and which
was made in the year 1869, descended to my grandfather. Upon my grandfather's death it descended
to me, it being then twenty-three years old. I wore
it with feelings of immense pride as if it had been—
and indeed was it not ?—the mantle of a prophet.
And such approbation did it meet with in my
young friends of that date that this identical garment
was copied seven times, and each time for the use
of a gentleman whose works, when Booksellers

Row still existed, might ordinarily be found in the Twopenny Box. So this garment spread the true tradition, and indeed, it was imperishable and indestructible, though what has become of it by now I do not know. I wore it for several years until it must have been aged probably thirty, when, happening to wear it during a visit to my tailor's, and telling that gentleman its romantic history, I was distressed to hear him remark, looking over his pince-nez :

" Time the moths had it ! "

This shed such a light upon the garment from the point of view of tailors that I never wore it again. It fell, I am afraid, into the hands of a family with little respect for relics of the great, and I am fairly certain that I observed its capacious folds in the mists of an early morning upon Romney Marsh some months ago, enveloping the limbs of an elderly and poaching scoundrel called Slingsby.

But indeed, the grey frieze apart, there was little enough in externals about the inner ring of the Pre-Raphaelites that was decorative. Rossetti wore grey frieze, because it was the least bothersome of materials; it never wanted brushing, it never wanted renewing, there it was. Madox Brown wore always an eminently un-Bohemian suit of black. Christina Rossetti affected the least picturesque of black garments for daily use, whilst on occasions of a festive nature she would go as far as a pearl-grey watered silk. Millais, of course, was purely conventional in attire, and so was Holman Hunt. I remember meeting Holman Hunt outside High Street, Kensington Station, on a rather warmish day. He was wearing an overcoat of extremely fine, light-coloured fur. To this he drew my attention and proceeded to lecture me upon the virtues of economy, saying with his prophetic air:

"Young man! observe this garment. I bought it in the year 1852, giving a hundred and forty pounds for it. It is now 1894. This overcoat has therefore lasted me forty-two years and I have never had another. You will observe that it has actually cost me per annum something less than £3 10s., which is much less, I am certain, than you spend upon your overcoats."

And here Mr. Hunt regarded Rossetti's garment, which was then aged thirty-three, and had cost £6 10s. when it was new. I did not, however, interrupt him, and the great man continued:

"And you will observe that I still have the coat, which is worth as much or more than its original sum, whilst, for all these years, it has enabled me to present a flourishing appearance whenever I had to transact business."

These are not, of course, Mr. Hunt's exact words, nor, perhaps, are the figures exactly right, but they render the effect of this dissertation. I never could understand why it was that whenever I came near Mr. Hunt he should always lecture me on the virtue of economy, yet this was the case. Nevertheless, in those days, following what I considered to be the rules of Morrisian Socialism, I certainly dressed with an extreme economy and I doubt whether all the clothes I had on could have cost so much as the £3 10s. which Mr. Hunt allotted for a yearly expenditure on overcoats. There was Rossetti's garment aged thirty-three, there was a water-tight German forester's pilot jacket, which I had bought in the Bavarian Spessart for four-and-sixpence, there were some trousers which I imagine cost eighteen shillings, a leather belt, an old blue shirt which, being made of excellent linen, had already served my grandfather for fifteen years, and a red satin tie which probably cost one shilling. But these facts, I imagine, were hidden from Mr. Hunt, who had no particular sympathy with the æsthetic movement or with advanced ideas. Mr. Holman Hunt, of course, was a Pre-Raphaelite of pure blood, and anything more hideous, anything more purely early-Victorian than in their day the Pre-Raphaelites put up with in the matter of furniture and appointments I do not think it possible to imagine.

Holman Hunt and Millais separated themselves early from the other Pre-Raphaelites, and their furniture remained normal, following the fashions of the day. And this remained true for all the disciples of the first Pre-Raphaelite group. Thus if you will look at Robert B. Martineau's " The Last Day in the Old Home," you will perceive a collection of the horrors of furnishing as it was understood in the days when Victoria was queen—a collection rendered by the painter with a care so loving as to show that he at least had no idea of salvation having to be obtained by curtain-serge and simplicity.

The first impulses towards the new furnishing came when Rossetti acquired, during a visit to Oxford, two disciples called William Morris and Algernon Charles Swinburne. These two young men made Rossetti's acquaintance whilst he was painting the frescoes in the Union—frescoes which have now almost disappeared. Swinburne, and more particularly Morris, must have exercised the most profound of influences over Dante Gabriel, and later over Madox Brown. For I have no doubt whatever that it was these two who pushed this great figure into the exaggerated and loose mediævalism that distinguished his latest period. I do not mean to say that Rossetti had fallen under no mediæval influences before this date, since obviously he had been enormously impressed by Sir Walter Scott. I used to posses a yellow-bound pamphlet entitled *Sir Hugh the Heron* and printed by Rossetti's grandfather when Rossetti himself was seven or eight. *Sir Hugh the Heron* contained the following spirited verse, which always lingers in my memory:

" And the shrieks of the flying, the groans of the dying
 And the battle's deafening yell,
 And the armour which clanked as the warrior rose,
 And rattled as he fell."

This first-printed poem of Rossetti's has always seemed to me symbolical of what, by himself, he did for mediævalism. Scott made it merely romantic, he suggested—I don't mean to say that he ever gave it as such—but he suggested that William Wallace went into battle in black velvet short hose, with in one hand a court sword and in the other a cambric pocket handkerchief. Rossetti before he came under the influence of Morris and Burne Jones went much deeper into mediævalism than ever Scott did. He looked as it were into the illuminated capitals of missals and so gave the world little square wooden chambers all gilded, with women in hennins, queer musical instruments, and many little pretty quaint conceits. Madox Brown, of course, in his peculiar manner carried the quaintnesses still further. With his queer knotted English mind he must give you an Iseult screaming like any kitchen wench, a Sir Tristam expiring in an extraordinary stiff spasm because armour would not bend, a King Marc poking a particularly ugly face into a grated window; and of all things in the world, a white Maltese terrier yapping at the murderers. This picture was of course designed to *épater les bourgeois*—touch them on the raw. And as such it need not be considered very seriously. But between them, Madox Brown and Rossetti invented a queer and quaint sort of mediævalism that was realistic always as long as it could be picturesque. Morris, Swinburne, and Burne-Jones however invented the gorgeous glamour of mediævalism. It was as if they said they must have pomegranates, pomegranates, pomegranates all the way. They wanted pomegranates not only in their pictures but in their dining-room and on their beds. I should say that Rossetti was a man without any principles at all, who earnestly desired to find some means of salvation along the lines of least resistance. Madox Brown on the other hand was ready to make a principle out of anything that was at all picturesque. Thus whilst Rossetti accepted the pomegranate as the be-all and end-all of life, Madox Brown contented himself with playing with a conventionalized daisy pattern such as could grow behind any St. Michael or Uriel of stained glass.

Neither Rossetti nor Madox Brown had the least desire to mediævalize their homes. Rossetti wanted to fill his house with anything that was odd, Chinese or sparkling. If there was something gruesome about it, he liked it all the better. Thus at his death, two marauders, out of the shady crew that victimized him and one honest man, each became possessed of the dark lantern used by Eugene Aram. I mean to say that quite lately there were in the market three dark lanterns each of which was supposed to have come from Rossetti's house at his death, only one of which had been bought with honest money at Rossetti's sale. Even this one may not have been the relic of the murderer which Rossetti had purchased with immense delight. He bought in fact just anything or everything that amused him or tickled his fancy, without the least idea of making his house resemble anything but an old curiosity shop.

This collection was rendered still more odd by the eccentricities of Mr. Charles Augustus Howell, an extraordinary personage who ought to have a volume all to himself. There was nothing in an odd jobbing way that Mr. Howell was not up to. He supported his family for some time by using a diving bell to recover treasure from a lost galleon off the coast of Portugal, of which country he appears to have been a native. He became Ruskin's secretary and he had a shop in which he combined the framing and the forging of masterpieces. He conducted the most remarkable of dealers' swindles with the most consummate ease and grace, doing it indeed so lovably that when his misdeeds were discovered he became only more beloved. Such a character would obviously appeal to Rossetti, and as, at one period of his career, Rossetti's income ran well into five figures, whilst he threw gold out of all the windows and doors, it is obvious that such a character as Rossetti's must have appealed very strongly to Mr. Charles Augustus Howell. The stories of him are endless. At one time whilst Rossetti was collecting chinoiseries, Howell happened to have in his possession a nearly priceless set of Chinese tea-things. These he promptly proceeded to have duplicated at his establishment, where forging was carried on more wonderfully than seems possible. This forgery he proceeded to get one of his concealed agents to sell to Rossetti for an enormously high figure. Coming to tea with the poet-artist on the next day, he remarked to Rossetti :

" Hallo, Gabriel, where did you get those clumsy imitations ? "

Rossetti of course was filled with consternation, whereupon Howell remarked comfortingly : " Oh, it's all right, old chap, I've got the originals, which I'll let you have for an old song."

And eventually, he sold the originals to Rossetti for a figure very considerably over that at which Rossetti had bought the forgeries. Howell was then permitted to take away the forgeries as of no value, and Rossetti was left with the originals. Howell, however, was for some time afterwards more than usually assiduous in visiting the painter-poet. At each visit he brought one of the forged cups in his pocket and whilst Rossetti's back was turned he substituted the forgery for one of the genuine cups which he took away in his pocket. At the end of the series of visits therefore, Rossetti once more possessed the copies and Howell the genuine set which he sold, I believe, to M. Tissot.

So that whatever Rossetti did possess he never could be really certain of what it actually was. He could not, even, as I have elsewhere pointed out, be certain that the pictures on his own easels were by his own hand. But in any case he went through life with a singular collection of oddments and the catalogue of his effects at his death is one of the most romantic documents of the sort that it is easy to lay one's hands on.

Madox Brown, on the other hand, had very much of Rossetti's passion for picking up things. But he cared very little for the wares or the value of the objects which he purchased. He would buy black Wedgewood or he would buy a three-penny pot at a little shop round the corner, or he would buy gilt objects from the palace of George IV at Brighton—in short, he would buy anything that would add a spot of colour to his dining-room. But I fancy the only bargain he ever made was once when he discovered a cartoon in red chalk amongst the débris of a rag-and-bone shop. For this he exchanged two old bonnets of my grandmother's. Sometime afterwards he observed—I think at Agnew's—another red chalk cartoon which was an authenticated Boucher. This second cartoon was so obviously the other half of the design he had already in his possession that he had no hesitation in purchasing it for a comparatively small sum. At the sale of his effects, in 1894, this panel fetched quite a considerable price and in the meantime it had looked very handsome upon the walls of his drawing-room.

The Madox Brown sale, apart from its note of tragedy for myself in the breaking up of a home that had seemed so romantic—that still after many years seems to me so romantic—had about it something extremely comic. Madox Brown's rooms had always seemed to me to be as comfortable and as pretty as one could desire. It was true that they had about them no settled design. But of an evening, many candles being lit, the golden wall paper shining with a subdued glow, the red curtains, the red couch, the fireplace with its Turkey-red tiles, the large table covered with books, the little piano of a golden wood with its panels painted and gilded by William Morris himself—all these things had about them a prettiness, a quaintness. And with the coming of the auctioneer's man it all fell to pieces so extraordinarily.

I do not think I shall ever forget Madox Brown's quaint dismay and anger when Mr. Harry Quilter "discovered" him. During his long absence in Manchester, while he was painting the twelve frescoes in the Town Hall—frescoes which were of great size, each of which occupied him a year and were paid for very insignificantly—the frescoes which the Manchester Town Council afterwards desired to whitewash out—after this long absence from London Madox Brown as a painter and as a man had become entirely forgotten. So that when he returned to London, he seemed to have almost no friends left and no one to buy his pictures. The old race of Northern merchant princes who had bought so

liberally were all dead, and shortly after his return
he sold to Mr. Boddington of Wilmslow fourteen
early pictures for four hundred pounds. Most of
these were lately exhibited at the Dudley Gallery,
where one of them sold for more than half the price
that had been given for the fourteen. This picture
is now, I believe, in the possession of Mr. Sargent.
Nevertheless in his rather dismal circumstances
Madox Brown set cheerfully to work to get together
a new home, and a new circle of friends. He went
about it with a remarkable and boyish gaiety, and
having got it together with its gilt leather wall
paper, its red tiles, its furniture from the palace
of George IV at Brighton and its other oddments,
he really considered that he had produced a sort of
palace. Then came Mr. Quilter. Mr. Quilter discovered the phrase, " Father of Pre-Raphaelism "
which so disturbed Mr. Holman Hunt. He discovered that this great artist whom he compared
to Titian, Botticelli, Holbein, Hogarth, and to
Heaven knows whom, was living in our midst, and
he proclaimed this astounding discovery to one
of the evening papers with the additional circumstance that Madox Brown was living in a state of
the most dismal poverty. He described Madox
Brown's studio—the only room in the house to
which he had been admitted—as a place so filled
with old fragments of rusty iron, bits of string, and
the detritus of ages that it resembled a farrier's
shop. He described a lay figure with the straw
sticking out of all its members, easels covered with
dust that tottered and perpetually threatened to
let their pictures fall, curtains so threadbare that

they were mere skeleton protections against the sun and draughts. In short he described a place half way between the Old Curiosity Shop of Dickens and a marine store in a suburb of Portsmouth. Madox Brown read this picturesque narrative with a face of exaggerated bewilderment. He pulled his biretta impatiently off his snow-white head, and gazed over his spectacles at the bits of string, the fragments of old iron, the tottering easels, the lay figure, with straw sticking out of every joint that in an attitude of dejection hung from its supports, like a man that has been executed three centuries before. With an air of extreme satisfaction he regarded all these objects which Mr. Quilter had so picturesquely and accurately described. Then he put on his biretta once more with great care and speaking solemnly and deliberately, let fall the words:

"God damn and blast my soul! What does the fellow want?"

Madox Brown had for long been away from London, and came of a generation of artists incomparably older in tradition than any that were then to be found alive—he the erstwhile disciple of David, the pupil of Baron Wappers, who had had his first training at the hands of the Grand School, a whole of a lifetime before. Madox Brown had simply never heard that a studio was a place where, amidst stuffed peacocks, to the tinkling of harmonious fountains falling into marble basins half hidden by orange trees, beneath an alcove of beaten copper and with walls of shining porphyry, you sat about in a velvet coat and had eau de Cologne squirted over your hair by a small black page. A studio for him was a comfortable place that no housemaid dare enter, a place to which you retired to work, a place in which you treasured up every object you had ever painted, from a rusty iron candlestick to half-a-dozen horse's teeth—a place with a huge table on which stood all the objects and implements that you had ever used, waiting amidst tranquil rust and dust until it should be their turn again to come in handy. So that he could not for the life of him imagine what it was Mr. Quilter did want. He didn't in fact know what advertisement was. Mr Quilter, on the other hand, had come across artists who mostly knew nothing else. In the matter of the studio they were thus at cross purposes. It wasn't a sign of poverty, it was just a symptom of an unbusiness-like career.

Madox Brown in fact was the most unbusiness-like of men, and he had less sense of the value of money than any person I have ever met. He had indeed a positive genius for refusing to have anything to do with money that came at all easily. When my mother was granted a pension from the Civil List upon the death of my father, Madox Brown greeted the two gentlemen who rather timidly brought the news with such a torrent of violent and indignant refusals, that one of them, poor dear Mr. Hipkins, the most beloved of men, to whose efforts the allowance was mainly due, became indisposed and remained ill for some days afterwards. Thus my mother never received a penny from her grateful country. A number of gentlemen, all of them artists, I be-lieve, subscribed a considerable sum amounting to several thousand pounds, in order to commission

Madox Brown to paint a picture for presentation to the National Gallery. Such an honour they very carefully pointed out, had been paid to no English painter with the exception of Maclise, though it was frequent enough in France. The ambassadors on this occasion approached Madox Brown with an almost unheard-of caution. For three days I was kept on the watch to discover the most propitious moment when my grandfather's humour after the passing away of a fit of the gout was at its very sunniest. I telegraphed to Mr. Frederick Shields, who came at his fastest in a hansom cab—a vehicle which I believe he detested. And then an extraordinary row raged in the house. Madox Brown insisted—as he had insisted in the case of my mother's pension—that it was all a plot on the part of the damned academicians to humiliate him. He insisted that it was a confounded charity. He swore incessantly and perpetually, upset all the fire-irons which Mr. Shields patiently and silently replaced. The contest raged for a long time; it continued through many days. I cannot imagine how Mr. Shields supported it, but, the most self-sacrificing of men, he triumphed in the end by insisting that it was an honour, an unprecedented honour. The four or five Academicians who had humbly begged to be allowed to share in the privilege of subscribing, had each solemnly and separately mentioned the precedent of Maclise. In short, pale and exhausted, Mr. Shields triumphed, though my grandfather did not live to complete the picture.

Of the many devoted friends that Madox Brown had, I think that Mr. Shields was the most devoted

and the best. Honoured as he is as the painter
of the mural decorations in the Chapel of Ease near
the Marble Arch—Sterne, by-the-by, is buried in
the graveyard behind the Chapel, *his* tombstone
having been provided by subscription of Free-
masons, though I do not know whether this is the
first honour of its kind ever paid to an author and a
clergyman—I should still like to relate one fact which
does much honour to this painter's heart, an honour
which I believe is unshared and unequalled in the
annals of painting. When Madox Brown, by the
efforts of Mr. Shields and Mr. Charles Rowley, was,
after many storms, commissioned to paint six of
the panels in the great hall at Manchester Mr.
Shields, himself a native of that city, was nominated
to paint the other six. He accepted the commission,
it was signed, sealed, settled and delivered. Madox
Brown began upon his work; he finished one panel;
he finished two; he finished three, the years rolled
on. But Mr. Shields made no sign. And Manchester
was in a hurry. They began to press Mr. Shields,
Mr. Shields said nothing. They threatened him with
injunctions from the Court of Chancery; they writted
him, they began actions, being hot-headed and
masculine men, for the specific performance of
Mr. Shield's contract. All the while Mr. Shields
lay absolutely low. At last in despair of ever getting
the Town Hall finished the city of Manchester commissioned Madox Brown to complete the series
of frescoes. This again was Mr. Shield's triumph.
For from the first he had accepted the commission
and he had remained silent through years of bullying,
having in his mind all the time the design that the

work should fall to my grandfather whom he considered an absolutely great artist. Had he at first refused the commission it would have been taken by some painter less self-sacrificing. He took it therefore and bore the consequences, which were very troublesome.

I was once walking with this fine gentleman when he became the subject of a street boy's remark which should not, I think, be lost to the world. That Mr. Shields is of this opinion I feel fairly certain, for I have many times heard him repeat the anecdote. A deeply religious man, Mr. Shields was at the time of which I am writing eminently patriarchal in appearance. His beard was of great length and his iron-grey hair depended well on to his shoulders. This attracted the attention of an extremely small boy who scarcely came up to the painter's knee. Both his eyes and mouth as round as three marbles, the child trotted along, gazing up into the artist's eyes until he asked :

" What is it, my little man ? "

Then at last the boy answered :

" Now I knows why it was the barber hung hisself ! "

Mr. Shields was not in any way embarrassed, but when I was extremely young and extremely self-conscious, he once extremely embarrassed me. Being of this picturesque appearance he was walking with myself and Mr. Harold Rathbone, the almost more picturesque originator of Della Robbia ware pottery. This was a praiseworthy enterprise for the manufacture amongst other things of beautiful milk jugs, which, at ten-and-sixpence a piece, Mr. Rathbone considered would be so handy for the Lancashire mill girls when they went on a day's outing in the country. We were in the most crowded part of Piccadilly; the eyes of Europe seemed to be already more than sufficiently upon us to suit my taste. Mr. Rathbone suddenly announced that he had succeeded in persuading the Liverpool Corporation to buy Mr. Holman Hunt's picture of "The Triumph of the Innocents." Mr. Shields stopped dramatically. His eyes became as large and round as those of the street child:

" You *have*, Harold ! " he exclaimed, and opening his arms wide he cried out: " Let me kiss you, Harold ! "

The two artists, their inverness capes flying out and seeming to cover the whole of Piccadilly, fell into each other's arms. As for me I ran away at the top of my speed and hid myself in the gloomy entrance under the steps of the orchestra at the back of St. James's Hall. But I wish now I could again witness an incident arising from another such occasion.

VIII

THE earliest Pre-Raphaelites bothered themselves very little therefore with politics, Rossetti himself less than any of the others, though most of the Rossettis had always views of an advanced character. How could it be otherwise, with Italians whose earliest ideas were centred around the struggle for Italian freedom ? It has always seemed to me a curious conjunction that Napoleon III, when he was a pauper exile in London, was a frequent visitor at the little house in Charlotte Street where the Rossettis lived in an odour of Italian conspiracy. And it has sometimes occurred to me to wonder whether the germs of Napoleon's later policy—that Utopian and tremendous idea that was his of uniting all Latin humanity in one immense alliance under the ægis and hegemony of the eagle of France—that tremendous idea that, appearing amidst the smoke of Solferino and Sadowa, fell so tragically upon the field of Sedan—whether that idea did not find its birth in the little room where Rossetti the father sat and talked continuously of Dante and of *Italia una*.

I remember hearing an anecdote concerning Mazzini that has nothing to do with Pre-Raphaelites—but it is one that amuses me. In the time of Mazzini's exile in London, he was in circumstances of extreme poverty. One of the sympathizers with the cause of the liberation of Italy allowed the refugee to live in the attic of his office. He was a Mr. Shaen, a solicitor of distinction, and his offices were naturally in Bedford Row. He rented the whole house but used only the lower rooms.

Years passed; Mazzini went away, died, and was enshrined in the hearts of his liberated countrymen. More years passed; Mr. Shaen died; the firm which Mr. Shaen founded grew larger and larger. The clerks invaded room after room of the upper house, until at last they worked in the very attics. One day one of the partners was dictating a difficult letter to a clerk in such an attic. He stood before the fire, and absent-mindedly fingered a dusty spherical object of iron that stood upon the mantelpiece. Getting hold of the phrase that he wanted, he threw, still absent-mindedly, this iron object into the fire. He finished dictating the letter and left the room. Immediately afterwards there was a terrific explosion. The round object was nothing more nor less than a small bomb.

With such objects Mazzini had passed his time whilst, years before, he had dreamed of the liberation of Italy. He had gone away; the bomb, forgotten upon the mantelpiece, had remained undisturbed until at last it found its predestined billet in the maiming of several poor clerks. I do not know that there is any particular moral to this story. It certainly does not bear upon what was the great moral of the Pre-Raphaelites, as of the Æsthetes.

146

It is true that this great moral is nothing more nor less than the mediæval proverb: " Let the cobbler stick to his last."

Indeed, it was in exactly those words that my grandfather replied to O'Connell when that ardent champion of the cause of United Ireland requested Madox Brown, Rossetti and Holman Hunt to stand for Irish constituencies. O'Connell's idea was that if the cause of Ireland could be represented in the House of Commons by Englishmen of distinction in the world of arts and intellect, the cause of Ireland would become much more acceptable in English eyes. In this he was probably wrong, for England has a rooted distrust for any practitioner of the arts. Rossetti, in any case, replied that his health would not allow him to go through the excitement of a parliamentary election.

This was probably true, for at the time Rossetti was at the lowest pitch of his nervous malady. Madox Brown, however, answered in a full-dress letter which was exceedingly characteristic of him. He refused emphatically to stand, whilst pointing out that his entire heart went out to the cause of Ireland, and that he sympathized with all uprisings, moonlightings, boycottings, and any other cheerful form of outrage. This was Madox Brown the romantic ! Immediately afterwards, however, he got to business with those words : " Let the cobbler stick to his last."

He continued—that the affairs of Ireland were exceedingly complicated, that in Ireland itself were many factions, each declaring that the other would be the ruin of the nation, and that he had to pay too much attention to his brushes and paints ever to tackle so thorny a question. He sympathized entirely with freedom in all its forms, he was ready to vote for Home Rule and to subscribe to the funds of all the Irish parties, but he felt that his was not the brain of a practical politician. What Mr. Holman Hunt wrote I do not precisely remember, though I have seen his letter. It put—as it naturally would—Madox Brown's views in language much more forcible and much less polite.

And indeed, until William Morris dragged across the way of Æstheticism the red herring of socialism, the Pre-Raphaelites, the Æsthetes, painters, poets, painter-poets and all the inhabitants of the drawing-rooms that Du Maurier illustrated in *Punch*—all this little earnest or posing world—considered itself as a hierarchy, as an aristocracy entirely aloof from the common sort.

It lived under the sanction of the arts and from them it had alike its placidity and its holiness. When poor Oscar Wilde wandered down Bond Street in parti-coloured velvet hose, holding a single red flower in his hand, he was doing what in those days was called "touching the Philistine on the raw." In France this was called *épater le bourgeois*. Maxime du Camp, whom I have always considered the most odious and belittling of memoirists—who has told us that, but for his illness, Flaubert would have been a man of genius—this Du Camp does in his carping way give us a picture of a sort of society which in many ways resembled that of the Æsthetes

148

towards the end of the last century. In Flaubert, Gautier, even in Mérimée, and in a half-score of French writers just before the fall of the Second Empire, there was this immense feeling of the priesthood of the arts. I do not mean to say that it was limited to the côterie that surrounded Flaubert. Victor Hugo had it; and even Alexandre Dumas *qui écrivait comme un cocher de fiacre*. Du Camp, the whole of whose admiration was given to the author of Monte Cristo, ought by rights to have been an English critic.

Indeed it was only yesterday, that I read in my daily paper an article by the literary critic who to-day is most respected by the British middle classes. Said this gentleman : " Thank Heaven, that the day of Flaubert and the Realists is passed for England and that the market is given over to writers of the stamp of Mr. A—— to writers who, troubling their heads nothing at all about the subtleties of art, set themselves the task of writing a readable story without bothering about the words in which it is written."

These words might well have been written by *ce cher Maxime !* The same English writer, in reviewing the Memoirs of Mme. de Boigne, goes out of his way to poke fun at the duchess who surrounded Chateaubriand with an atmosphere of adoration. This seemed ridiculous to Mr. ——. It would not have seemed ridiculous to Du Camp.

But be these matters how they may, it is pretty certain that, outside this æsthetic circle, we have never had in England any body of people, whether artists or laity, who realized that art was a thing that it was in the least worth putting oneself out for; and when Oscar Wilde wandered down Bond Street in a mediæval costume, bearing in his hand a flower, he was doing something not merely ridiculous. It was militant.

Wilde himself I met only in his later years. I remember being at a garden party of the Bishop of London, and hearing behind me a conversation so indelicate that I could not resist turning around. Oscar Wilde, very fat, with the remainder of young handsomeness—even of young beauty—was talking to a lady. It would be more precise to say that the lady was talking to Wilde, for it was certainly she who supplied the indelicacies in their conversation, for as I knew Wilde he had a singularly cleanly tongue.

But I found him exceedingly difficult to talk to, and I only once remember hearing him utter one of his brilliancies. This was at a private view of the New Gallery. Some one asked Wilde if he were not going to the soirée of the O. P. Club. Wilde, who at that time had embroiled himself with that organization, replied: " No. Why, I should be like a poor lion in a den of savage Daniels."

I saw him once or twice afterwards in Paris, where he was, I think, rather shamefully treated by the younger denizens of Montmartre and of the Quartier Latin. I remember him as, indeed, a tragic figure, seated at a table in a little cabaret, lachrymosely drunk, and being tormented by an abominable gang of young students of the four arts.

Wilde possessed a walking-stick with an ivory head, to which he attached much affection—and, indeed, in his then miserable poverty it was an object of considerable intrinsic value. Prowling about the same cabaret was one of those miserable wrecks of humanity, a harmless, parasitic imbecile, called Bibi Latouche. The young students were engaged in persuading poor Wilde that this imbecile was a dangerous malefactor. Bibi was supposed to have taken a fancy to Wilde's walking-stick, and the young men persuaded the poet that if he did not surrender this treasure he would be murdered on his way home through the lonely streets. Wilde cried and protested.

I do not know that I acted any heroic part in the matter. I was so disgusted that I went straight out of the café, permanently cured of any taste for Bohemianism that I may ever have possessed. Indeed, I have never since been able to see a student, with his blue béret, his floating cloak, his floating tie, and his youthful beard, without a feeling of aversion.

One of Wilde's French intimates of that date assured me, and repeated with the utmost earnestness and many asseverations, that he was sure Wilde only sinned *par pure snobisme,* and in order to touch the Philistine on the raw. Of this I am pretty well satisfied, just as I am certain that such a trial as that of Wilde was a lamentable error of public policy on the part of the police. He should have been given his warning, and have been allowed to escape across the Channel. That any earthly good could come of the trial, no one, I think, would be so rash as to advance. I did not like Wilde, his works seemed to me derivative and of no importance, his humour thin and mechanical, and I am lost in amazement at the fact that in Germany and to some extent in France, Wilde should be considered a writer of enormous worth. Nevertheless, I cannot help thinking that his fate was infinitely more bitter than anything he could have deserved. As a scholar he was worthy of the greatest respect. His conversation, though it did not appeal to me, gave, as I can well believe, immense pleasure to innumerable persons; so did his plays, so did his verse. Into his extravagances he was pushed by the quality of his admirers, who demanded always more and more follies; when they had pushed him to his fall, they very shamefully deserted this notable man.

On the afternoon when the sentence against Wilde had been pronounced, I met Dr. Garnett on the steps of the British Museum. He said gravely: "This is the death-blow to English poetry." I looked at him in amazement, and he continued: "The only poets we have are the Pre-Raphaelites, and this will cast so much odium upon them that the habit of reading poetry will die out in England."

I was so astonished that I laughed out loud. I had hardly imagined that Wilde could be called a Pre-Raphaelite at all. Indeed, it was only because of the confusion that existed between Pre-Raphaelism and Æstheticism that the name ever became attached to this group of poets. Pre-Raphaelism as it existed in the 'forties and 'fifties was a sort of Realism inspired by high moral purpose.

Æstheticism, which originated with Burne-Jones and Morris, was a movement that concerned itself with idealizing anything that was mediæval. It may be symbolized by the words, "long necks and pomegranates." Wilde carried this ideal one stage further. He desired to live upon the smell of a lily. I do not know that he ever did, but I know that he was in the habit of sending to young ladies whom he admired a single lily flower, carefully packed in cotton-wool. And the cry from the austere realism of my grandfather's picture of *Work*, or Holman Hunt's *Saviour in the Temple*, was so far that I may well be pardoned for not recognizing Wilde at all under the mantle of a *soi-disant* Pre-Raphaelite.

But looking back I recognize how true Dr. Garnett's words were. For certainly at about that date English poetry died. It is really extraordinary the difference that has arisen between those days and now—a matter of not twenty years. The literary life of London of the early nineteenth century was extraordinarily alive and extraordinarily vivid. To be a writer then was to be something monumental. I remember almost losing my breath with joy and astonishment when Mr. Zangwill once in a railway carriage handed me a cigarette; to have spoken to Mr. William Watson was as glorious a thing as to have spoken to Napoleon the Great. In those days writers were interviewed; their houses, their writing desks, their very blotting pads, were photographed for the weekly papers. Their cats, even, were

153

immortalized by the weekly press. Think of that, now !

But when Swinburne died—to our lasting shame— we did not even bury him in Westminster Abbey. To our lasting shame I say—for Swinburne was, without exception, the best-known Englishman in the world. I do not think that it was the trial of Wilde that alone brought this about. Two other factors conduced.

In the glorious 'nineties Mr. John Lane and Mr. Elkin Mathews founded a romantic and wonderful publishing business. This was called the Bodley Head. It attracted all the young poets of the nest of singing birds that England then was. There never was such an excitement.

Little volumes of poems were published in limited editions, and forty, fifty or sixty pounds would be paid at auction for a single copy. There appeared to be no end to it, and then the end came. I do not know why Mr. Lane and Mr. Mathews parted : I do not know why the Bodley Head died down. No doubt the fate of Wilde had a great deal to do with it. Probably the public, with its singular and muddle-headed perspicacity, inseparably connected in its mind the idea of poetry with ideas of vice. I do not know. At any rate, all these glories died away as utterly as the radiance is said to vanish from the dying flying-fish.

And then came the Boer War which appears to me like a chasm separating the new world from the old. Since that period the whole tone of England appears to me to have entirely changed, principles having died out of politics, even as the

spirit of artistry has died out amongst the practitioners of the arts.

As it is in the political world, so in the artistic. I
do not mean to say that the Pre-Raphaelites were
any very great shakes. But they cared intensely
about their work; they talked about it and about
little else. They regarded themselves, indeed, as
priests. And without some such beliefs, how can
an artist be hardened to do good work ? There is
no being so solitary, there is no being with so little
power of gauging where he stands in the estimation
of the world.

I—and when I write " I " I mean every writer who
ever used a hyphen—am told sometimes that I am the
finest—or let us say the most precious—stylist now
employing the English language. That may be so
or it may not. What means have I of knowing ?
For the very paper which says that such and such
a work of mine is the finest of the sort that was
ever written, will say to-morrow that a book by
Miss —— is a work almost inconceivably fine—the
finest thing since Shakespeare; and this is constantly happening to me.

A weekly paper last year wrote of one of my
books : " This is undoubtedly the finest historical
novel that has appeared since the days of Scott."
Next week in the same column, written by the same
hand, there appeared the review of a novel by a
female connection of the critic. " This," he said,
" is undoubtedly the finest historical novel that has
appeared since the days of Scott." Where, then, do
I stand, or to whom shall I go to find out ? Is it to
my sales ? They are satisfactory, but they might be

larger. Is it to my publisher ? He will inevitably tell me—and every writer who ever used a hyphen—that he loses money over my books.

It is twenty years since I published my first novel, and every year or so since then the publisher of that early work has written to tell me that he lost one hundred pounds by that book, and why will I not give him another ? And I ask myself why, if this gentleman once lost so largely over me—why does he wish to publish me again ? Or why should any one wish to publish my work ? Yet I have never written a line that has not been published.

This, of course, is only the fortune of war; but what strikes me as remarkable was that my grandfather was as anxious to embark me upon an artistic career as most parents are to prevent their children from entering into a life that as a rule is so precarious.

My father's last words to me were : " Fordie, whatever you do, never write a book." Indeed, so little idea had I of meddling with the arts that, although to me a writer was a very wonderful person, I prepared myself very strenuously for the Indian Civil Service. This was a real grief to my grandfather, and I think he was exceedingly overjoyed when the doctors refused to pass me for that service on the ground that I had an enlarged liver. And when then I seriously proposed to go into an office, his wrath became tempestuous.

Tearing off his nightcap—for he happened at the time to be in bed with a bad attack of gout—he flung it to the other end of the room.

" God damn and blast my soul ! " he exclaimed.

" Isn't it enough that you escaped providentially from being one kind of a cursed clerk, but you want to go and be another ? I tell you, I will turn you straight out of my house if you go in for any kind of commercial life." So that my fate was settled for me.

IX

POETS AND PRESSES

I THINK that there is no crime—literary or connected with literature—that nowadays an average,
fairly honest English writer will not commit for
the sake of a little money. He will lengthen
his book to suit one publisher, he will cut it
down to suit another. Nay, men otherwise honourable and trustworthy will, for the matter of that,
perjure themselves in the most incredible manner
as to financial arrangements thay may have come
to, or in the most cold-blooded style will break
contracts and ignore obligations. I suppose that
never before was the financial struggle amongst
the literary classes so embittered and so ignoble.
The actual circumstances of literary life may have
been more humiliating in the days when Johnson
waited upon the patron that he never found. Hazlitt
and the English essayists who seem to have existed
in an atmosphere of tallow candles and porter, and
to have passed their days in low pot-houses, may
have been actually worse off than writers of their
rank would be to-day. Hood starved, Douglas
Jerrold, Hannay or Angus B. Riach led existences of
extreme squalor with spirits of the most high. And
indeed, disagreeable as Bohemianism seems to me,

the somewhat squalid lives of writers and artists of
the 'forties and 'fifties had about them something
much more manly and even a little more romantic
than is to be found in the literary life of to-day. I
do not know that the artist of the 'forties troubled
himself much about social position? Cruikshank
was violently angry when Maclise, in his wonderful
series of pen-and-ink portraits in *Fraser's Magazine*,
gave to the world a likeness of the immortalizer of
Pickwick sitting upon a barrel in a boosing-ken,
his sketch block held before him, whilst his keen
and restless eyes surveyed what the commentator
in the text calls *this scene of tumult and crime.*
Mr. Cruikshank wrote indignantly to declare that it
was shameful to pillorize him for ever as sitting in
such low haunts. He wished to say that he was as
good a gentleman as the Duke of Wellington, and
passed his days as a gentleman should. And, indeed,
I dimly remember being taken to call at Cruikshank's
home in Mornington Crescent—though Cruikshank
himself must have been long dead—and seeing there
such Nottingham lace curtains, pieces of brain-
coral, daguerreotypes, silhouettes and engravings
after Cruikshank, as would have been found in any
middle-class home of early and mid Victorian days.
One of the principal of these engravings was the
immense caricature that Cruikshank made for the
Good Templars. This represented upon one hand
the prosperous and whiskered satisfaction that falls
to a man who has led a teetotal existence and, in
many terrible forms, what would happen to you if
you indulged in any kind of alcoholic beverage.

Dickens avowed quite frankly and creditably his

desire to have footmen in purple velvet small clothes
to hang behind his carriage, and Thackeray was never
quite easy as to his social position.   But on the other
hand there was as a general rule very little thought
about these matters.   You earned very little, so
you sat in a pot-house because you could not afford
a club.   And you got through life somehow without
much troubling to make yourself of importance by
meddling in politics.   Thus, for instance, there was
my grandfather's cousin Tristram Madox, who, being
along with Douglas Hannay, a midshipman, was
along with him cashiered and turned out of the
Service for breaking leave and going ashore at
Malta, and " violently assaulting Mr. Peter Parker,
Tobacconist."   Tristram Madox ran through several
subsequent fortunes, and ended by living on ten
shillings a week that were regularly sent him by
Madox Brown.   This allowance was continued for
many years—twenty or thirty, I should think.
One day it occurred to Madox Brown that he would
like some news of his poor relation.   I was accordingly sent down to the squalid cottage in a suburb
of Ramsgate, to which for so many years the weekly
postal orders had been addressed.   Upon my men-
tioning the name of Madox, consternation fell upon
a pale-faced household.   Tristram Madox had been
dead ten years; in the interval the cottage had
changed hands twice, but the incoming tenants had
always accepted gratefully the weekly ten shillings
that fell upon them from they knew not where.
 Hannay on the other hand—presumably because
he had no fortunes to run through—adopted the
life of a man of letters.   He wrote one sufficiently

bad novel, called *Eustace Conyers*, and lived that life which always seemed to lie beneath the shadow of the King's Bench prison. I never heard my grandfather say much that was particularly illuminating about this group of men; though his cousin took him frequently into their society. Their humour seems to have been brutal and personal, but only a bludgeon would suppress it. Thus, when Tristram Madox was talking about one of his distinguished ancestors of the tenth century, Douglas Jerrold shut him up by saying: "I know! The man who was hanged for sheep-stealing." Or, again, when Douglas Jerrold was uttering a flood of brilliant witticisms a very drunken woman, who had been asleep with her head upon the table opposite Jerrold, shut *him* up by raising a bleared face and exclaiming: "You're a bloody fool."

Nothing else would have shut Jerrold up. But I never heard my grandfather say that it was reprehensible or remarkable that they should sit in low pot-houses, or even that he should go there to meet them. They could not afford anything better; so they took what they could get. As for the social revolution, they never talked about it, and although Dickens wrote *Oliver Twist* and *Bleak House* it was done with a warm-hearted enthusiasm, and the last thing that he would have considered himself was a theoretic social reformer. Between this insouciance and the uneasy social self-consciousness of the present day literary man, there arose for a short time the priestly pride, as you might call it, of the Pre-Raphaelites.

These people undoubtedly regarded themselves

as a close aristocracy. They produced works of art of one kind or another, and no one who did not produce works of art counted. The laity in fact might not have existed at all. Indeed, even the learned and professional classes were not excluded from the general contempt. An Oxford Don was regarded as a foolish, useless, and academic person, and my grandfather would say for instance, of a doctor : " Oh, those fellows have nothing better to do than to wash their hands twelve times a day." It never, I think, entered his head to inquire why a doctor so frequently washed his hands. He regarded it as a kind of foppishness. And I can well remember that I entirely shared his point of view. So that to speak to any one who made money by commercial pursuits was almost not to speak to a man at all. It was as if one were communicating with one of the lower animals endowed with power of speech.

And to a certain extent the public of those days acquiesced. From the earliest mediæval times until towards the end of the nineteenth century there has always been vaguely in the public mind the idea that the man of letters was a sort of necromancer— as it were a black priest. In the dark ages almost the only poet that was known to man was the author of the *Æneid*. I do not suppose that many men had read this epic, but all men had heard of its author. Was not his fame worldwide ? Was he not Duke Virgil of Mantua ? Did he not build the city of Venice upon an egg ? Yes, surely, he indeed was the greatest of all magicians. He left behind him his books of magic. If you took a pin and stuck it into one of these books the line that it hit upon predicted infallibly what would be the outcome of any enterprise upon which you were engaged. These were the *Sortes Virgilianae*. Similarly, any one who could write or was engaged with books was regarded as a necromancer. Did he not have strange knowledges ? Thus you had Friar Bacon, Friar Bungay, or Dr. Faustus. The writer remained thus for centuries something mysterious, some one possessing those strange knowledges. For various classes, by the time of Johnson his mystery has gradually been whittled down. The aristocracy, in the shape of patrons, came to regard him as a miserable creature, something between a parasite and a pimp. To his personal tradesman he was also a miserable creature who did not pay his bills and starved in a garret. By the nineteenth century the idea that he was a sort of rogue and vagabond had spread pretty well throughout the land. A middle class father was horrified when his daughter proposed to marry an artist or a writer. These people were notorious for marital infidelities and for the precariousness of their sources of livelihood. Nevertheless, a sort of mysterious sanctity attached to their produce. There can hardly have been a single middle-class household that did not have upon its drawing-room table one or two copies of books by Mr. Ruskin. I remember very well being consulted by a prosperous city merchant as to what books he should take with him upon a sea voyage. I gave him my views, to which he paid no attention. He took with him, *Sesame and Lilies*, *Notes upon Sheep Folds*, Carlyle's *Life of Frederic the Great*, Tennyson's *Idylls of the King*, and Swinburne's *Atalanta*. With this singular library my portly friend set sail. He had not the slightest idea of what any of these books might be about, but he said: "Ah! they'll do me a great deal of good." As if, in his cabin, these volumes would act as a spiritual lifebuoy and float him, supposing the ship should founder, if not to land, at least to Heaven. That was the trace of the old necromantic idea that something mysterious attached to the mere possession of books. But the same gentleman would introduce a writer to his friends with a sort of apologetic cough, rather as if he had been found in the company of a prostitute, and when revelations of Carlyle's domestic misfortunes were published he manifested a calm satisfaction. He had always suspected that there must be something wrong because Carlyle was an author. But he still expected that his soul was saved because he possessed the *Life of Frederic the Great*.

Thus in the 'seventies and 'eighties things were at a very satisfactory pass. Artists regarded themselves as an aristocracy set apart and walled off. The rest of the world regarded them as dangerous beings producing mysterious but, upon the whole, salutary works. There was no mixing and there was no desire to mix. As far as the arts were concerned, there was in those days a state of affairs very much such as has subsisted in France since the time of the French Revolution. It is true that in France somewhat more social importance attaches to the man of letters. That is largely because of the existence of the French Academy. At the time when there is a vacancy in the ranks of the immortal

Forty you may observe a real stir in what is known as All Paris. Duchesses get out their carriages and drive candidates round to pay their calls upon the electors; nay, duchesses themselves canvass energetically in favour of the particular master whose claims they favour, and the inaugural speech of an elected Academician is a social function more eagerly desired than were the drawing-rooms of Her late Majesty Victoria. But otherwise the worlds of letters and of arts mix comparatively little with commercial society in France.

And this has always seemed to me to be a comparatively desirable frame of mind for the practitioner of the arts to adopt. For, unless he do consider himself—rightly or wrongly—as something apart he must rapidly lose all sense of the dignity of his avocation. He will find himself universally regarded, no longer, perhaps, as anything so important as a dangerous rogue and vagabond, but as something socially negligible. And all respect for literature as literature he will find to have died out utterly and for ever.

Flaubert was obsessed by the idea that literature was a thing hated by the " bourgeoisie"; that was the dominant idea of his life. And in his day I think he was right. That is to say, that the common man hated violently any new literary form that was vital, unusual and original. Thus Flaubert came to sit upon the criminal's bench after the publication of *Madame Bovary*. But nowadays, and in England, we have a singular and chilling indifference to all literature. Shakespeare, Homer and Dante might all put out their works to-day—for all I know writers as great may actually be amongst us—and the actual effects of their publishing would be practically nothing. It is all very well to say that the press is responsible for this state of affairs. We have a press in England that is, upon the whole, of the lowest calibre of any in the civilized world—I am, of course, speaking in terms intellectual, for our news organization is as good as it could be. But from the point of view of criticism of any kind, whether of the fine arts, of letters, of music or of life itself, all but the very best of our newspapers of to-day would disgrace a fourth class provincial town of France or Germany. And this is a purely commercial matter. When I was conducting a certain publication I was rung up on the telephone by the advertising managers of two of the largest and most respectable daily newspapers. The first one told me that if I would take a six-inch double column in his literary supplement once a week, he would undertake that a favourable notice of my publication should appear in his organ side by side with the advertisement. The advertising manager of the other newspaper asked me peremptorily why I had not advertised in his columns; I replied that it was because I disapproved very strongly of a certain action to which his newspaper had committed itself.

" Very well, then," he said, " you quite understand that no notice of your periodical will be taken in our literary columns."

I am bound to say that this gentleman was merely " bluffing," and that quite impartial notices of my publication did appear in his paper. Indeed, I

166

should imagine that the literary editor of the journal in question never spoke to an advertising manager. But just think of the state of affairs—though it *was* only a matter of bluff—when such a threat could be made ! I do not mean to say that there is any very actual or overt corruption in the London press of to-day, but the hunt for advertisements is a bitter and unscrupulous struggle. Advertisement canvassers are—or at any rate I have found them so— men entirely without scruples, and the editorial departments of newspapers are thoroughly slack in the supervision of their representatives. The advertisement canvasser will come into the editorial office and will say to the literary editor in a friendly but slightly complaining manner—I have heard this speech myself—

" Look here, Messrs. So-and-so say that they have spent forty pounds a week with us for the last three months and that you never give their books any space at all. Couldn't you see that they have a mention now and then ? "

The literary editor, knowing perfectly well—or feeling sub-consciously that his position as editor or perhaps even the very existence of his literary supplement depends upon its power to attract advertisements, will almost certainly look out for something amongst the works published by Messrs. So-and-so, and will then praise this work to the extent of a column or so. He will not always do this out of fear. Sometimes it will be because he desires to help the poor devil of an advertisement canvasser, who has a wife and family. Sometimes he will do it to oblige the publisher, who may be

the best of good fellows. But always the result
will be the same. And, armed with this achievement, the advertising canvasser will go round to
other publishers and assure them that, if they will
spend money on advertisements in his paper, he
will secure for them favourable notices upon the
day when the advertisement appears. All this is
very natural, a slow and imperceptibly spreading
process of corruption. But it is bitterly bad for
literature. Twenty-five years ago it would have
been impossible, fifteen years ago it would have
been impossible. Now, it *is*. There are exceptions,
of course, but every day they grow fewer.

The fine old newspaper whose advertisement manager proposed that I should give him every Monday
a six-inch double column and receive in exchange
my favourable notice—this fine old newspaper had
just a week before passed into " new hands." And
now-a-days alas! almost invariably new brooms
sweep very dirty ! Cataclysmic and extraordinary
changes take place every day in the world of newspapers. In one week two years ago I received visits
from just over forty beggars. Every one of these
introduced himself to my favour with the words :
" I am a journalist myself " ! One of these poor
men had a really tragic history. He bore a
name of some respectability in the journalistic
world. He had been a reporter upon a midland
daily paper; he had become the editor of a south-
west local journal. One day he was riding a bicycle
outside his town when a motor-car approached him
from behind, knocked him down, and, as he lay on
the ground spread-eagled, it ran over both his legs

and both his arms and broke them. The car went on without stopping, and this poor man lay for eighteen months in a hospital. When he came out he was penniless, and he found that the whole face of journalism had altered. The midland paper for which he had written had passed into the hands of Lord Dash, and the entire staff had changed; his south coast local paper had passed out of existence; so had the great London morning paper for which he had occasionally written. In another newspaper office with which he had been connected he found two editors, each properly engaged, quarrelling as to who should occupy the editorial chair, and neither one of these had been the editor of the paper when he had gone into the hospital. In the short space of eighteen months all the men he knew had lost their jobs and had disappeared from Fleet Street. That is why one will receive visits from forty beggars in one week, each of them introducing himself with the words : " I am a journalist myself."

It is this terrible insecurity of tenure that has so brought low—that is so bringing low—the journalism of England. And it is not so much the fact that the majority of our journals are written by shop-boys for shop-girls—for, after all, why should shop-girls not have their organs ?—or that they are directed by advertising managers for the benefit of shop-keepers. What is really terrible, is that the public is entirely indifferent to the fare that is put before it. It is as indifferent to the leading articles.

There is an old skit of Thackeray's representing the astonishment of an Oriental Pasha at the ordered routine and the circumstances of an English middle class household. He sees the white breakfast-table laid, the shining coffee and cream jugs, the eggs and bacon bubbling in their silver dishes. The family come down and range themselves in their places around the table. The Pasha utters the appropriate ejaculations and comments at the strangeness of the scene. Last of all comes down the master of the house. He puts his napkin across his knees, is helped to eggs and bacon and then—comfortably opens his newspaper.

"Bismillah!" the Pasha ejaculates, "will he read through that immense sheet before he applies himself to the work of the day? By Allah! it is as large as the mainsail of His Highness's yacht."

Mr. Thomlinson of the 'sixties and 'seventies probably did not read through the whole of his paper. But he did read the leaders and the foreign correspondence, and then took himself off to business, his wife with her key basket attending him to the hall, where she cast a glance at the hat-rack to see that her husband's hat was wel brushed and his umbrella properly folded. [These last words are not my own. They are suggested by the introductory direction to a lady of the house in the cookery book written by Mrs. Beeton—a work most excellent y shadowing that almost vanished thing, an English home.]

Mr. Thomlinson, if he d'd not ride down to his office in the City, drove there in his brougham. The remainder of his newspaper he reserved for a comfortable and half somnolent perusal after dinner, whilst Mrs. Thomlinson crocheted and the young ladies played "The Battle of Prague" upon the piano, or looked over the water-colour sketches that they had made at Ramsgate that summer. Then with his mind comfortably filled with the ideas of his favourite leader writers, Mr. Thom'inson would take his flat candlestick and go tranquilly to bed.

When I was a boy it used to be considered a reproach with which one could flatten out any " bourgeois " to say that his m nd was regulated by the leader in the newspaper. And the minds of most of the middle class in that day were indeed so regulated. Nowadays it would be almost a testimonial to say of a m'ddle class man that he read anything so solid and instructive as were the leaders of the 'seventies and 'eighties. That we do not read the leaders to-day is probably to our credit. A little time ago I was in the editorial room of one of our great organs. The editor was g'ving me his views upon something or other. A clerk came in with a note. The editor interrupted his flow of speech to say :

" Here, you ! the German journalists' deputation is coming to London to-morrow. Just write a leader about it. I am too busy. Be polite, but not too polite, you understand. If you have not time to write it get some one else to do it. Anybody will do. Tell them that—not to be too polite. Let them read the back files for what we have said already. I want the copy in half-an-hour."

You will observe that it would be incorrect to say that this leader was going to be written by a shop-boy for shop-girls. It was going to be written by just any clerk, for nobody at all in England. Unfortunately, if nobody at all in

England to-day reads leaders, this is not the case in foreign countries. There was once a time when the *Standard* had an immense reputation abroad. Continental papers hung upon its lips and attached to its utterances on foreign politics an enormous and deserved importance. And some such importance is still attached on the Continent to the utterances of English newspapers, though the *Standard* itself no longer monopolizes attention. Thus the utterances of our "Gutter Press," written by any clerk for nobody, and carefully observing the editor's direction to be not too polite—these utterances find attached to them an all too great importance in the newspapers of the particular country which for the time being the proprietor of the newspaper has made up his mind to bait. In England they produce no impression at all, but abroad unfortunately they do a great deal of harm, because the foreigner can never really get it out of his head that a newspaper represents officially the views of the State. This same editor once gave one of his departmental sub-editors a fortnight's holiday. In this fortnight he was to study the works of Flaubert and Maupassant—in order to acquire the quality that is called "snap."

This may appear impossible, yet it is perfectly true. But what would have happened in the days of Delane? One is a little tired of hearing of Delane, yet there is no doubt that Delane was one of the greatest editors of papers and one of the great forces of the day. He indeed earned for *The Times* the name of "The Thunderer." And this he did by means of enormous industry and enormous rectitude. He paid unsleeping attention to the quality of the paper in all its departments. If the musical editor wrote too often or with too much enthusiasm of any given *prima donna*—or if he suspected that it was being done, he would himself take the opportunity of visiting the opera and forming an estimate. Or, if he suspected the art editor of too much partiality for a living painter, Delane would take a great deal of trouble to discover what was the general consensus of opinion of the art world concerning the claims of that painter. This, of course, was not an ideal method of directing criticism of art. Delane himself was not an authority on music, and the general consensus of opinion on any given painter will tell as a rule very hardly against originality or new genius. Nevertheless, it was a conscientious thing to do, and quite the most practical in a world where log-rolling is a dangerous factor.

And if there was only one Delane, there were in London of that day at least twenty editors of daily and weekly papers to whom Delane's ideals were ideals too. An editor of that day regarded himself as discharging a very responsible and almost sacred duty. He discharged it autocratically, and his position was of the utmost security and tenure. He would have about him, too, a force of august anonymity, and to be in the same room with Delane was to feel oneself hushed, as if royalty had been about. Indeed, merely to take " copy " to *The Times* office was to feel oneself infinitely humble as regarded that newspaper, but nevertheless a functionary of importance in the rest of the world.

And, as with the editors, so with the leader writers.

173

These also were august and serious gentlemen. They appeared to be of the rank of editors of the great Quarterlies; or at least, they were contributors to these revered organs. They would debate the topics of the day with the editor-in-chief, and they would demand two days to reflect about and to write their article if it was one of any importance. In those days, in fact, no editor could call to him his clerk and say that he wanted a not too polite leader in half-an-hour.

I do not mean to say that the actual conditions of the English press up to the date of the Boer War were altogether ideal. But when a newspaper got its hand upon a writer of ability, of genius, or of rectitude, it knew what to do with him. It gave him plenty of space, it kept occasionally an eye upon him, and it left him very much alone. Thus there arose such really great journalistic critics as W. E. Henley, the late R. A. M. Stevenson, or G. W. Steevens, though Steevens lived into and died at the hands of the new journalism. And these men were really great in their own way. I do not mean to say that Henley was a great literary critic in the sense that Sainte Beuve was great, or that fifty Frenchmen are great. But he had at least some canons of art, and, right-headed, wrong-headed, or altogether beside the mark, he roared out gallantly enough the ideas which for the moment had possession of him. And I have always considered that the final proof that the Tory party is really the stupid party—the damning and final proof was that it never subsidized Henley and never provided him with an organ. Had Henley been a Liberal, he

174

would have had half-a-dozen papers at his feet.
The Tory party without a qualm let die alike
the *National Observer* and the *New Review* as it
would have let die fifty periodicals of as fine a
genius had Henley had the strength or the money
to start them.   But Henley was a very great man,
and the circle of writers with whom he surrounded
himself was very valuable and very vital until the
death of Henley, and the coming of that never to be
sufficiently accursed war set as it were an iron door
between the past and the present.

To Henley and his circle I will return; they took
as it were the place of Pre-Raphaelism after Pre-
Raphaelism had degenerated into a sort Æstheticism,
and Æstheticism into a sort of mawkish flap-doodle.
But the point was that the older journalism did
afford place and space for such vigorous authentic
and original writers.   Its trouble was that unless
an editor was very vigorous these strong critics,
getting a too free hand, would go off into riots of a
perfectly tremendous log-rolling.

Thus for instance one had the *Athenæum* under
the editorship of Mr. Maccoll.   Mr. Maccoll was one
of the most charming and esoterically erudite of
men, but his mind, I think, was entirely immersed
in what is called Symbolic Logic.   As to what
Symbolic Logic was or may be I have not the faintest
idea.   One evening when I was walking home with
Mr. Maccoll from Dr. Garnett's at the British
Museum, Mr. Maccoll with his gentle voice, large
person, black kid gloves—I never in my life saw him
without the black kid gloves either indoors or out—
and abstract manner, kindly tried to explain to me

what this science was. But all my mind retained
was a vague idea that if you called a dog a tree and
a tree R, and if you worked it out as an algebraic
proposition, you would solve the riddle of the uni-
verse. At any rate he was a very gentle, kind and
abstracted man, and it was a genuine pleasure to
see him standing, tall, blond and bald in the middle
of a drawing-room holding in his black kid gloves his
cup of tea, and his eyes wandering always round and
round the frieze just below the ceiling. And I have
this much to say of gratitude to Mr. Maccoll, that
although he entertained the deepest hostility to
my father—a hostility which my father vigorously
returned—of all the friends and enemies that my
father and grandfather had between them, the
editor of the *Athenæum* was the only one—if I
except Dr. Garnett and Mr. Watts-Dunton—who
ever tried to do me a good turn.

But under this amiable and scholarly personage
the *Athenæum* was a wildly uncontrolled journal.
The chief pages which were supposed to be given up
to literary criticism were actually given over to the
control of one or two antiquarians and archæologists
who used them for the purpose of battle-axing all
their rival archæologists and antiquarians. Pure
literature as such was almost entirely left out in
the cold, except when Mr. Watts-Dunton chose to
take a hand. Novels were dismissed with a few
sniffy words nearly always dictated by the personal
feelings of the contributor. Then there would come
endless pages of discussions as to the author of
Junius—discussions that spread out over years
and years. Then there would be the late Mr. F. G.

Stephens battle-axing *his* personal enemies in the columns devoted to art criticism, and then would come Mr. Joseph Knight, genially and amiably praising his dramatic friends. Thus under the captaincy, but certainly not under the control, of Mr. Maccoll the *Athenæum* drifted magnificently along its way. It would have done credit as an archæological organ to a German university town; its scientific notes were excellent; its accuracy in matters of fact was meticulous beyond belief. It would condemn as utterly useless a history of the world if its author stated that Sir John Glenquoich of Auchtermuchty was the twenty-seventh instead of the twenty-sixth baronet. It was, in fact, a paradise for bookworms, but regarded as the chief organ of literary, artistic, musical and dramatic criticism of the chief city of the world, it was really extraordinary.

X

A LITERARY DEITY

The log-rolling of the 'seventies, 'eighties and 'nineties might be sedate and scientific as in the case of the older organs, or it might be uproarious and truculent as it was when Henley and his gang of pirates came upon the scene ; but at any rate it meant that some sort of interest was taken in the literary world, and that the literary world expected that some sort of interest would be taken in it. It certainly did. I remember my amazement—and I must add my admiration—when I first read through Rossetti's voluminous and innumerable letters to my grandfather at about the time when he was publishing his first volume of poems. They were really magnificent—these letters. I think that no author ever in such a splendid way set about securing favourable notices from the Press. It was not that the author of *The Blessed Damozel* was not ashamed to corrupt the Press; he simply gloried in it as if it were a game, or a thrilling adventure. He might have been Napoleon conducting a successful battle; and my grandfather might have been his chief of staff.

Not a single organ was neglected. It was : Tell Watts to get at so-and-so. Nobody that I know

knows Dash, but you might reach him through Blank.
And so on through many letters and many hurried
notes as ideas came up in the great man's mind. I do
not know whether anything of the sort had ever been
done before, but I am pretty certain it can never have
been done more thoroughly. It could not have been
done; there would not have been room. *No* stone
was left unturned. And I do not know that I see any
harm in all this.

The Press responded magnificently, and Rossetti
is Rossetti. Had he been "Satan" Montgomery
the Press would probably have responded as magnificently and Montgomery would still have been
nothing. The fact is that the great thing—for
literature—is to get the public to read books at all.
In that case the good book will live and the bad book
will die after it has served its puffed purpose. For
that reason I think we should never grudge a popular
writer his success. If a man may make a large
fortune out of quack medicines, why should another
not have his little prosperity from quack books?
Probably some percentage of his readers will go on
to read something better; the great majority of
them would never otherwise read anything at all,
so that their tastes can not be spoken of as having
been debauched.

The only thing which is fatal is indifference, and
of that we have to-day a large quantity. We have
indeed nothing else, so that a fatal lethargy has
settled down upon publishers as upon authors,
upon the press, and above all upon the public. In
the good old days when log-rolling was a frequent
and profitable adventure, it was entirely different.

Those were fine days to have lived through. There remained the Pre-Raphaelites throning it on their altitudes, their spies and vedettes making thunder in all the journals when Mr. Rossetti or Mr. Swinburne or Mr. Ruskin, or even when any of the lesser lights, turned over as it were in his olympian slumbers and produced a new volume. There was Mr. Meredith beginning to come into his own. *The Amazing Marriage* or *Lord Ormont and his Aminta* was appearing as a serial in the *Universal Review*—that fine enterprise for which Mr. Harry Quilter was never sufficiently praised or thanked. There, too, Mr. Meredith's *Jump-to-Glory Jane* was mystifying us not a little. Mr. Thomas Hardy also was coming into his own. His *Pair of Blue Eyes* was in all our mothers' mouths. The enormous glory of *Lorna Doone* was still illuminating thousands of middle-class homes. This book I remember to have read over and over again when I was a boy. I fancy I know it nearly all by heart, so that now if any one would start me with : *If any one would hear a plain tale told plainly I, John Ridd of the Parish of Oare* . . . or *Now the manner of a winkie is this* . . . I could go on with the quotation for pages. Yet I cannot have looked at *Lorna Doone* for twenty years. *John Inglesant* was also having its reputation made by means of Mr. Gladstone's post cards. So with many other books. Was there not *The Story of an African Farm ?* Did not *Ships that pass in the Night* bring tears into the eyes of innumerable Young Persons ? Mr. Anthony Hope's *Dolly Dialogues* were appearing in the *Westminster Gazette*. The *Westminster Gazette* itself startled the enthusiastic world by appearing on green paper. It told us all that this green paper would be the salvation of all our eyes. I know I ruined mine by reading of Lady Mickleham night after night in the dimly lit carriages of the glamorous Underground. For in those days there was a glamorous Underground. It smelled of sulphur as hell is supposed to smell; its passages were as gloomy as Tartarus' were supposed to be, and smokes and fumes poured from all its tunnels whilst its carriages were lit by oil lamps so that little pools of oil swayed and trembled in the bottoms of the globe-like lamp-glasses. And standing up, holding my green paper up against the lamp I used to read those Dialogues whilst the train jolted me along through the Cimmerian gloom. Why, I remember going up to Manchester with my grandfather, and in the train sat a publisher whom my grandfather spoke of as young Heinemann. He was relating with the utmost enthusiasm that he had had a MS. sent him called, I think, *The Scape Goat*. This, young Heinemann said, was the finest novel that had ever been written. It was not for some time afterwards that my grandfather realized that the author of this work was who he was, and that he himself had given this author, as it were, his literary baptism and an introduction to Dante Gabriel Rossetti.

My grandfather, I remember, regarded *The Scape Goat* as a work of " genius." His literary tastes were peculiar. Thus, during the last nights of his life, when I used to go into his bedroom to see if he were sleeping in safety, I should perceive, resting in the flat candle-stick beside his bed, not only his watch and his spectacles, but a copy of Eugène Sue's *Mystères de Paris*. This book he was re-reading at the suggestion of Mr. W. M. Rossetti, and he considered it also to be a work of genius. He did not live to finish it, but died in the night shortly after he had laid it down. Rossetti, too, I think, regarded Sue's work as "of genius." And then the two painters would never be tired of reading Meinhold's *Amber-witch* and *Sidonia the Sorceress*. But then Rossetti regarded Flaubert as morbid and too cynically immoral to be read by any respectable painter-poet—such a queer thing is literary taste.

And such a queer thing too is the ascription of morbidity. Thus Dr. Garnett, a high functionary of the British Museum, a very learned man, and the writer of the only volume of really scholarly and ironic tales that exists in the English language, found that Christina Rossetti, who had the mind of a mediæval ascetic, was "morbid." Yet, upon the whole, the lesson of Christina Rossetti was that, although life is a sad thing, we must put up with it and regard the trials it brings us as being a certain preparation for a serene and blessed immortality. Whereas upon the whole, Dr. Garnett's message to the world was one of scholarly negation of a sort of mellow cynicism. Or again we find Rossetti, a man of as many irregularities as one man could reasonably desire in one earthly existence, a man whose poetry, if it has any lesson at all, teaches no lesson of asceticism—we find Rossetti in 1870 saying that it was no wonder that France danced and stumbled into disaster when it could produce a work so morbid as *Madame Bovary*.

A Literary Deity

Yet Flaubert was a man of the utmost personal chastity, of the most bourgeois honesty, and of the most idealistic patriotism when his sympathies were aroused by the tragic downfall of his country. And *Madame Bovary* is a work which surely more than any other points out how disastrous from a material point of view is marital infidelity. Yet it shocked Dante Gabriel Rossetti.

Flaubert, on the other hand, considered that if France had read *L'Education Sentimentale* France would have been spared the horrors of the *débâcle*. Maxime du Camp grins and giggles over this idea of Flaubert's. But, reading and re-reading as I do this, the greatest of all modern romances, I can understand very well what this blond and gigantic writer, with his torrents of Berserker rage over the imbecilities of the common mind—I can understand very well what he meant. For *L'Education Sentimentale* is romantic in that it depicts life as being the inverse of the facile romance of the cloak and sword and catchword—the romance of easy victory and little effort. And France, from the downfall of Napoleon I. to the downfall of Napoleon III., was above all other lands that of the catchword and the easy victory. Governments fell at the mere shaking of the head of a purely selfish bourgeoisie. Charles X. fled, Louis Philippe fled, the Second Republic fell before risings that were mere flocking together of idle spouters of catch-words. Victories over trifling foes, victories in Algiers, in the Crimea, over the Austrians, over the Mexicans, victories of the most easy, were supposed to add laurels to the eagles of Jena and Austerlitz. And all the while

in these easy revolutions the character of the French
people grew softer and more verbose; and under
the smoke of these easy victories the character of
the French army became softer and more a matter
of huge gestures. It was these facts that Flaubert
painted in *L'Education Sentimentale*. It was these
morals that his facts would have pointed out to the
French people if they had read his book. But indeed
L'Education Sentimentale is so inspired by contempt
for inanity and fine phrases, it so points the finger
towards the road of sanity and fine effort, that any
nation that really read and marked it might well find
itself mistress of the world. I am, however, as yet
unaware that any nation has betaken itself to the
study of the affairs of Frédéric Moreau and of Mme.
Arnoux. So we shall have to go on building Dread-
noughts until the arrival of a blessed time of which
no omens are very visible in our skies.

It is indeed a curious thing, the criticism that
one great artist will bestow upon another. Thus
Turgeniev acknowledges the receipt of *L'Education
Sentimentale*. He writes to Flaubert—"This is
indeed a work of genius" in the proper and conventional manner. And then growing really pleased,
he proceeds to tear to pieces the beautiful little
passage in which Flaubert describes Mme. Arnoux
singing :

"Elle se tenait debout, près du clavier, les bras tombants, le
regard perdu. Quelquefois pour lire la musique elle clignait ses
paupières, en avancant le front un instant. Sa voix de con-
tralto prenait dans les cordes basses une intonation lugubre qui
glacait, et alors sa belle tête aux grands sourcils s'inclinait sur
son épaule. Sa poitrine se gonflait, ses bras s'écartaient, son

cou d'où s'echappaient des roulades se renversait mollement comme sous des baisers . . . elle lança trois notes aigues, redescendit, en jeta une plus haute encore, et, après un silence, termina par un point d'orgue."

This struck Turgeniev as being supremely ridiculous, and it was the main thing which did strike him in this enormous and overpowering work. It was like the *Athenæum,* which condemned a history of the world because Sir John Glenquoich of Auchtermuchty was described as the twenty-seventh instead of the twenty-sixth baronet. I suppose this was because the *Athenæum* critic had got hold of a guide to Auchtermuchty. Similarly Turgeniev, living in the constant society of the Viardots, and more particularly in that of that great singer Pauline Lucca— Turgeniev had at the moment in his mind a meticulous admiration for musical exclusiveness. Pauline Lucca would have ended her songs with a dazzling cadenza—a shower of small notes.

Yes, it is impossible to say whether Turgeniev or Flaubert were the greatest of all novelists. They lived and unfolded their unprecedented talents in the same years, in the same city, in the same circle, filled with the same high ideals and high enthusiasms. And this is a very striking proof of how high effort in the arts flourishes by the mere contagion of contact. It is the custom of grudging Russophiles to declare that Turgeniev gained nothing by living in France. Or even it is their custom to declare that he lost a great deal. Nothing will be truer than to say that Turgeniev was born with a natural gift and a natural technique that made him at once the most gifted and the most technically perfect of all writers. His first story, which was written before he was twenty-one and before he had ever been to France, is as perfect as is *Fathers and Children* or *The House of the Gentlefolk*. And it would be as absurd to say that Flaubert or Gautier influenced the character of Turgeniev's works, as it would be to say that Turgeniev was an influence to Zola, Maupassant or the Goncourts. Great writers, or strong personalities, when they have passed their impressionable years, are no longer subject to influences. They develop along lines of their own geniuses. But they are susceptible to sympathy, to encouragement, to ideas of rivalry, to contagious ambitions. And only too frequently they have a necessity for a tranquil and sympathetic home-life. The one set of incentives Turgeniev found amongst the French masters. The other was given him in the home of the Viardots. Such an existence he could have found nowhere else in the civilized world of that day.

I remember Turgeniev personally only as a smile. He had been taken by poor Ralston, the first of his translators into English, to call upon Rossetti—Turgeniev was in England for grouse-shooting, to which he was passionately attached. And not finding Rossetti at home, Ralston had brought the Russian master to call upon my grandfather. Both Turgeniev and Ralston were men of gigantic stature —each of them six feet six in height, or something like it, and I cannot have been more than two feet two at the most—a small child in a blue pinafore. I must have been alone in the immense studio that had once been the drawing-room of Colonel Newcome.

A Literary Deity

At any rate it is recorded as the earliest incident of my chequered and adventurous career, and moreover as evidencing the exquisite politeness that at that time had been taught me—I hope I may not since have lost it—that my grandfather, coming into the studio, found me approaching the two giants and exclaiming in a high treble: "Won't you take a chair?" I must have been one, two or three years of age at the time.

I do not know that the anecdote is of any interest to anybody, but it pleases me to think that thus, in the person of Turgeniev, these two circles touched for a moment. For that other circle of Flaubert and his friends had aims very similar—had the same high views of the priestcraft of the arts. Each in its different way influenced very enormously the life and thoughts of their respective countries. The influence of the Pre-Raphaelites was certainly less extended than that of the great French realists, nevertheless, after the passage of half a generation or so in the form of Æstheticism, this influence also crossed the Channel, so that in France, in Belgium, in Russia, and perhaps still more in Germany, you will find many houses that might have been furnished by Morris & Company—houses where the cult of Burne-Jones and Rossetti, and perhaps still more that of Oscar Wilde, is carried on. These seeds have indeed been blown to the ends of the earth so that taking my walk the other morning through the streets of an obscure and sufficiently remote German town, the first thing that struck my eyes in a book-seller's window were two large and not very good reproductions of the *Salutation of Beatrice* and of *Beata Beatrix.*

In somewhat the same slow manner the influence of Flaubert, Turgeniev and their followers has crossed the Channel. And now, half a generation or so after their death, you will find a few English writers who have read a book or so of Flaubert, and perhaps a thousand or two of English men and women who have read something of Turgeniev. For this last, we have to thank in the first place Mrs. Constance Garnett, whose translation of Turgeniev's works has given me, I think, more pleasure than anything else in the world except, perhaps, the writings of Mr. W. Hudson. Whenever I am low, whenever I am feeble or very tired or pursued by regrets, I have only to take up one or the other of these writers. It does not much matter which. For immediately I am brought into contact with a wise, a fine, an infinitely soothing personality. I assimilate pleasure with no effort at all, and so weariness leaves me, regrets go away to a distance, and I am no more conscious of a very dull self. Mr. Hudson is of course the finest, the most delicate and the most natural of stylists that we have or that we have ever had. Perhaps I should except Mrs. Garnett, who has contrived to translate Turgeniev with all his difficulties into a language so simple and so colloquial. Each of these writers uses language as little complicated as that of a child. Word after word sinks into the mind, pervading it as water slowly soaks into sands. You are, in fact, unconscious that you are reading. You are just conscious of pleasure as you might be in the sunshine. And this for me is the highest praise, or let me say the deepest gratitude, that I have to bestow. If I could express it better I would, but I find no other words.

Turgeniev, as I have said, is little read in England. I think I remember to have heard the publisher of the English translation say that he had sold on an average fourteen hundred sets of his edition. Supposing, therefore, that each set has been read by five persons, we find that perhaps seven thousand of the inhabitants of the British Isles have an acquaintance with this writer. And since Turgeniev may be regarded as one of the greatest writers of the world—the writer who has done for the novel what Shakespeare did for the drama, Homer for the epic, or Heine for lyric verse—and since the population of the British Isles is some forty-eight millions, these figures may be said to be fairly creditable.

This is creditable, for it means that if you took a walk through London with a placard on your back bearing the words: " Have you read Turgeniev ? " you might during an afternoon's walk in South Kensington receive affirmative answers from possibly two people. In Hampstead the adventure would be more profitable. You would probably find at least ten who responded. That I think is about the proportion, for it must be remembered that South Kensington is the home of pure culture in our islands, whereas Hampstead is the home of culture plus progress, rational dress and vegetarianism. This of course is why Turgeniev is read at all in England.

Being a Russian he is supposed in some way to

help you towards being a better socialist—for in
England we do not read for pleasure, but, when we
read at all, we read in order to be made a better
something or other. That is why you will find ten
persons who have read Turgeniev for one who has
read Flaubert. In fact, having met, God knows,
hundreds and hundreds of English literary people, I
have met only one who has read the whole of Flaubert's works or began to understand what was
meant by the art of this great writer. And even he
found *L'Education Sentimentale* a tough proposition.
But then it is impossible to be made a better socialist
by reading Flaubert, and there is a general impression
amongst English writers that to read him, to be
influenced by him, would be to diminish your
" price per thou." Indeed, I was once begged by
the tearful, but charming wife of a distinguished
English man of letters to desist from advising her
husband to learn what lessons he could from the
French master. She said :

" Billy has such a struggle as it is. His work
isn't at all popular. We *do* want to have a motor-
car. And then there are the poor children." And
the poor lady, with her tear-swimming eyes, looked
agonizedly at me as if I were a monster threatening
the domesticity of her home. For the sake of the
poor children I am glad to say that Billy did not take
my advice. He never went to Mudie's for a second-
hand copy of *Un Cœur Simple,* his short stories
are becoming increasingly popular in the sixpenny
magazines. I believe he has his motor-car, but I
do not know, for his wife made him take the opportunity to quarrel with me shortly afterwards. She

would, I think, have encouraged him to lend me money in large sums; she would have trusted me to take her children out for walks. But I had threatened the most sacred thing of the literary domestic hearth; I had given her husband wicked counsel. Almost I had endangered his price per thousand words. I must go.

This story, which is perfectly true, has a moral of the deepest. For the gradual elevation of " price per thou." to the estate of the sole literary god in England has come about in many and devious manners. In the old days there was a thing that was called a pot-boiler. This was an occasional piece of inferior work which you produced in order to keep yourself from starvation, whilst you meditated higher and quite unprofitable flights. Your mind was set upon immortality and from posterity you hoped to receive the ultimate crown. A quarter of a century ago this feeling was absolutely dominant. It was so strong, is was so dinned into me that still, when I really analyse my thoughts, I find I am writing all the while with an eye to posterity. I am ashamed of myself. Anxious to be a modern of the moderns, anxious to be as good a man of business as the latest literary knight, or the first member of the British Academy of Letters, whoever they may be, I find myself still thinking that I am writing for an entirely unprofitable immortality. I desire fervently to possess a motor-car, a country seat, a seat in the House of Commons, the ear of the Home Secretary, and a bath of cut crystal with silver taps that flow champagne or eau de Cologne. I desire immensely to be influential, expensive and all the rest of it. But still I go on writing for posterity.

It is, I presume, in the blood, in the training. My great-great-grandfather Brown was the first anti-lancet surgeon. He was a person of expensive and jovial tastes. He loved port wine and he died insolvent in the King's Bench prison. Frederick the Great invited him to be his body surgeon, Napoleon the Great always released any English surgeon he might take prisoner if he could prove that he was a pupil of Dr. John Brown. Napoleon considered that the pupils of Brown were benefactors to humanity. But Dr. John Brown died in a debtor's prison because he invented and stuck to the surgery of posterity. Ford Brown his son, an ardent politician of a Whig complexion, quarrelled violently with his relative and patron, Commodore Sir Isaac Coffin, who was a Tory, and lost alike all chance of promotion in the service, and all chance of patronage for his son Ford, who had been inscribed as a midshipman on the books of the *Arethusa* frigate. Ford Brown therefore died in reduced circumstances, an embittered man because of his devotion to the political principles of posterity. And Ford Madox Brown, his son, died in reduced circumstances, still painting away at pictures, the merit of which he hoped that posterity would see.

But I do not mean to say that he was above painting the humble pot-boiler. On the contrary, his efforts to do so were frequent and pathetic. Thus, for quite a long time for a guinea a day he worked at enlarging daguerreotypes and painting posthumous portraits in the portrait factory of

192

Messrs. Dickinson. At the same time he was giving twelve years of toil to his one large picture called " Work." During the Crimean War he tried desperately to get commissions for a series of twelve popular designs with titles like " The Bugle Calls," " The Troopship Sails," " In the Trenches before Sevastopol," " Wounded," and " The Return Home," which represented a gentleman with only one arm and one leg, coming back to the embraces of a buxom English matron and five children of varying sizes. But he never got any commission for any such work. Mr. Gambart and the print-sellers were much too wise. Later, he attempted to paint pictures of the dog-and-child order, made famous by the late Mr. Burton Barber. In this attempt he was eminently unsuccessful.

Rossetti, on the other hand, was as successful with pot-boilers as Madox Brown was the reverse. He drew in pastel or charcoal innumerable large heads of women with plentiful hair and bare necks and shoulders. These he sold for huge sums, giving them Latin or Italian titles. Sometimes the occupation palled upon him. Then he wrote : " I can't be bothered to give the thing a name. A head is a head, and that is an end of it." But generally he found names like *Aurea Catena*. Millais of course occupied the latter years of his life with practically nothing but pot-boilers, except that towards his very end he repented bitterly, and tried once more to paint as he had done when he was still a Pre-Raphaelite Brother. Holman Hunt was as unsuccessful as Madox Brown in turning out real pot-boilers, though " The Light of the World " had as much success as if it had been painted in that spirit.

The point is that none of these painters and none of the writers who surrounded them had any contempt for money as such. They wanted it, but it was not the end and aim of their existence. And " price per thou." not having been invented in those days, they did not become agonized, thrilled or driven mad at the thought of this deity.

Nor indeed did this Goddess so much perturb the writers for whom Mr. Henley was the centre. His disciples desired money perhaps a little more than the Pre-Raphaelites, and revered their work perhaps a little less. On the other hand, perhaps again they really tried more to make a good job of their work. There was less of panoply, mysticism and aloofness; they expected less of the trimming of their work and put more power into their elbows. They had too, none of the feeling of standing apart from the common herd of life. They wanted as much as anything to be men—upon the whole quite commonplace men, indulging in orgies of tobacco, whisky and the other joys of the commercial traveller. About love as they handled it there was nothing mystic; passion justified nothing. It was kiss and pay and go, and when you married you settled down. Dante, in his relations with Beatrice, they voted a bore, but on the other hand they admired the tortures that he invented for his adversaries in hell.

It was an entirely different atmosphere. There was about it nothing Italianate. Most of Henley's gang saw no shame in indulging in occasional bouts of journalism. Many of them were content to be called journalists, and did not mind a damn as long as they turned out jolly good stuff.

I confess that had I known of their attitude of mind in those days it would have shocked and pained me. Nowadays I think they were rather fine fellows, and that it does not much matter what they did. In those days they seemed to me to be strange and rough.

I came out of the hot-house atmosphere of Pre-Raphaelism where I was being trained for a genius. I regarded that training with a rather cold distaste. On the other hand Henley and his friends seemed to me to be unreasonably boisterous and too loudly cocksure. Henley, who presented the appearance of a huge, mountainous, scaly, rough-clothed individual, with his pipe always in his hand and his drink always at his elbow, once damned my eyes up hill and down dale for half-an-hour because I sustained the argument that *Il Principe* was written not by Aretino but by Machiavelli. Henley had suffered from some slip of the tongue and, although he must have been perfectly aware of it in the next second, he chose to stand to his guns, and as I have said, swore at me for quite a long time. At last this seemed to grow monotonous, and I said : " God damn *you*, Mr. Henley. If Machiavelli did not write *Il Principe* I will give a pound to the first beggar I meet in the street."

I expected to die, but Henley suddenly grinned, passed his tobacco-jar over to me, said, " Of course he did," and began again to talk of Stevenson. He talked of Stevenson with an extraordinary mixture of the deepest affection and of the utterance of innumerable grudges. It was about the time—or just after it—that his article on Robert Louis appeared in small type at the end of the *Pall Mall Magazine,* and that article was setting the whole town agog. I do not know that the conversation with Henley added anything to my comprehension of the matter. But the repetition of Henley's grudges was a much pleasanter thing in words than in small type. You had the man before you, you were much better able to appreciate from his tone of voice where he exaggerated and where he meant you to know that he exaggerated.

XI

DEATHS AND DEPARTURES

LITERARY quarrels such as separated Henley and Robert Louis Stevenson are always rather tragic, are always rather comic. They have about them a flavour of regret such as distinguishes the older French music. That they are usually bitter in the extreme is due to the fact that the writer possesses a pen and the power to express himself. He possesses also an imagination. So that not only does his mind make mole-hills of grievance assume the aspect of mountains of villany, but, with his pen going forty to the dozen, he sets down in wounding words the tale of his griefs. His griefs may be nothing at all—generally they are so. Sometimes they may amount to real treachery, for the artist with his stretched nerves easily loses any sense of right or wrong where his personal affairs are concerned. Not infrequently new wives will break up old friendships, the wines being too strong for an otherwise well-tried bottle. Nowadays money sometimes comes in ; in the olden times it did, too, but much less often. I remember my grandfather laying down a rule of life for me. He said :

"Fordie, never refuse to help a lame dog over a stile. Never lend money : always give it. When you give money to a man that is down, tell him that it is to help him to get up; tell him that when he is up he should pass on the money you have given him to any other poor devil that is down. Beggar yourself rather than refuse assistance to any one whose genius you think shows promise of being greater than your own."

This is a good rule of life. I wish I could have lived up to it. The Pre-Raphaelites, as I have tried to make plain, quarrelled outrageously—as you might put it, about their boots or their washing. But these quarrels as a rule were easily made up, they hardly ever quarrelled about money, and they never, at their blackest moments, blackened the fame of each other as artists. One considerable convulsion did threaten to break up Pre-Raphaelite society. This was caused by the dissolution of the firm of Morris, Marshall, Faulkner & Company. Originally in this firm there were seven members, all either practising or aspiring artists. The best known were William Morris, Rossetti, Burne-Jones and Madox Brown. The "Firm" was founded originally by these men as a sort of co-operative venture. Each of the artists supplied designs which originally were paid for in furniture, glass or fabrics. Each of the seven partners found a certain proportion of the capital—about £100 a-piece, I think. As time went on they added more capital in varying proportions, Morris supplying by far the greater part. Gradually the "Firm" became an important undertaking. It supplied much furniture to the general public; it supplied a great number of stained glass windows to innumerable churches and cathedrals. It may be said to have revolutionized at once the aspect of our homes and the appearance of most of our places of worship. But, whilst the original partnership existed, the finances of the " Firm " were always in a shaky condition. It paid its artists very little or next to nothing. I happen to possess my grandfather's book of accounts with the " Firm." It shows that he supplied them with something more than 300 designs—of which perhaps a hundred and fifty were cartoons for stained glass and the others for tables, chairs, sofas, water-bottles, wine-glasses, bell-pulls, and who knows what. For these he was credited with sums that at first were quite insignificant—£1 10s. for a stained glass cartoon, ten shillings for a table, half-a-crown for a drinking-glass. And these sums were paid in kind. Later the sums paid became somewhat larger, but were still quite inadequate, if they were to be considered as ordinary transactions of the open market. I think that the largest sum that Madox Brown received for any cartoon was £5. The other artists received exactly similar prices, whether they were Rossetti, Mr. Philip Webb or Mr. Peter Paul Marshall.

As the years went by the " Firm," though it extended its operations enormously, showed no signs of becoming financially prosperous. William Morris supplied more and more capital until, although for those days and for that set he was a very wealthy man, his financial position was rapidly becoming precarious. The position was thus extremely complicated. Morris had supplied a great quantity of money; the other artists, and more particularly

Madox Brown and Rossetti, had supplied a really immense amount of work, partly for the love of the thing and partly because they thought that they would ultimately receive adequate payment. A certain amount of irritation was caused by the fact that Morris, as the head of the " Firm," ordered gradually more and more work from Burne-Jones and his particular friends, and less and less from Madox Brown and Rossetti. This was perfectly reasonable, for Burne-Jones was a popular artist for whose designs there was much demand, whilst Madox Brown and Rossetti in the nature of things were comparatively little in request. It was natural and legitimate, but it could not fail to be wounding to the neglected artists.

The day came when Morris perceived that the only way to save himself from ruin was to get rid of the other partners of the " Firm," to take possession of it altogether, and to put it in a sound and normal financial position. There was here the makings of a very pretty financial row. I have only stated this case—which has already been stated several times—in order to make it clear how nicely balanced the position was. There was no doubt that the " Firm " could be made a great financial success. Indeed, it afterwards became so, and so I believe it remains. Madox Brown, and to a less degree Rossetti, considered that they had devoted the labours of many years to contributing to this success. They knew that the reconstituted and successful " Firm " would commission no work of theirs, and all their labours had been very inadequately paid for. Morris, on the other hand, had to consider that he had supplied by far the greater amount of the capital which for so many years had kept the "Firm" going, and, if at that date it was at the point of success, this was due to the popular quality of the designs which he and Burne-Jones supplied. The legal agreements which constituted the "Firm" were of the haziest kind. Nowadays I take it there would be the makings of a splendid and instructive lawsuit. But Morris & Company passed into the hands of William Morris; Rossetti, Madox Brown and the rest were displaced and there was practically no outcry at all. This was very largely due to the self-sacrificing labours of Mr. Watts-Dunton—surely the best of friends recorded in histories or memoirs. How he did it I cannot begin to imagine; but he must have spent many sleepless nights and have passed many long days in talking to these formidable and hot-blooded partners. Of course he had to aid him the fact that each of these artists cared more for their work than for money, and more for the decencies of life and good fellowship than for the state of their pass-books.

A certain amount of coldness subsisted for some time between all the parties, and indeed I have no doubt that they all said the most outrageous things against each other. Some of them, indeed, I have heard, but in the end that gracious and charming person, Lady Burne-Jones, succeeded in bringing all the parties together again. William Morris sent Madox Brown copies of all the books he had written during the estrangement, Madox Brown sent William Morris a tortoise-shell box containing a dozen very brilliant bandana pocket-handkerchiefs, and joined the Kelmscott House Socialist League. Indeed, one of the prettiest things I can remember was having seen Madox Brown sitting in the central aisle of the little shed attached to Morris's house at Hammersmith. Both of them were white-headed then; my grandfather's hair was parted in the middle and fell, long and extremely thick, over each of his ears. It may interest those whose hair concerns them to know that every morning of his life he washed his head in cold water and with common yellow soap, coming down to breakfast with his head still dripping. I don't know if that were the reason; but at any rate he had a most magnificent crop of hair. So these two picturesque persons re-cemented their ancient friendship under the shadow of a social revolution that I am sure my grandfather did not in the least understand, and that William Morris probably understood still less. I suppose that Madox Brown really expected the social revolution to make an end of all "damned academicians." Morris, on the other hand, probably expected that the whole world would go dressed in curtain-serge, supplied in sage-green and neutral tints by a "Firm" of Morris & Company that should constitute the whole State. Afterwards we all went in to tea in Kelmscott House itself—Morris, my grandfather and several disciples. The room was large and, as I remember it, white. A huge carpet ran up one of its walls so as to form a sort of dais; beneath this sat Mrs. Morris, the most beautiful woman of her day. At the head of the table sat Morris, at his right hand my grandfather, who resembled an animated King of Hearts. The rest of the long table was crowded

in a mediæval sort of way by young disciples with
low collars and red ties, or by maidens in the inevitable curtain-serge, and mostly with a necklace of
bright amber. The amount of chattering that went
on was considerable. Morris, I suppose, was tired
with his lecturing and answering of questions, for
at a given period he drew from his pocket an enormous
bandana handkerchief in scarlet and green. This
he proceeded to spread over his face, and leaning
back in his chair he seemed to compose himself to
sleep after the manner of elderly gentlemen taking
their naps. One of the young maidens began asking my grandfather some rather inane questions :
What did Mr. Brown think of the weather, or what
was Mr. Brown's favourite picture at the Academy ?
For all the disciples of Mr. Morris were not equally
advanced in thought.

Suddenly Morris tore the handkerchief from
before his face and roared out :

"Don't be such an intolerable fool, Polly!"
Nobody seemed to mind this very much—nor,
indeed, was the reproved disciple seriously abashed,
for almost immediately afterwards she asked :

"Mr. Brown, do you think that Sir Frederick
Leighton is a greater painter than Mr. Frank
Dicksee ? "

Morris, however, had retired once more behind
his handkerchief, and I presume he had given up in
despair the attempt to hint to his disciple that
Mr. Brown did not like Royal Academicians. I do
not remember how my grandfather got out of this
invidious comparison, but I do remember that when,
shortly afterwards, the young lady said to him : "You

paint a little too, don't you, Mr Brown ? " he
answered : " Only with my left hand."

This somewhat mystified the young lady, but it
was perfectly true, for shortly before then Madox
Brown had had a stroke of paralysis which rendered
his right hand almost entirely useless. He was
then engaged in painting with his left, the enormous
picture of " Wycliffe on his Trial," which was to
have been presented by subscribing admirers to the
National Gallery.

This was the last time that Madox Brown and
Morris met. And they certainly parted with every
cordiality. Madox Brown had indeed quite enjoyed
himself. I had been rather afraid that he would
have been offended by Morris's retirement behind
the pocket-handkerchief. But when we were on
the road home Madox Brown said :

" Well, that was just like old Topsy. In the Red
Lion Square days he was always taking naps whilst
we jawed. That was how Arthur Hughes was able
to tie Topsy's hair into knots. And the way he
talked to that gal—why, my dear chap—it was just
the way he called the Bishop of Lincoln a bloody
bishop ! No, Morris isn't changed much." It was
a few days after this, in the evening, that Madox
Brown, painting at his huge picture, pointed to the
top of the frame that already surrounded the canvas.
Upon the top was inscribed " Ford Madox Brown,"
and on the bottom, *Wycliffe on his Trial before John
of Gaunt. Presented to the National Gallery by a
Committee of Admirers of the Artist."* In this way the
" X " of Madox Brown came exactly over the centre
of the picture. It was Madox Brown's practice to

begin a painting by putting in the eyes of the central figure. This, he considered, gave him the requisite strength of tone that would be applied to the whole canvas. And indeed I believe that, once he had painted in those eyes, he never in any picture altered them, however much he might alter the picture itself. He used them as it were to work up to. Having painted in those eyes he would begin at the top left-hand corner of the canvas, and would go on painting downwards in a nearly straight line until the picture was finished. He would of course have made a great number of studies before commencing the picture itself. Usually there was an exceedingly minute and conscientious pencil-drawing, than a large charcoal cartoon, and after that, for the sake of the colour scheme, a version in water-colour, in pastels and generally one in oil. In the case of the Manchester frescoes almost every one was preceded by a small version painted in oils upon a panel, and this was the case with the large Wycliffe.

On this, the last evening of his life, Madox Brown pointed with his brush to the " X " of his name. Below it, on the left-hand side the picture was completely filled in; on the right it was completely blank—a waste of slightly yellow canvas that gleamed in the dusky studio. He said :

" You see I have got to that ' X.' I am glad of it, for half the picture is done and it feels as if I were going home."

Those, I think, were his last words. He laid his brushes upon his painting cabinet, scraped his palette of all mixed paints, laid his palette upon his brushes and his spectacles upon his palette. He took off the biretta that he always wore when he was painting—he must have worn such a biretta for upwards of half-a-century—ever since he had been a French student. And so having arrived at his end-of-the-day routine which he had followed for innumerable years, he went upstairs to bed. He probably read a little of the *Mystères de Paris*, and died in his sleep, the picture with its inscriptions remaining downstairs, a little ironic, a little pathetic, and unfinished.

I haven't the least idea of where Madox Brown's fame as an artist to-day may stand. It is impossible to form an estimate. I am certain that he is far better known in France and Belgium than in the United Kingdom. The other day an American art-critic, who did not know who I was but was anxious to impress me with the fact that British art was altogether worthless, said vehemently— I had been trying to put in a word for Constable, Gainsborough and Turner—said vehemently:

" There was only one English painter who could ever paint. His name was Brown, and you probably never heard of him. He painted a picture called ' Work.' "

I retired from that discussion with decent discomfiture.

On the other hand, when I was hanging the pictures at the Madox Brown Exhibition at the Grafton Galleries, the late R. A. M. Stevenson came in and, clutching my arm, proceeded to whirl me round in front of the walls. He poured out one of his splendid floods of talk—and I think that he was the best talker that ever was, better than his cousin Robert Louis, or better even than Henley, many of whose expletives and mannerisms " Bob " Stevenson retained. He poured out a flood of words before each of the pictures, going to prove in the most drastic manner that Madox Brown ought never to have been a painter at all—he ought to have been an historical novelist. On the following day, which was Press Day, I was doing my best to explain the pictures to a crowd of journalists when I was once more seized vehemently by the elbow, and there was Stevenson. He whirled me round the galleries and poured out a flood of talk before picture after picture. This time he proved as completely, as drastically, that Madox Brown was the only real English painter since Hogarth—the only national one, the only one who could paint, the only one who had any ideas worth the snuff of a candle. And pointing to the little picture called " The Pretty Baa-Lambs," with the whole of his brown being, his curious earnest, rather beaver-like face illuminated by excitement, he exclaimed :

" By God ! the whole history of modern art begins with that picture. Corot, Manet, the Marises, all the Fontainebleau School, all the Impressionists, never did anything but imitate that picture."

So that Mr. Stevenson left me in a confusion that was odd and not so very unpleasant. I considered him at that time—and perhaps I still consider him— the finest critic of art that we ever produced. On the one day he said that Madox Brown " could not paint for nuts "; on the next he asseverated that Madox Brown was greater than all the Italian primitives, French modernists, or than Prometheus who first brought fire from Heaven. And as I cannot imagine that Mr. Stevenson had any particular desire to please me I can only leave the riddle at that.

Shortly after the death of Madox Brown I left London only to re-enter it as a permanent resident when twelve or thirteen years had gone by. And, gradually, all that " set " have died off, along with all the Victorian great figures. Ruskin died, Morris died, Christina and my aunt Lucy died, and Burne-Jones ; only Mr. Holman Hunt remained of the painters. And yet it is odd how permanent to me they all seemed. Till the moment of Swinburne's death, till the moment of Meredith's, I had considered them—I found it when I heard of their deaths—as being as permanent as the sun or the Mansion House. Thus each death came as a separate shock. So it was with the last death of all which I read of—only a few days ago whilst I was travelling in a distant country.

It had been a long and tiresome journey, in a train as slow as the caravan of a Bedouin. We had jolted on and on over plain after plain. And then with a tired and stertorous grunt, in a sudden and how much needed shaft of sunshine, the train came to a standstill, wearily and as if it would never pluck up spirits again to drag along its tale of dusty carriages. The station was bright pink, the window frames were bright emerald green; the porters wore bright blue uniforms; and one of them a bright scarlet cap. In the background—but no, under the shafts of sparkling light there was no background; it all jumped forward as if it were a flat, bright pattern covering a high wall—there was a landscape in chequers of little plots of ground. The squares of bare earth were of brighter pink than anything you will see in Devonshire; where the newly cut fodder had stood, the green was a pale bright emerald. The patches of tobacco were of a green more vivid; the maize more vivid still. The very cocks of hay, dotted about like ant-heaps, were purple. The draught oxen, bright yellow, stood before the long carts, painted bright blue, and panted in the unaccustomed heat. Peasant women in short green petticoats with blue velvet bodices and neckerchiefs of bright green, of sky-blue, of lemon yellow, bore upon their heads purple baskets, or beneath coifs of sparkling white linen raked the purple hay on the green fields, or lifted up into the blue wagons bundles of fodder with forks that had bright red shafts. And all this colour, in the dazzling, violent light was hung beneath an absurd blue sky. It was the colour of the blue houses one sees in the suburbs of Paris, and contained, blotted all over it, absurd pink and woolly German clouds.

I closed my eyes. It was not that it was really painful, it was not that it was really disagreeable. All this richness, all this prosperity seemed so stable and so long-established that in our transient world it suggested a lasting peace. But coming out of our greys and half-tints of London, where nothing vivid ever occurs to disturb the eye, it was too overwhelming. It was—and the words came on to my lips at the very moment—too brave, too

Pre-Raphaelite! It was just as if Nature had set herself to do the thing well, and had done the thing so well that the eye couldn't possibly stand it. Pre-Raphaelite! That was what it all was.

Desiring to rest my eyes, I turned them upon one of those newspapers that are so difficult to read, and there was conveyed to my mind the message :

Es wird uns telegraphiert aus London dass der Mahler Holman Hunt, der Vater des englischen Pre-raphaelismus, im 83ten. Jahre seines Lebens, gestorben ist.

" It is telegraphed to us out of London that the painter Holman Hunt, the father of English Pre-Raphaelism, to-day, in the eighty-third year of his life, is dead."

I do not know whether there was something telepathic about Nature that she gave this brave Pre-Raphaelite show in Hesse-Nassau to frame for me an announcement that called up images so distant and so dim of a painter—of a set of painters who in their own day decided to do the thing well—to do the thing so well that most beholders of their pictures still close their eyes and say that it is too much. For the odd thing is that these Pre-Raphaelites painted in the dim and murky squares of Bloomsbury. There was nothing Hessian about their environment; if they were not all Cockneys, they were townsmen to a man.

And the most immediate image of Mr. Holman Hunt that comes to my mind is enshrined in a lamp-lit interior. There was Mr. Holman Hunt, resting after the labours of his day, with the curious, vivid, rugged head, the deep-set, illuminated eyes that were perpetually sending swift glances all over the room. There was also, I know, one of Her Majesty's judges poring over the reproductions of some Etruscan vases; and there may have been other people. It was a tranquil interior of rather mellow shadows, and Mr. Holman Hunt, with the most ingenuously charming manner in the world, was engaged in damning—as it were in musing asides—all my family and their connections and myself. He was talking of the old times, of the 'forties and 'fifties, when he was known as Old Hunt and Millais as The Lamp Post, because he was so tall. And uttering many things which may be found now in his auto-biography, Mr. Hunt would let drop sentences like :

" The Brotherhood used to meet pretty often at Rossetti's rooms, but, of course, Rossetti was a common thief. . . ."

" Your grandfather was then painting a picture called ' The Pretty Baa-Lambs,' but, of course, Madox Brown was a notorious liar. . . ."

" These details may be interesting to you when you come to write the life of your grandfather, but, of course, you, as a person of no particular talent, setting out upon an artistic career, will die ignominiously of starvation. And so Millais and I, having discovered the secret of the wet white ground, proceeded to swear an oath that we would reveal it to none other of the brethren."

And so distractedly—so amiably, for the matter of that, were these damning " of courses " dropped into the great man's picturesque narrative, that it was not until after I had for two or three hours left the dim and comfortable lamplight of the room that I really realized that Mr. Hunt had stated that he considered Rossetti a thief, my grandfather a liar, and myself doomed to an infamous and needy death. How Mr. Hunt had arrived at this last conclusion, I do not know, for this happened twenty years ago, between the death and burial of Madox Brown, I having been sent to ask this friend of my grandfather's early years to attend his funeral. I was just nineteen at the time, so that I know quite well that what the great painter meant was not that he perceived traces of incipient villany upon my countenance or of decadence in my non-existent writings, but that he really desired to warn me against the hardships of the artistic life, of which in middle life he tasted for so long and so bitterly. Similarly, when he said that Rossetti was a thief, he meant that the author of *Jenny* had borrowed some books from him and never returned them, so that they were sold at the sale of Rossetti's effects. And when he called my grandfather, not yet in his grave, a notorious liar, that signified that he was irritated by the phrase, " grandfather of Pre-Raphaelism," which was applied to Madox Brown in his obituaries. These had been circulated to the halfpenny evening press by a news agency. An industrious hack-writer had come upon this phrase in a work by Mr. Harry Quilter, no other writer at that date having paid any attention at all to Madox Brown's career. The phrase had afforded Madox Brown almost more explosive irritation than its repetition thus caused Mr. Holman Hunt. For, rightly or wrongly, just as Mr. Hunt considered himself the father and grandfather of Pre-Raphaelism, as well as the only

Pre-Raphaelite that counted, so Madox Brown considered himself much too great an artist to have been mixed up in a childish debating society called a Brotherhood, and invented by a set of youths very much his juniors. But now, indeed, with the announcement, *Heute wird aus London telegraphiert*, which the wires so generously flashed to the ends of the civilized earth, the Father of Pre-Raphaelism had passed away. For of all the Pre-Raphaelite brothers, Mr. Hunt was the only one who fully understood, who fully carried out, for better or for worse, for richer or for poorer, the canons of Pre-Raphaelism. It was Madox Brown who first painted bright purple haycocks—yes, bright purple ones—upon a bright green field. But he painted them like that because he happened to notice that when sunlight is rather red and the sky very blue, the shadowy side of green-grey hay is all purple. He noticed it, and he rendered it. It was a picturesque fact appealing to an imagination that looked out for the picturesque. Mr. Holman Hunt rendered things with the avid passion of a seeker after truth; it was a hungry desire; it was a life force pushing him towards the heroic, towards all of the unexplored things in human experience that are as arid and as bitter as the unexplored fields of ice around the Pole. Just as the explorer, robbing these august regions of their mystery with his photographs and his projections, is inspired by the passion for those virgin mysteries, just as he earns at once our dislike by penetrating mysteries that should remain mysteries, if we are to remain comfortable, so with Mr. Holman Hunt. Inspired with the intense, unreasoning faith of the

ascetic for the mysteries of revealed religion—
inspired, too, with the intense and unreasoning
desire of the ascetic for the rendering of truth, since
he believed that truth and revealed religion were as
much identical as are the one in three of the Trinity,
so Mr. Holman Hunt supported the fiery suns of
the desert, the thirsts of the day, the rigours of the
night, the contempt of his compatriots, and the
scorn of his time. He was endeavouring to prove that
our Lord was a Semitic boy or an adult Jew inspired
with the ecstasy of a modern French anarchist, that
His Mother was a Bedouin woman of no particular
distinction, or that the elders in the Temple were a
set of Semitic sheikhs dressed in aniline-dyed, Manchester goods, burnouses, packed together in wooden
tabernacles beneath a remorseless sun. This was
the message of Mr. Holman Hunt to his generation,
a message surely very salutary and very useful.
For of its kind, and as far as it went, it meant clearness of thought, and clearness of thought in any
department of life is the most valuable thing that a
man can give to his day. The painter of " The Light
of the World " dealt a very hard blow to the fashion-
able religion of his day. This the world of his youth
understood very well. It declared Mr. Hunt to be
an atheist, and, with Charles Dickens at its head,
cried to the government for the imprisonment of
Mr. Hunt and his Brethren.

These things are, I suppose, a little forgotten now
—or perhaps they all repose together on that hill
where grows the herb Oblivion. I don't know.
But round the romantic home of my childhood, the
opponents of Pre-Raphaelism seemed still to stalk

like assassins with knives. There was a sort of Blue Beard called Frank Stone, R.A.—God alone knows nowadays who Frank Stone, R.A., was! But Frank Stone said, in the *Athenæum* of the year of grace 1850, that the flesh of Pre-Raphaelite pictures was painted with strawberry jam. There was a veritable Giant Blunderbore called Grant, P.R.A.—who in the world was Grant, P.R.A.?—who, with forty thieves, all R.A.'s, immolated the innocent pictures of Holman Hunt, Millais, D. G. R., Brown and Collinson—who sent them home ripped up with nails, who never returned them at all, or who hung them next the ceiling in gloomy rooms one hundred and forty feet high. That, at least, was my early picture of the horrors that the Pre-Raphaelites had to endure.

And the public certainly took its share, too. The good, indolent public of that day was not too indolent to take an interest in pictures, and it certainly very hotly disliked anything that had P.R.B. attached to it, perhaps because it was used to things with P.R.A. (Who *was* Grant, P.R.A.?) People in those days, like people to-day, had tired eyes. They wanted nice, comfortable half-tones. They wanted undisturbing pictures in which flesh, trees, houses, castles, the sky and the sea alike appeared to have been painted in pea-soup. Consequently, hay that appeared purple in the shadows, and flesh that seemed to have been painted with strawberry jam, upset them very much. They were simple, earnest people, those early Victorians, and had not yet learnt the trick of avoiding disturbing thoughts and sights. Perhaps it was that the picture postcard had not yet been invented. It is incredible nowadays to think that any one would be in the least disturbed if a painter as great as Velasquez should come along and paint you a scarlet landscape with a pea-green sky. We should care nothing at all. Only if he pushed himself really well he would find himself elected A.R.A at the third attempt, and his pictures would be bought by a doctor in Harley Street. He would be celebrated in a small afternoon-tea circle. But the great public would never hear of him, and would never be disturbed by his scarlet grass and green sky. We should not indeed really care two pins if the President of the Royal Association should declare that the grass is bright scarlet and the sky green. We should just go on playing Bridge.

But the public of the Pre-Raphaelites was really worried. It felt that if these fellows were right, its eyesight must be wrong, and there is nothing more disturbing ! It desired, therefore, that these painters should be suppressed. It didn't want them only to be ignored. They were disturbers of great principles. If they began by declaring that flesh looked like strawberry jam, when all the world knew that it looked like pea-soup, they would begin next to impugn the British Constitution, the morality of the Prince Consort, *The Times* newspaper, the Nonconformist conscience, the bench of Bishops, and the beauty of the crinoline. There would be no knowing where they wouldn't get to.

And indeed the worried public was perfectly right. Pre-Raphaelism may or may not have been important in the history of modern art; it was all-important in the development of modern thought. The amiable muddle-headedness of the crinoline period was perfectly right to be horribly worried when Millais exhibited a picture showing Christ obedient to His parents. You have to consider that in those days it was blasphemous, indecent and uncomfortable to consider sacred personages at all. No one really liked to think about the Redeemer, and Millais showed them the Virgin kissing her Son. According to Victorian Protestant ideas the Mother of Our Lord was a person whom you never mentioned at all. But Millais dragged her right into the foreground. You couldn't get away from her. She was kissing her little Son, and her little Son was obedient to her. Adolescence, family affection, subjection to His Mother and father, or early occupations—all these things were obviously logical, but were very disturbing. They meant all sorts of revisions of judgment. It was not only that flesh looked like strawberry jam, but that the Saviour was a man with the necessities, the craving for sympathy, and the vulnerability of a man. These facts Millais forced upon the attention of the public.

And not being of the stern temper of Mr. Hunt, Millais bent before the storm of popular opinion. He was afraid that Charles Dickens would get him imprisoned. He changed the figure of the Virgin so that no longer does she comfort her Son with a kiss. Millais could alter his picture, but nothing in this world could ever have forced Mr. Hunt to bend. In consequence, Millais, a very great painter,

17

climbed an easy road to affluence, and died in the chair once occupied by Grant, P.R.A. Mr. Hunt pursuing his sterner course, seeking avidly for truth as it must have appeared, was for long years shunned by patrons, and hard put to it to live at all. There have, I think, been few such struggles in the cause of any conscience, and never with such a fierce and iron determination has any painter, in the teeth of a violent opposition, fettered his art so to serve the interests of religion and of truth.

This religiosity which Mr. Holman Hunt, before even Darwin, Huxley, and other Victorian figures, so effectively destroyed, was one of the scourges of the dismal period which to-day we call the Victorian era. And if Mr. Hunt destroyed the image of Simon Peter as the sort of artist's model that you see on the steps of Calabrian churches, furtively combing out, with the aid of a small round mirror, long white hairs depending from his head and face —these hairs being the only portion of him that has ever been washed since his birth—if Mr. Hunt destroyed this figure, with its attitudes learnt on the operatic stage, its blanket revealing opulently moulded forms, and its huge property keys extended towards a neo-Gothic Heaven—if Mr. Hunt gave us instead (I don't know that he ever did, but he may have done) a Jewish fisherman pulling up dirty-looking fish on the shores of a salt-encrusted and desolate lake—Mr. Hunt in the realms of modern thought, enormously aided the discovery of wireless telegraphy and in no way damaged the prestige of the occupant of St. Peter's Chair.

This truism may appear a paradox. And yet

nothing is more true than that clearness of thought
in one department of life stimulates clearness of
thought in another. The great material developments of the end of last century did not only succeed
the great realistic developments that had preceded
them in the arts. The one was the logical corollary
of the other. Just as you cannot have a healthy
body in which one of the members is unsound, so
you cannot have a healthy national life in the
realms of thought unless in all the departments of
life you have sincere thinkers, and this is what
Mr. Hunt undoubtedly was—a sincere thinker. To
say that he was the greatest painter of his day might
be superfluous; he was certainly the most earnest
beyond all comparison. That we should dislike
the vividness of his colour is perhaps the defect of
our degenerate eyes, which see too little of the sunlight. And such a painting as that of the strayed
sheep on the edge of the Fairlight Cliff, near Pitt—
such a painting is sufficient to establish the painter's
claims to gifts of the very greatest. You have the
sunlit sheep, you have the dangerous verge of the
hill; you have the sea far below, and from these
things you find awakened in you such emotions as
Providence has rendered you capable of. This, without doubt, is the province of art—a province which
perhaps Mr. Hunt, in his hunger and thirst after
righteousness, unduly neglected.

Of pictures of his at all in this absolute *genre*, I
can recall otherwise only one, representing the deck
of a steamer at night. Mr. Hunt, in fact, set himself
the task of being rather a pioneer than an artist.
His fame, the bulking of his personality in the eyes

of posterity, as with all other pioneers, will no
doubt suffer. But when he gave Mr. Gambart what
Mr. Gambart complained was " a great ugly goat "
instead of a pretty, religious picture, with epicene
angels, curled golden hair and long night-gowns,
Mr. Hunt was very certainly benefiting the life of
his day. And, indeed, this is a terrifying and sug-
gestive picture. But this great man cared very
little for beauty, which is that which, by awakening
untabulated and indefinite emotions, makes, indefi-
nitely, more proper men of us. Had he cared more
for this he would have been a greater artist; he might
have been a smaller man. Beauty, I think, he never
once mentions in his autobiography. But truth
and righteousness, as he understood it, were always
on his lips as they were always in his heart. In
spite of the acerbity of his utterances, in spite of
the apparent egotism of his autobiography, which to
the unthinking might appear a bitterly vainglorious
book, I am perfectly ready to declare myself certain
that Mr. Holman Hunt was, in the more subtle sense,
an eminently unselfish man. The " I " that is so
eternal in his autobiography is not the "I" that was
William Holman Hunt. It was all that he stood
for—the principles, the hard life, the bitter endur-
ance, the splendid record of young friendships, the
aims, the achievement. It was this that Mr. Hunt
desired to have acknowledged. In his autobiography
he did himself perhaps less than justice; in his
paintings, too, he did himself perhaps less than justice;
but in the whole course of his life, from his strugglings
away from the merchant's stool to his death, which
was " telegraphed to us " in the obscurest of Hessian

" AND THERE WAS ONLY ONE PRE-RAPHAELITE—THAT WAS
MR. HOLMAN HUNT"

villages, he never betrayed his ascetic's passion. It was to this passion that his egotism was a tribute. From his point of view, Rossetti was not a good man because he was not a religious painter who had journeyed into Palestine in search of truth. He never even went to Florence to see where Beatrice lived. If Mr. Hunt called Rossetti a thief, it was because he desired to express this artistically immoral fact, and he expressed it clumsily as one not a master of words. And similarly, if he called Madox Brown a liar, it was because Madox Brown was not a painter of his school of religious thought. His aim was not to prevent other persons buying pictures of Madox Brown or Rossetti; his aim was not to prevent Madox Brown or Rossetti prospering, or even becoming presidents of the Royal Academy. He desired to point out that the only way to æsthetic salvation was to be a believing Pre-Raphaelite. And there was only one Pre-Raphaelite—that was Mr. Holman Hunt. Any one without his faith must, he felt, be a bad man. And in a dim and muddled way, he tried to express it. At other times he would call these rival painters the best and noblest of fellows, or the one man in the world to whom to go for advice or sympathy. And this indeed was the main note of his life, he himself having been so companionable, as fine a fellow, and as good to go to for advice. But being a painter, he had to look for shadows, and not being much of a hand with the pen or the tongue, if he could not find them, he had to invent them. That, in the end, was the bottom of the matter.

I permit myself these words upon a delicate

subject, since Mr. Hunt's autobiography, which must necessarily be his most lasting personal memorial, does so very much less than justice to the fineness of his nature. This hardly all his hardships and privations could warp at all. And I permit them to myself the more readily since I may, without much immodesty, consider myself the most vocal of the clan which Mr. Hunt dimly regarded as the Opposition to his claim to be regarded as the Founder of Pre-Raphaelism. But I think I never did advance —it was never my intention to advance—any suggestion that the true inwardness of Pre-Raphaelism, the exact rendering, hair for hair of the model; the passionate hunger and thirst for even accidental truth, the real *caput mortuum* of Pre-Raphaelism, was ever expressed by any one else than by the meticulously earnest painter and great man whose death was telegraphed from the dim recesses of London into the chess-board pattern of sunlit Pre-Raphaelite Hessian harvest lands. May the fields to which he has gone prove such very bright places where, to his courageous eyes, his Truth shall be very vivid and prevail !

Madox Brown has been dead for twenty years now, or getting on for that. I would not say that the happiest days of my life were those that I spent in his studio, for I have spent in my life days as happy since then; but I will say that Madox Brown was the finest man I ever knew. He had his irascibilities, his fits of passion when, tossing his white head, his mane of hair would fly all over his face, and when he would blaspheme impressively after the manner

of our great-grandfathers. And in these fits of temper
he would frequently say the most unjust things.
But I think that he was never either unjust or
ungenerous in cold blood, and I am quite sure that
envy had no part at all in his nature. Like Rossetti
and like William Morris, in his very rages he was
nearest to generosities. He would rage over an injustice to some one else to the point of being bitterly
unjust to the oppressor. I do not think that I
would care to live my life over again—I have had
days that I would not again face for a good deal—
but I would give very much of what I possess to
be able, having still such causes for satisfaction as
I now have in life, to be able to live once more some
of those old evenings in the studio.

The lights would be lit, the fire would glow between
the red tiles; my grandfather would sit with his
glass of weak whisky-and-water in his hand, and
would talk for hours. He had anecdotes more
lavish and more picturesque than any man I ever
knew. He would talk of Beau Brummel, who had
been British Consul at Calais when Madox Brown
was born there, of Paxton who built the Crystal
Palace, and of the mysterious Duke of Portland
who lived underground, but who, meeting Madox
Brown in Baker Street outside Druce's, and hearing
that Madox Brown suffered from gout, presented
him with a large quantity of colchicum grown at
Welbeck. . . .

Well, I would sit there on the other side of the
rustling fire, listening, and he would revive the
splendid ghosts of Pre-Raphaelites, going back to
Cornelius and Overbeck and to Baron Leys and

Baron Wappers, who taught him first to paint in the romantic grand manner. He would talk on. Then Mr. William Rossetti would come in from next door but one, and they would begin to talk of Shelley and Browning and Mazzini and Napoleon III, and Mr. Rossetti, sitting in front of the fire, would sink his head nearer and nearer to the flames. His right leg would be crossed over his left knee, and, as his head went down, so, of necessity, his right foot would come up and out. It would approach nearer and nearer to the fire-irons which stood at the end of the fender. The tranquil talk would continue. Presently the foot would touch the fire-irons and down they would go into the fender with a tremendous clatter of iron. Madox Brown, half dozing in the firelight, would start and spill some of his whisky. I would replace the fire-irons in their stand.

The talk would continue, Mr. Rossetti beginning again to sink his head towards the fire, and explaining that, as he was not only bald but an Italian, he liked to have his head warmed. Presently, bang! would go the fire-irons again. Madox Brown would lose some more whisky and would exclaim :

"Really, William!"

Mr. Rossetti would say :

"I am very sorry, Brown."

I would replace the fire-irons again, and the talk would continue. And then for the third time the fire-irons would go down. Madox Brown would hastily drink what little whisky remained to him, and jumping to his feet would shout :

" God damn and blast you, William, can't you be more careful ? "

To which his son-in-law, always the most utterly calm of men, would reply :

" Really, Brown, your emotion appears to be excessive. If Fordie would leave the fire-irons lying in the fender there would be no occasion for them to fall."

The walls were covered with gilded leather; all the doors were painted dark green; the room was very long, and partly filled by the great picture that was never to be finished, and, all in shadow, in the distant corner was the table covered with bits of string, curtain knobs, horse-shoes and odds and ends of iron and wood.

XII

HEROES AND SOME HEROINES

ABOUT six months after Madox Brown's death I went permanently into the country, where I remained for thirteen years, thus losing almost all touch with intellectual or artistic life. Yet one very remarkable pleasure did befall me during the early days of that period of seclusion. Mr. Edward Garnett, at that time literary adviser to the most enterprising publisher of that day, came down to the village, bringing with him a great basket of manuscripts that had been submitted to his firm. It was a Sunday evening. We were all dressed more or less mediævally, after the manner of true disciples of socialism of the William Morris school. We were drinking, I think, mead out of cups made of bullock's horn. Mr. Garnett was reading his MSS. Suddenly he threw one across to me.

"Look at that," he said.

I think that then I had the rarest literary pleasure of my existence. It was to come into contact with a spirit of romance, of adventure, of distant lands, and with an English that was new, magic and unsurpassed. It sang like music; it overwhelmed me like a great warm wave of the sea, and it was as clear

226

as tropical sunlight falling into deep and scented forests of the East. For this MS. was that of *Almayer's Folly*, the first book of Mr. Joseph Conrad, which he had sent up for judgment, sailing away himself, as I believe, for the last time, upon a ship going towards the East. So was Joseph Conrad " discovered."

But that was the day of discoveries. It was an exciting, a wonderful time. In those years Mr. Rudyard Kipling burst upon the world with a shower of stars like those of a certain form of rocket. Mr. Zangwill was " looming large." *To-day* was a wonderful periodical; it serialized the first long novel of Mr. H. G. Wells. Mr. Anthony Hope was going immensely strong. Mr. J. M. Barrie was beginning to " boom." Mr. Crockett was also " discovered," and Mrs. Craigie and the authors of the Pseudonym Library, with its sulphur yellow covers that penetrated like a fumigation into every corner of Europe. " Mademoiselle Ixe " must have found millions of readers. And it was *really* the talk of the town. Mr. Gladstone, I think, wrote a postcard about it. Then there was Olive Schreiner, who was a prophetess, wrote wonderfully well about South Africa, and lectured the Almighty for the benefit of Hampstead.

The tone of all this new literature was of course very different from that of Pre-Raphaelism. It was in many ways more vivid, more actual, and more of every day, just as it was certainly less refined and less precious. And I must confess that I at least revelled in this new note. Being very young and properly humble, all these appearances filled me with delight and with enthusiasm. It was as entrancing to me to read the *Wheels of Chance* in the badly printed columns of *To-day* as it was to read the *Dolly Dialogues* on the green paper of the *Westminster*, and it was only a more wonderful thing to be able to read *The Nigger of the Narcissus*, which was the last serial to appear in Henley's *New Review*. I was ready to accept almost anybody and anything, though, at the one end of the scale I could not swallow *Three Men in a Boat* or, at the other, *Dreams*, by Olive Schreiner. What was called in those days the New Humour appeared to me as vulgar as the works of Albert Smith and not half so funny. On the other hand, the New Seriousness appeared to me to be more funny than either, particularly when Miss Schreiner took to arguing with God. I remember saying as much to a young Hampstead lady who came near to being my first— and who knows whether she would not have been my only—love. I had seen her home from my grandfather's, and we walked up and down before her garden gate discussing this work, which struck me as so comic. She ended by saying that I was as vulgar as I was stupid. So there, that romance came to an end! She was a very earnest and charmingly ridiculous person, and is now married to an eminent stockbroker. But from this tender reminiscence I gather that I must have had limits in my appreciations of the bubbling literature of that day. But the limits must have been singularly wide. I suppose those works really took me out of the rather stifling atmosphere of Pre-Raphaelism, just as in earlier days I used to lock myself in the coal-cellar in order to read *Dick Harkaway* and *Sweeney Todd the Demon Barber* and other penny dreadfuls. Then, I was reacting—and I am sure healthily—against being trained for the profession of a genius.

But I can remember with what enormous enthusiasm I used to read the little shilling, paper bound, bluish books which contain the first stories of Mr. Rudyard Kipling. Mr. Kipling himself is of an origin markedly Pre-Raphaelite. He is a nephew of Burne-Jones and I suppose that the writings of poor " B. V. Thomson," the very Pre-Raphaelite author of *The City of Dreadful Night*—that these works more profoundly influenced the author of *The Man who would be King* than any other pieces of contemporary literature. I do not know whether I knew this at the time, but I can very well remember coming up by a slow train from Hythe and attempting at one and the same time to read the volume of stories containing *Only a Subaltern* and to make a single pipe of shag last the whole of that long journey. And I can remember that when I came at almost the same moment to Charing Cross and the death of the subaltern I was crying so hard that a friendly ticket collector asked me if I was very ill, and saw me into a cab.

What, then, has become of all these fine enthusiasms—for assuredly I was not the only one capable of enthusiasms ? What has become of the young men with the long necks and the red ties; what has become of all the young maidens with the round shoulders, the dresses of curtain-serge and the amber necklaces ? Where are all those of us who admired

Henley and his gang ?   Where are all the adorers
of the Pre-Raphaelites ?   Where are all the poets
of the Rhymers' Club ?   Where are all the authors
of *To-day,* of *The Idler,* and *The Outlook* in its
brilliant days ?   Somebody—I think it was myself—
made a couplet running :

> "Let him begone," the mighty Wyndham cried.
> And Crosland vanished and *The Outlook* died.

One had such an enthusiasm for the work of
Mr. Crosland in those days, and a little later.

And where is it all gone ?   And why ?   I do not
know—or perhaps I do.   I went, as I say, for
thirteen years into the country.   I lived entirely, or
almost entirely, amongst peasants.   This was of
course due to that idealizing of the country life which
was so extraordinarily prevalent in the earlier
'nineties amongst the disciples of William Morris
and other Cockneys.   It was a singularly unhealthy
frame of mind which caused a number of young men,
totally unfitted for it, to waste only too many good
years of their lives in posing as romantic agricul-
turists.   They took small holdings, lost their hay-
crops, saw their chickens die, and stuck to it with
grim obstinacy until, William Morris and Morrisism
being alike dead, their feelings found no more support
from the contagion of other enthusiasms.   So they
have mostly returned to useful work, handicapped by
the loss of so many good years, and generally with
ruined digestions; for the country with its atrocious food and cooking is, in England, the home of
dyspepsia.

I suppose that is why England is known abroad

as *das Pillenland—le pays des pilules*—the land of patent medicines.

So that although I must write it down—*atque ego in Arcadia vixi*—I am able to see, having returned after this interval to a city where the things of the spirit have as much place as can be found in the country of " price per thou."—I am able, as the French would say, to *constater* how enormous a change has come over the face of the only city in the world where, in spite of everything, life is worth living. For, after all, London is the only place in the world where there is real freedom and real solitude, where no man's eye is upon you, since no man cares twopence what you are, where you may be going, or what will become of you. And there we have it, the reason why London is so good a place for mankind, and a place so bitter bad at once for the arts and ideas. Rushing about as we do in huge crowds, we have no time for any solidarity; faced as we are by an incredible competition we have no heart in us for self-sacrifice, and at it as we are all day and half the night we have no time for reflection. Yet it is only of reflection that ideas are born, and it is only by self-sacrifice and by self-sacrifice again that the arts can flourish. We must write much and sacrifice much of what we have written; we must burn whole volumes; deferring to the ideas of our brother artists whom we trust, we must sacrifice other whole volumes, to achieve such a little piece of perfection that, if that too were burnt, the ashes of it would not fill a doll's thimble. Yet before us hangs always now the scroll with the fateful words, " price per thou."

The mention of this wonderful contrivance will extort from a French or a German writer a look of utter incredulity. They will think that you are " pulling their legs." And then gradually you will observe to be passing into their faces an expression of extremely polite, of slightly ironical admiration :

" Ah, yes," they will say. " You English are so practical."

And indeed we are very practical. But it is only on the material side that we even begin to consider ways and means. Thus, lately we had an enlightening and lively discussion as to the length a " book " should have. [By " book " a six-shilling novel should, I suppose, be understood.] We were instructed that the public desires, nay, insists on, a certain fixed amount of reading matter. You might weigh a book in scales, you might measure its lines of *bourgeois* or *pica* type with a foot-rule. But your book must be able to be assayed either by weight or by measure. Indeed, nowadays your publisher when he commissions a novel, insists in his agreement that it shall be 75,000 words in length. Just imagine ! You might want to write the chronicle of a family as Thackeray did in *The Newcomes*, and you must do it all in 75,000 words, or you might want to write the story of how a young man got engaged to a young woman during five accidental meetings in omnibuses. And, if you cannot do it in 4,000 words, so as to make it a " short story " for one of the popular magazines, you must extend it to 75,000 or there will be, every publisher will tell you, " no market for it." In the earlier 'nineties the publisher cheated his authors as a rule tyrannically enough, and, since no author ever looked at an agreement in those days, things went smoothly. The publisher on the other hand considered sometimes the quality of the work that he published, and seldom thought about the length of the book. Indeed, everything was then made more easy for the author's activities. When I published, at the age of eighteen, my first novel, it was borne in upon me that there was no need to be acquainted with the mysteries of grammar—or rather of syntax, since in England there is no such thing as grammar—of syntax, of spelling or of punctuation. The author of that day could write exactly as he pleased; he could make mistakes as to dates; he could re-christen his heroine by inadvertence four times in as many chapters. But he knew that he would have three succeeding sets of proofs and revises, and that each proof and each revise would be gone through with an almost incredible care by a proof-reader who would be a man of the highest education and of a knowledge almost encyclopædic. I once by a slip of the pen wrote the name of the painter of the " Primavera," Buonarotti. Sure enough the proof came back marked in the margin : " Surely there is no picture of this name by Michael Angelo. Query Botticelli ? " So that indeed in the 'nineties, and before that, one had a sense not only of dignity and luxury but of security. And this was very good for writing.

Consider where we are now ! In the case of the last novel but one that I published I received from the publisher the most singular and the most insolent document that I think an author could possibly

receive. This requested me to mark with red
ink any printer's error and with black my own
changes in the text. Just think of what this means !
An author when he is correcting his proofs, if he is
anywhere near worth his salt, is in a state of the most
extreme tension. It is his last chance for getting
his phrases musical or his words exactly right; it is
an operation usually more trying than the actual
writing of a book. And into this intense abstraction
there is as it were to come the voice of a damned
publisher exclaiming: "Red ink, if you please; that
hyphen is a printer's error." Nowadays indeed
the publisher only allows his author one proof and
no revises unless the author make a horrible row
about it. And the publisher's proof-reader seems
to have disappeared altogether. Last March I
received three sets of proofs—forty-eight pages—in
which the printer had uniformly spelled the word
receive wrong. Now I know how to spell receive,
and so does my typist. Yet it is a matter as to which
one always has a lingering doubt. So that when
nine times in forty-eight pages I found the " i "
preceding the " e " I was frightened and turned to
a dictionary. But do you imagine that the " reader
for the press " had once noticed this ? Not a bit
of it. The whole forty-eight pages were guiltless of
a speck from his pen, and after that I had my nerves
perpetually on the stretch to find out and to examine
all words like believe or deceive. My mind was in
a woful state of jangle and exasperation, and the one
critic who appeared to carefully have read the book
remarked that I had split an infinitive. It is not
that this particular thing so particularly matters;

234

it is that the whole spirit is so atrocious and so depressing. The half-ruined libraries, we are told, badger the unfortunate publisher; the unfortunate publisher has beaten down the unfortunate printer until, I am told, the printing schedule of to-day is only 55 per cent. of what it was in 1890. As a consequence the printer will only send one set of proofs and no revises. He sacks any proof-reader whose competence commands a decent wage, so that all the really efficient " readers for the press " are said to be employed by the newspapers.

And along with all this there has gone the tremendous increase in the cost of living and the enormous increase of the public indifference to anything in the nature of the arts. This last—and possibly both of these factors—began with the firing of the first shot in the Boer War. That was the end of everything— of the Pre-Raphaelites, of the Henley gang, of the New Humour, of the Victorian Great Figures, and of the last traces of the mediæval superstition that man might save his soul by the reading of good books.

Africa has been called the grave of reputations. South Africa has bitterly revenged itself upon us for our crimes. It was undoubtedly the Rand millionaire who began to set the pace of social life so immensely fast. And the South African War meant the final installation of the Rand millionaire in Mayfair, which is the centre of English—and possibly of European and American—socia life. The Rand millionaire was almost invariably a Jew; and whatever may be said for or against the Jew as a gainer of money, there is no doubt that having got it he spends it with an extraordinary lavishness, so that the whole tone of English society really changed at about this time. No doubt the coming of the motor-car, of the telephone, of the thousand and one pleasant little inventions of which no one had any idea in the nineteenth century—no doubt the coming of all these little things that have rendered life so gay, so sensuous, and so evanescent—all these little things have played their part in adding immensely to the cost of life if one has to live at all as pleasantly as one's neighbours. But they are the accident; it is the people who set the measure of the amount to which these luxuries are to be indulged in; it is those people who, in essence, rule our lives.

It is all very well to say that luxury—which is the culture of life—is neither here nor there in the world of the arts or the ideas. My German great-grandmother, the wife of the Bürgermeister of one of the capital cities of Germany, could never get over what appeared to her a disastrous new habit that was beginning to be adopted in Germany towards the end of her life, about 1780. She said that it was sinful, that it was extravagant, that it would lead to the downfall of the German nation. This revolutionary new habit was none other than that of having a dining-room. In those days Germany was so poor a country that even though my great-grandparents were considered wealthy people they were always accustomed to eat their meals in the bedroom. There was, that is to say, only one room and a kitchen in their house. The beds of the whole family were in niches in the walls surrounding the living room, and it was here that they ate, slept, changed their clothes, or received their guests. The families of merchants less wealthy even cooked in their bedrooms. This appeared to my great-grandmother the only virtuous arrangement. And it was no doubt in the same spirit that, Madox Brown considered it a proof of decadent luxury to wash one's hands more than three times a day. Nowadays, I suppose, we should consider my great-grandmother's virtue a disgusting affair, and one that because it was insanitary was also immoral, or at least anti-social; whilst my grandfather who washed his hands only three times a day —before breakfast, lunch and dinner—would be considered as only just scraping through the limits of cleanliness. Yet the price of soap is increasing daily.

It may well be said : Why could my German grandfather when he married not have gone on eating his meals in his bedroom after the patriarchal manner ? But to say so would argue a serious want of knowledge of the creature that man is. He would have been intolerably miserable; his wife would have been intolerably miserable; his children would have been miserable and crest-fallen amongst their playmates, for by that time—say a hundred years ago —all the neighbours had dining-rooms. So that the problem before my grandfather was to set his printing-presses to work with redoubled speed and so to earn money enough to build for his wife and his children a sufficiently large house. And so he did, so that when he died he had not only bought the very large town house of a Westphalian nobleman, but he was able to leave to each of his fourteen children the sum of £3,750—which taken in the aggregate represented a very large fortune for a German of the 'forties. But then, £400 a year in the 'eighties was considered sufficient for a man to marry on in London. It is not enough for a bachelor nowadays, if he is to live with any enjoyment.

And the artist *must* live with enjoyment if his work is to be sound and good. He ought, if he is to know life, to be able to knock at all doors; he ought to be able to squander freely upon occasion; he ought to be able to riot now and then. It is no good saying that he ought to be able to live with his muse as with his love, in a cottage. *L'un et l'autre se disent*, but though it is very well to live with love in a cottage in your young years when the world is a funny place, and the washing-up of dishes such a humorous incident as makes of life a picnic, the writer who passes his life at this game will be in the end but a poor creature, whether as a man or a writer. Or no, he may make a very fine man of the type of little St. Francis of the Birds. But he will be a writer purely doctrinaire. And for a writer to be doctrinaire is the end of him as an artist. He may make an excellent pamphleteer.

This is very much what has happened to English literary life. The English writer appears to me— in the pack, for obviously there are the exceptions, mostly of an old-fashioned order—in the pack like a herd of hungry wolves. Yet, unlike the wolf, he is incapable of herding to any sensible purpose. The goodness of the Pre-Raphaelite movement was its union in a common devotion to the arts. Its actual achievements may have been very small. I should not like if I were put upon my critical judgment to say that either Rossetti or Holman Hunt, either Swinburne or William Morris, Millais or Burne-Jones, or, for the matter of that, my grandfather, were first-rate artists. But their effect in heightening the prestige and the glamour of the arts was very wonderful, and remains, for the Continent if not for England, a wonderful thing too. Similarly with Henley's crowd of friends. Their union was very close, though not so close as that of the Pre-Raphaelite circle. Their devotion to a sort of practical art was very great too, though it was not so conscious as that of Flaubert and his ring. Henley, at least subconsciously, taught his followers that the first business of art is to interest, and the second to interest, and the third again—to interest. And I think that nearly all that is vital, actual and alive in English work of to-day is due to the influence of Henley and his friends, just as I am perfectly certain that the two first-class purely imaginative writers of England of to-day—Mr. Henry James and Mr. Joseph Conrad—are the direct products artistically of Turgeniev and of Flaubert. It is mortifying to have to consider that each of these great writers is a foreigner. But so it is, and I should rather imagine that neither of these distinguished foreigners has ever heard the phrase that I have in this place so often used.

And great though Pre-Raphaelism was as an influence, great though Henleyism is as an influence, yet each of these influences left behind it a curse that has miasmatically affected the English world of letters.

I remember—years ago before I went into the country—sitting in one of those distressingly unpleasant French restaurants of Soho that even in those days these superior and Morris-influenced writers considered as being at once romantic and satisfactory—I remember sitting listening to a group of my fellow-socialists of that type. I was always frightened of my companions, they were so bitterly contemptuous of me if I failed to know exactly what was the proper doctrine about any point of the Ideal Commonwealth, or as to what sort of clothes Dante wore at Ravenna. Yes, I was frightened; and suddenly it came into my head to understand that a temporal tyranny might be a bad thing, but that the intellectual tyranny that my young friends would set up, when their social revolution came round the corner like the three-horse omnibus—that this intellectual tyranny would be infinitely worse than anything that Ivan the Terrible could ever have devised. For these young men, my companions, would keep all the good things of life for those who understood what would happen to babies in the Ideal State, for those who knew what Beatrice ate on the morning before she met Dante for the first time, for those who had the *Cuchullain Saga*, the *Saga of Grettir the Strong* and possibly *Ossian* and *News from Nowhere* by heart. As for me I never could understand anything at all about the economic conditions of the Ideal State. Most of the Celtic and Scandinavian epics appeared to me to be intolerably long and amateurish productions of dull peasants who occasionally produced passages of brilliancy accidentally surpassing anything that was ever written or ever will be. And, as for *News from Nowhere* . . .

240

Heroes and Some Heroines

So, looking at my contemptuous young companions, each with his soft frieze coat, the pockets
of which suggested that they contained many
apples, each with his low collar, each with his
red tie, and looking at the dirty table-cloths, the
common knives, the cheap and poisonous claret, I felt
suddenly guilt, humility and intense dread; I felt
that I was a Philistine! I felt that every moment
that I sat there I might be found out and conveyed
swiftly to the chilling dungeons of the Ideal State.
I seemed to hear from round the corner the rattle
of the three-horse 'bus. I seemed to catch in the eyes
around that table a threatening gleam as if they
suspected that I was a sort of spy at that banquet
of conspirators.

I fled—into the country. Looking at the matter
now, I perceive that Henley was responsible for this—
Henley and his piratical gang. These people had
struck me as rough and unduly boisterous when I
went to them out of a Pre-Raphaelite household.
But, my grandfather being dead, I suddenly reacted.
I did not know then, but I know now that my brain
was singing to me:

> " Under the bright and starry sky
> Dig my grave and let me lie."

Only I wanted to have some tussles with the
" good brown earth " before that hill-top should
receive me. Well, we have most of us found the
" good brown earth " part of a silly pose—but I am
not sorry. It was Henley and his friends who introduced into the English writing mind the idea that a
man of action was something fine and a man of

R   241

letters a sort of castrato. *They* went jumping all over the earth, they " jumped the blind baggage " in the United States, they played at being tramps in Turkey; they died in Samoa, they debauched the morals of lonely border villages. You see what it was—they desired to be men of action, and certainly they infected me with the desire, and I am very glad of it, just as I am very glad that the intolerable boredom of a country life without sport or pursuit taught me better in time.

With the idea that a writer should have been a man of action before he begins to write I am cordially in agreement; indeed, I doubt whether any writer has ever been thoroughly satisfactory unless he has once had some sort of normal existence. No greater calamity could befall one than to be trained as a genius. For the writer looks at life and does not share it. This is his calamity; this is his curse. If Shakespeare had not held horses outside a theatre or taken an interest in commercial enterprises, or whatever it was of a normal sort that he did before he wrote his first play, I think it is certain that the Baconians would not to-day be troubling their heads about him. He would have remained a poet of about the calibre of Fletcher, who was a very beautiful and poetical soul. Shakespeare had a soul not a bit more poetic, but he was of his world and he knew life. Hence he had not only the gifts of a poet but the knowledge of how to invent along the lines of probability, and the one faculty is as essential to the perfect work of art as is the other. And Shakespeare had the immense advantage of belonging to a circle—to a circle that

praised art high, that troubled its head about the
technical side of things, and a circle that troubled
itself very little about its social position. Shakespeare—or whoever it was—wrote the ballad beginning :

> " It was a lordling's daughter,
> The fairest one of three."

in which a learned man and a soldier contend for the
favour of an earl's daughter. They put up a fairly
equal fight of it so that for the moment I do not
remember which got the upper hand. But do you
imagine that an English writer of to-day would give
a man of letters a show if he had to picture him as the
rival of an officer in the Guards, or on the other hand
as the rival of a colonial pioneer ? Not a bit of it !
The modern English writer—and he would not be
of necessity a traitor to his cloth—would argue in
this way : A writer has in England no social position; an officer in the Guards is at the top of the tree.
Therefore the heroine would take the officer in the
Guards. Or again he would say a man of letters is
regarded as something less than a man, whereas any
sort of individual returning from the colonies is
regarded inevitably as something rather more than
two supermen rolled into one. So that the heroine
would inevitably take the returned colonist.

No, this writer would not be a traitor to his cloth.
It does not matter that officers in the Guards are
mostly rather silly fools without conversation or any
interests beyond the head of their polo mallets, or
that nearly every returned colonial can do nothing
better than talk of the affairs of his dull colony
in the language at once of a bore and a prig—for

of necessity his mind is occupied with a civilization of a low kind. But still, the poor depressed writer will see that the heroine—being a bright and beautiful English girl—will prefer money or social position to any of the delights of communing with giants of the intellect. And to marry a lieutenant in the Guards is to have duchesses on your visiting list or to go yearly to Ascot in the smartest of frocks, though there may be some difficulty in meeting the bills sent in by Madame Somebody. Or again, to marry a colonial administrator or one of those rather sketchy gentlemen from Australia who are always lecturing us as if they were so many Roosevelts by the grace of God—to marry some such gentleman is in all probability to become the wife at least of a K.C.M.G., possibly of a peer, to have eventually a palace in Park Lane and the country estate of an impoverished earl.

So the writer of fiction would estimate the chances, and I do not know whether he would be right or wrong; for certainly the ordinary man of letters has precious little to offer anybody and none too much for himself. Poor devil, he is between the necessity for an expenditure that would have seemed vast to his grandfather and a buying public that day by day shows less desire to buy books. For this too the South African War was partly responsible. I had a young connection who lately went up for the preliminary examination at the Admiralty. Said the examining admiral :

"Now, my man, what papers does your father read ? And what do you judge from that that his politics are ? "

"CHRIST WASHES PETER'S FEET"

(From the picture by Madox Brown in the Tate Gallery)

This was not an invidious political question on the admiral's part; the object of the examination is to test a boy's powers of observation. The boy's answer was :

" Oh, my governor's a Tory. He reads the *Daily Chronicle*, the *Daily News*, the *Westminster Gazette*, the *Manchester Guardian*. . . ."

" But," said the admiral, aghast, " those are all Liberal papers. You said your father was a Tory."

" Oh yes," the boy answered with assurance, " he takes in *The Times*, the *Saturday Review*, the *Spectator*, and *Field*, to give his side a show—to put the money into their pockets. But he never reads any of them except now and then, and the *Field* always on Sunday. He says he can do all the lying that is wanted on his side for himself, without reading the Tory papers. But he wants to know what lies the other side are telling, because he can't make *them* up for himself."

The admiral laughed and passed the boy, but the admiral was old-fashioned. He had a pre-Boer-War habit of mind as regarded the newspapers. In his prime he took *The Times* or the *Morning Post*, and that was all he had in the way of a paper. But with the coming of the South African War we acquired the habit of skimming through from seven to ten papers a day—to get a little hope. I don't blame us. The man who could go through the period of Spion Kop without rushing anywhere to read the latest bulletin, or could keep in his pocket one single penny that might give him some glimmer of hopeful news, was something less than a man. I suppose I was as hot a pro-Boer as any one well could be, but I know I came very near to crying with joy when

Mafeking was relieved. I remember that that night I had been up to Highgate. I was coming back very late and I asked the tram-driver if there was any news. He said there was none. Suddenly the conductor came running out of the fire-station shouting:

" The relief-party is in ! "

Immediately he scrambled on board the tram, the driver whipped his horses to a gallop, and we went tearing madly down that long hill into the darkness, the conductor standing on top of the tram and shouting at the top of his voice that Mafeking was relieved. And, in those black and grim streets, shining with the wet, suddenly every window lit up and opened, and from each there came out a Union Jack. It was as if we entered a city given over to night, to the tears of the rain, to merciless suspense, and as if we left behind us streets gay, triumphant, illuminated, imperial. Or perhaps imperial is not the word. I don't know.

Farther down in the town we came upon places where the news was already. I went towards St. Paul's to see if there was not some sort of inspiring demonstration. But in Holborn I was knocked down. A fat and elderly gentleman, bearing over his shoulder a long pole on which were nailed about twenty little flags, turned suddenly round and the end of the pole caught me under the ear.

Imperial ? No, I think not. We were more like a nation of convicted murderers, suddenly reprieved when the hangman's cap was over our eyes. I think I was as glad as any one else. But the Nemesis remains. Still, every day I read my five newspapers. And, in common with the rest of England, I don't believe a single word that I read in any one of them. Like the father of the boy who was up for examination, I prefer to read papers of the shade of politics that for the moment may happen to be not my own. I can lie so much more skilfully than any journalist upon my own side.

But this enormous and unimpressed reading of newspapers has given the last kick to the writer of books. It is the end of him. He has gone out. Before the War a rich man occasionally bought a book. The other day I owned a periodical. Said a man to me—*he* owned seven motor cars :

"I wish your paper did not cost half-a-crown. If it was only a shilling I would certainly buy it. But times are so hard that I have to put down my book bill."—"And he had great possessions."

Before the War this gentleman would have been forced, by sheer hypocrisy, to pay that particular cock to Æsculapius. But the War gave us our excuse for "putting down" anything—book bills coming of course first—and since the War my friend has had to keep it up against a Rand magnate of his immediate circle. At that moment this other gentleman owned six motor-cars. My friend had therefore to have his seven. I believe he was the second richest man in England.

I cannot, however, say that the poor come any better out of that particular struggle. Thus at about the same time I received a whining letter from a working men's club in the north of London. They said that they numbered exactly thirty, that my periodical was absolutely necessary to them, and that they could not possibly afford half-a-crown.

They were mostly school-teachers. I answered perfectly seriously that if my periodical was so absolutely necessary to the saving of their souls, there were exactly thirty of them, so that to purchase a copy for their club would cost each of them exactly one penny per month. I suggested that if each one of them would once a month walk a penny tram fare, or smoke 1-64th of a pound less tobacco, or drink one quarter of a pint less beer, or go for one day without a daily paper, their club might very well purchase monthly a copy of my so necessary periodical. I received in reply a note from the secretary of that club stating that my letter was ribald, insulting and utterly unsympathetic to the woes of the poor who had paid me an undeserved compliment.

No. I do not think that the workman, the school-teacher and the rest of them will be any better masters for literature which is falling under their dominance. And I do not see any hope of improvement until the state supplies literature free. That of course is coming, but I have no doubt that the state will sweat the author even more mercilessly than do, in effect, the millionaire, the shopkeeper, the school-teacher and the workman of to-day. For all these people demand such literature as they have time, or deign, to consume—they demand it at derisorily cheap rates. And you cannot have good new literature cheaply. It cannot be done, simply because the author, too, has the right to live. Of course you may have cheap reprints of the works of dead authors—as cheaply as you like, for the state, with its contempt for all things of the mind, steals the only property which is really created by any man. So the heirs of Shakespeare and of Dickens may go starve whilst their non-copyright editions contribute to the starvation of succeeding authors.

That authors themselves have contributed to the want of interest in literature that the public displays is also true. That is a legacy of Pre-Raphaelism— the worst legacy that any movement ever left behind it. For those young men from whom I fled into the country invented later, or had already invented, the dreary shibboleth that literature must be written by those who have read the *Cuchullain Saga* or something dull and pompous, for those who have read similar works. Literature, these people say, is of necessity abstruse, esoteric, far-fetched and unreadable. Nothing is less true, nothing more fatal. Great literature always is and always has been popular. It has had, that is to say, its popular appeal. Homer was a popular writer, Virgil was a popular writer, Chaucer wrote in what was then called the vulgar tongue for the common people. This, too, Dante did. I believe that Shakespeare deliberately " wrote down " in order to catch the ear of the multitude. Goethe was one of the most populars authors of his day, and the most popular author of to-day or any time was also the finest artist of his own or any day. This was Guy de Maupassant.

Who, I wonder, in England will ever realize that literature, besides being " elevating," is a gay thing, is a pleasant thing, is a thing made for the increase of joy, of mirth, of happiness, and of those tears which are near to joy ? It is the business of a book to be easy to read—to be as easy to read as any book upon its given subject can possibly be. I do not mean to say that a book about the Treaty of Tilsit can ever be as easy for a water-side labourer or for me to read as a work about things that I or the water-side labourer know perfectly well. But it is the duty of the author to capture attention, and then to make his subject plain; there is no other duty of an author.

It is not for him to pose as a priest dwelling amongst obscurities. If his readers, if his lovers will regard him as priest it is very well. Or, if his readers, if his lovers will find and seek to cast light upon obscurities in his pages it will be still better, for that will mean that in them he has awakened thought and emotions. And when an author— when any artist has awakened in another person thoughts and emotions, he is, to the measure of the light vouchsafed him, blessed indeed. This author will have told his tale in language as simple as his personality will permit him to use, in thoughts as simple as God will give him.

Here stand I, the man in the street. I have no special knowledge, I have no special gifts. I desire to be interested as I was interested when I read in the coal-cellar the adventures of Harkaway Dick. I desire to be interested as I was interested when I first read *Ivanhoe, Lear, Nicholas Nickleby, La Maison Tellier, Fathers and Children, The Trial of Joan of Arc, The Arabian Nights,* or —twenty years ago—*The Dolly Dialogues* or *Daisy Miller.* You see, the poor man in the street is catholic enough in his tastes. And he has a passionate desire to be interested. This is indeed the noblest and the finest of all desires, since it means that he desires to enter into the fortunes, the hopes, the very hearts of his fellow-men, and it is in this way and in no other that literature can render a man better. I once lent a book to an old and quite ignorant cottage woman who had always had a taste for reading novels. And there are few cottage people who will not read novels with avidity. Some days afterwards I went in to see this old woman. The tears were dropping down her cheeks, and she was wiping them away as fast as she could. She had just finished the book in question. She said :

" Ah ! aw do jest love yon book. It does me all the good in the world. Aw feels a score of years leeter for the cry ! "

This book was *Fathers and Children.* Yet what was Bazarow to her or she to Bazarow ?

And there the matter is in a nutshell. Here I stand and cry for such a writer, and when such a writer, with such a purpose, disregarding all shibboleths, considering himself not as a priest who has to express *himself* but as quite a humble man who has before him the task of interesting me and the millions that I represent—when this writer comes he will sweep away all barriers. No markets will be closed to him, and no doors; there will be no hearts that he will not enter and no hearth that will not welcome him as its guest. He will be honoured by emperors, and ploughmen will desire to take his hand. Wealth will be his beyond belief, and power. And he will be such a priest as Moses was, or those who were greater than Moses. But I do not think that he will have the *Cuchullain Saga* by heart.

XIII

CHANGES

I was walking the other day down one of the stretches of main road of the west of London. Rather low houses of brownish brick recede a little way from the road behind gardens of their own, or behind little crescents common to each group of houses. Omnibuses pass numerously before them and there is a heavy traffic of motor vehicles, because the road leads out into the country towards the west. But since this particular day happened to be a Sunday, the stretch of road, perhaps half a mile in length, was rather empty. I could see only two horse 'buses, a brougham and a number of cyclists. And at that moment it occurred to me to think that there were no changes here at all. There was nothing at that moment to tell me that I was not the small boy that thirty years ago used, with great regularity, to walk along that stretch of road in order to go into Kensington Gardens. It was a remarkably odd sensation. For the moment I seemed to be back there, I seemed to be a child again, rather timid and wonderingly setting out upon tremendous adventures that the exploring of London streets then seemed to entail.

And having thus dipped for a moment into a past

as unattainable as is the age of Homer, I came
back very sharply before the first of the horse 'buses
and the fourth small band of cyclists had passed me
—I came back to wondering about what changes the
third of a century that I can remember had wrought
in London and in us. It is sometimes pleasant, it
is nearly always salutary, thus to take stock. Considering myself, it was astonishing how little I seemed
to myself to have changed since I was a very little
boy in a velveteen coat with gold buttons and long
golden ringlets. I venture to obtrude this small
piece of personality because it is a subject that has
always interested me—the subject, not so much of
myself, as in how far the rest of humanity seem to
themselves to resemble me. I mean that to myself
I never seemed to have grown up. This circumstance
strikes me most forcibly when I go into my kitchen.
I perceive saucepans, kitchen spoons, tin canisters,
chopping boards, egg - beaters and objects whose
very names I do not even know. I perceive these
objects and suddenly it comes into my mind—though
I can hardly believe it—that these things actually
belong to me. I can really do what I like with them
if I want to. I might positively use the largest of
the saucepans for making butter-scotch, or I might
fill the egg-beater with ink and churn it up. For
such were the adventurous aspirations of my childhood, when I peeped into the kitchen, which was
a forbidden and glamorous place inhabited by a
forbidding moral force known as *Cook*. And that
glamour still persists, that feeling still remains. I
do not really very often go into my kitchen although
it, and all it contains, are my property—I do not go

into it because lurking at the back of my head I have always the feeling that I am a little boy who will be either "spoken to" or spanked by a mysterious *They*. In my childhood *They* represented a host of clearly perceived persons: my parents, my nurse, the housemaid, the hardly ever visible cook, a day-school master, several awful entities in blue who hung about in the streets and diminished seriously the enjoyment of life, and a large host of unnamed adults who possessed apparently remarkable and terrorizing powers. All these people were restraints. Nowadays, as far as I know, I have no restraints. No one has a right, no one has any authority, to restrain me. I can go where I like: I can do what I like: I can think, say, eat, drink, touch, break, whatever I like, that is within the range of my own small empire. And yet till the other day I had constantly at the back of my mind the fear of a mysterious *They*—a feeling that has not changed in the least, since the day when last I could not possibly resist it, and I threw from an upper window a large piece of whitening at the helmet of a policeman who was standing in the road below. Yesterday I felt quite a strong desire to do the same thing when a bag of flour was brought to me for my inspection because it was said to be mouldy. There was the traffic going up and down underneath my windows, there was the sunlight, and there, his buckles and his buttons shining, there positively, on the other side of the road, stalked the policeman. But I resisted the temptation. My mind travelled rapidly over the possibilities. I wondered whether I could hit the policeman at the distance, and presumed I could. I wondered whether the policeman would be able to identify the house from which the missile came, and presumed he would not. I wondered whether the servant could be trusted not to peach, and presumed she could. I considered what it would cost me, and imagined that, at the worst, the price would be something less than that of a stall at a theatre, whilst I desired to throw the bag of flour very much more than I have ever desired to go to a theatre. And yet, as I have said, I resisted the temptation. I was afraid of a mysterious *They.* Or again, I could remember very distinctly as a small boy, staring in at the window of a sweet-shop near Gower Street Station and perceiving that there brandy balls might be had for the price of only fourpence a pound. And I remember thinking that I had discovered the secret of perpetual happiness. With a pound of brandy balls I could be happy from one end of the day to the other. I was aware that grown-up people were sometimes unhappy, but no grown-up person I ever thought was possessed of less than fourpence a day. My doubts as to the distant future vanished altogether. I knew that whatever happened to others I was safe. Alas! I do not think that I have tasted a brandy ball for twenty years. When I have finished my day's work I shall send out for a pound of them, though I am informed that the price has risen to sixpence. But though I cannot imagine that their possession will make me happy even for the remaining hours of this one day, yet I have not in the least changed, really. 1 know what will make me happy and perfectly contented when I get it—symbolically I still desire only my little pound of sweets. I have a vague, but very strong, feeling that every one else in the world around me, if the garments of formality and fashion that surround them could only be pierced through—that every one else who surrounds me equally has not grown up. They have not in essentials changed since they were small children. And the murderer who to-morrow will have the hangman's noose round his neck—I am informed at this moment that criminals are nowadays always executed on Tuesdays at eleven o'clock—so let us say that a criminal who will be executed next Tuesday at that hour will feel, when the rope is put round his throat, an odd, pained feeling that some mistake is being made, because you do not really hang a child of six in civilized countries. So that perhaps we have not any of us changed. Perhaps we are all of us children, and the very children that we were when Victoria celebrated her first Jubilee at about the date when Plancus was the consul. And yet we are conscious, all of us, that we have tremendously changed since the date when Du Maurier gave us the adventures of Mr. Cimabue Brown.

We have changed certainly to the extent that we cannot, by any possibility, imagine ourselves putting up for two minutes with Mr. Brown at a friend's At Home. We could not possibly put up with any of these people. They had long, drooping beards: they drawled : they come back to one as being extremely gentle, and their trousers were enormous. Moreover the women wore bustles and skin-tight jerseys. (I have a friend the top cushions of whose ottomans are entirely filled with her discarded bustles. I cannot imagine what she could have been doing with so many of these articles. After all, the fashion of wearing them did not last for ten years; and the bustle was itself a thing which, not being on view, could hardly have needed to change its shape month by month. So that although the friend in question already possesses nine Chantecler hats and may, in consequence, be said to pay some attention to her personal appearance, I cannot imagine what she did with this considerable mass of unobtrusive adornments).

In those days people seem to have been extraordinarily slow. It was not only that they dined at seven and went about in four-wheelers; it was not only that they still asked each other to take pot luck —I am just informed that no really modern young person any longer understands what this phrase means—it is not only that nowadays if we chance to have to remain in Town in August we do not any longer pull down the front blinds, live in our kitchen, and acquire by hook or by crook a visitor's guide to Homburg, with which we could delude our friends and acquaintances on their return from Brighton into the idea that in the German spa we had rubbed shoulders with the great and noble. It is not only that our menus now soar beyond the lofty ideal of hot roast beef for Sunday, cold for Monday, hash for Tuesday, leg of mutton for Wednesday, cold on Thursday and so on; it is that we seem altogether to have changed. It is true that we have not grown up, but we are different animals. If we should open a file of *The Times* for 1875 and find that the leader writer agreed with some of our sentiments to-day,

we should be as much astonished as we are when we
find on Egyptian monuments that the lady who set
snares for the virtue of Joseph was dissatisfied with
the state of her linen when it came home from the
wash.

Now where exactly do these changes, as the phrase
is, come in ? Why should one feel such a shock of
surprise at discovering that a small slice of High
Street, Kensington, from the Addison Road railway
bridge to the Earl's Court Road has not " changed " ?
Change has crept right up to the public-house at
the corner. Why, only yesterday I noticed that the
pastrycook's next door to the public-house was " to
let." This is a great and historic change. As a
boy I used to gaze into its windows and perceive a
model of Windsor Castle in icing-sugar. And that
castle certainly appeared to me larger and more like
what a real castle ought to be than did Windsor
Castle, which I saw for the first time last month. I
am told that at that now vanished confectioner's you
could get an excellent plate of ox-tail soup and a cut
off the joint for lunch. Let me then give it the alms
for oblivion of this tear. Across the front of another
confectioner's near here is painted the inscription,
" Routs catered for." What was a rout ? I suppose
it was some sort of party, but what did you do when
you got there ? I remember reading a description
by Albert Smith of a conversazione at somebody's
private house, and a conversazione in those days
was the most modern form of entertainment.
Apparently it consisted in taking a lady's arm and
wandering round amongst show-cases. The host
and hostess had borrowed wax models of anatomical

dissections of a most realistic kind from the nearest hospital, and this formed the amusement provided for the guests, weak negus and seed biscuits being the only refreshment. This entertainment was spoken of in terms of reprobation by Mr. Albert Smith—in the same terms as we might imagine would be adopted by a popular moralist in talking of the doings of the smart set to-day. Mr. Smith considered that it constituted a lamentably wild form of dissipation and one which no lady, who was really a lady, ought to desire to attend.

Yes, very decidedly we have changed all that. Though we have not grown up, though we are still children, we want something more exciting than anatomical dissections in glass cases when we are asked out of an evening. We have grown harder, we have grown more rapid in our movements, we have grown more avid of sensation, we have grown more contemptuous of public opinion, we have become the last word.

But if we are more avid of sensations, if we are restless more to witness or to possess, to go through or to throw away always a greater and greater number of feelings or events or objects, we are, I should say, less careful in our selections. The word "exquisite" has gone almost as completely out of our vocabulary as the words "pot luck." And for the same reason. We are no longer expected to take pot luck because our hostess, by means of the telephone, can always get from round the corner some sort of ready-made confection that has only to be stood for ten minutes in a *bain-marie* to form a course of an indifferent dinner. She would do that if she were mildly old-fashioned. If she were at all up to date she would just say, " Oh, don't bother to come all this way out. Let's meet at the Dash and dine there." In either case pot luck has gone as has " dropping-in of an evening." Social events in all classes are now so frequent; a pleasant, leisurely impromptu foregathering is so seldom practicable that we seldom essay it.

Dining in restaurants is in many ways gay, pleasant and desirable. It renders us on the one hand more polite, it renders us on the other less sincere, less intimate with our friends and less exacting. We have to be tidier and more urbane, but on the other hand we cannot so tyrannically exact of the cook that the dishes shall be impeccable. We are democratized. If in a restaurant we make a horrible noise because the fish is not absolutely all that it should be, we shall have it borne in upon us that we are only two or three out of several hundred customers, that we may go elsewhere, and that we shall not get anything better anywhere else. If the tipping system were abolished it would be impossible to get a decent meal anywhere in London.

At present it is difficult. It is difficult, that is to say, to get a good meal anywhere with certainty. You may patronize a place for a month and live well, or very well. Then suddenly something goes wrong, everything goes wrong, a whole menu is uneatable. The cook may have gone; the management, set on economizing, will have substituted margarine for real butter in cooking; the business may have become a limited company with nothing left to it but the old name and redecorated premises. And five hundred customers will not know any difference. Provided that a book has a binding with a sufficiency of gilt; provided that a dinner has its menu; provided that a picture has its frame, a book's a book, a dinner's a dinner, a picture will cover so much wall-space, and, being cheapened, will find buyers enough.

And this tendency pervades every class of establishment; it is not only that French cookery is everywhere very risky to set out upon. Always repulsive in appearance and hopelessly indigestible, English plain cooking is dead. At my birth I was put up for election at an old club that has now disappeared. My name came up for election when I was eighteen, and I was allowed, with proper restrictions—when, as it were, I was accompanied by a nurse—I was allowed the use of the premises. The members were almost all Anglo-Indians of considerable age, and many were of a fine stinginess. They used to find the club prices for meals unthinkable, and it was their habit, about lunch-time or towards seven, to toddle off to an eating-house in the immediate neighbourhood. Here, for the sum of eightpence, they would obtain a plate of meat and a piece of bread. There were no table-cloths on the tables that were covered with black leather wiped clean with a wet cloth; table-napkins cost a penny, and the floors were sanded. But the food was splendid of its kind, and the company consisted entirely of venerable clubsmen. There was a special brew of ale, the best in the world; the cheese was always the finest October, and a really wonderful port was to be had. My venerable fellow-members, however, as a rule limited themselves

to their plate of meat, after which they would walk
back to the club. Here they could have bread and
cheese and a glass of ale for nothing. (I wonder if
there is still in London any club like this ? I know
there is one yet where your change is washed and
wrapped in tissue paper). But there was the club
and there was the Dash Eating-house.

The other day I was anxious to prove to a stranger
that London was the cheapest city in the world, and
casting about in my mind for a means of proof I
remembered the Dash. It was still there. The
low rooms were the same; the leather-covered tables
were the same. The menus were the same; but
dismay came upon me when I observed that every
item on the menu was a penny cheaper. And nap-
kins were handed to us gratis !

And then the meat. Oh dear ! And the old
special ale was no more to be had; the place was tied
to a London brewery. And the cheese was *Canadian !*
The place, you see, had been discovered by the
city clerk. There was not one old face, not one
bald head there. The new management had taken
in many more rooms. I do not know if anywhere
there was written Ichabod on the walls, and no
old waiter sadly deplored the changes, for we
were waited upon by girls. The food was tepid
and tough, but as I paid my ridiculously tiny bill
the voice of a clerk behind me remarked, " Quite
the good old times." So that there we are.

If I try to illustrate my meaning in terms of eating
rather than by illustrations less material it is not
that exactly similar processes are not observable
everywhere else. We grow more rapid, but our

senses are coarsened : we grow more polite, we grow even more tolerant, but we seek less earnestly after the truth. In the 'seventies and 'eighties men were intolerably slow, but they had enthusiasms. A writer thought more about writing, a painter thought more about painting, a preacher, for the matter of that, more about preach'ng. A quixotic act to-day is regarded as something almost criminal if it entails loss of money. It is not so long since the word quixotic meant foolish but fine, whereas nowadays, so seldom does any action really quixotic occur, that it is almost invariably regarded with suspicion, and the person indulging himself in such an action is apt to find himself avoided. His friends may think that he is " going to get something out of it " that they cannot see, and they dread lest that something be got out of themselves. Probably we have not gained much, probably we have not lost much. Probably the thinker has a worse time of it; the unthinking certainly have an immensely better one. The squalor and the filth of the existence of the poor in the 'seventies and 'eighties are almost unthinkable to-day. I am physically and mentally in the most wretched state when I happen to travel by one of the London " tubes." The noise is barbaric, the smell of humanity sickening, and the sight of the comparatively imbecile faces of my fellow towns-men of the middle and lower classes is sometimes more depressing than I can stand. For what can be more depressing than to sit with 40 or 50 of one's fellow-beings in a strong light, all of them barbar-ously and unbecomingly clad and each of them with a face dull, heavy, unvivacious, to all appearances incapable of a ray of human intelligence, of a scintilla of original thought? So, at least, I imagine the late Mr. Herbert Spencer thinking if his ghost could come once more from the shades of the billiard-room of the Athenæum Club, and, paying his twopence, descend into the lift and take the tube from Shepherd's Bush to Tottenham Court Road. (This, by the bye, would pretty exactly have represented Mr. Spencer's attitude. That gentleman once sat at table next to a connection of my own for three consecutive days. He sat in deep silence. Upon the fourth day he took from his ears two little pads of cotton wool. He exhibited them to the lady and remarking, " I stop my ears with these when I perceive there is no one at the table likely to afford rational conversation," he put them back again.)

But if the thinker, if the man with a taste for the exquisite, have to-day a pretty bad time of it unless he stops at home, all we humbler people get through our little lives and accomplish our ultimate end in becoming the stuff that fills graveyards, upon the whole much more agreeably. If exquisite editions of books are not at our hand, we get them plentifully in editions of an extreme cheapness. If we desire to see pictures, it will no longer be an expedition of a day to go from Hammersmith, which is now called West Kensington Park, to the National Gallery.

I can remember very well the time when it meant a tenpenny 'bus fare and an hour's slow drive to go from Hammersmith to Trafalgar Square, and it cost as much and took as long to go from Shepherd's Bush to Oxford Circus. And these sums and these spaces of time, when they come to be doubled, require to be seriously thought about. Nowadays we do not think at all. Life is much fuller, and I fancy we value a visit to the National Gallery much less. But if we value it less still it is more agreeable. I remember travelling in an odious horse-box of grimy yellow wood in an intolerable stench of sulphur and shag tobacco along with eleven navvies in the horrid old underground trains. The conditions were unspeakable, the fares relatively high. This occurred to me perhaps once or twice, but they must have been the daily conditions of how very large a class ! Nowadays our friend the workman steps into a clean lift and descends into cool, white, brilliantly lit tunnels that twenty-five years ago would have been things entirely beyond his experience or his dreams. And because of them, too, he can live further out, in a cleaner air, in conditions immeasurably superior. Routs are no longer catered for, leisure is an unknown thing, and the old-fashioned confectioner's shop will be pulled down to make way for a cheap-jack of some sort, inhabiting a terra-cotta palace with great plate-glass windows and white, soft stone facings. There will be about the new man something meretricious, flashy, and not altogether desirable. I do not know that I shall ever want to go into such a shop, but to many people the little pictures on tickets that are given away with little packets of cigarettes—to a great many hundreds of simple and kindly people, the arms of the City of Bath or the portrait of the infant son of the king of Spain, will afford great and harmless joy and excitement. I do not mean to say that in the pockets of this great alluvial world of humanity the old order will not remain in an even astonishing degree.

I was talking the other day to a woman of position when she told me that her daughters were immeasurably freer than she had been at their age. I asked her if she would let her daughters walk about alone in the streets. " Oh dear yes," she said. I asked her whether she would allow one of them to walk down Bond Street alone. " Oh dear, certainly not Bond Street ! " she said. I tried to get at what was the matter with Bond Street. I have walked down it myself innumerable times without noticing anything to distinguish it from any other street. But she said no, the girl might walk about Sloane Street or that sort of place, but certainly not Bond Street. I should have thought myself, from observation, that Sloane Street was rather the haunt of evil characters, but I let the matter drop when my friend observed that, of course, a man of my intelligence must be only laughing when I pretended that I could not see the distinction. I pursued therefore further geographical investigations. I asked her if she would permit her daughter to walk along the Strand. She said, " Good gracious me ! The Strand ! Why, I don't suppose the child knows where it is ! " I said, " But the Strand ! " " My dear man," she answered, " what should she want to walk along the Strand for ? What could possibly take her to the Strand ? " I suggested timidly, theatres. " But you only go to them in a brougham, muffled up to the eyes. She wouldn't see which way she was going." And she called to her daughter, who was on the other side of the room : " My dear, do you know where the Strand is ? " And in clear, well-drilled tones she got her answer, " No, mamma," as if a private were answering an officer. The young lady was certainly twenty-five. So that perhaps the old order does not so much change. Reflecting upon the subject of Bond Street, it occurred to me that it would not be so much a question of the maiden's running the risk of encountering evil characters as that since every one walks down Bond Street, every one would see her walking there alone. You have got to make the concession to modern opinion, you have got to let your daughter go out without an attendant maid, but you do not want to let anybody know that you have done it. And that, after all, is the fine old British spirit gallantly manifesting itself in an unfriendly day. No doubt, in spite of the constant planing that we are undergoing, in spite of the constant attrition that constantly ensues when man rubs against man all day long in perpetual short flights, each flight the flight of a battalion ; in spite of the perpetual noises by which we are deafened, in spite of the perpetual materialism to which we are forced in order to find the means for all this restlessness—in spite of it all the " character " still flourishes amongst us. Perhaps we are each and every one of us characters, each and every one of us outwardly cut to pattern but inwardly as eccentric as an old gentleman friend of mine who will not go to bed without putting his boots upon the mantel-piece ? In one thing I think we have changed. I had a very elderly and esteemed relative who once told me that whilst walking along the Strand he met a lion that had escaped from Exeter Change. I said,

"What did you do?" and he looked at me with contempt as if the question were imbecile. "*Do!*" he said. "Why, I took a cab." I imagine that still in most of the emergencies of this life we fly to that refuge. But I believe that the poor Strand has changed in another respect. I was once walking along the south side—the side on which now stand the Cecil and Strand Hotels—when my grandfather happened to drive past in a hansom, sprang suddenly out, and addressing me with many expletives and a look of alarm, wanted to know what the devil I was doing on that side. I really did not know why I should not be there or how it differed from the north side, but he concluded by saying that if he ever saw me there again he would kick me straightway out of his house. So I suppose that in the days of Beau Brummel there must have been unsavoury characters in that now rigid thoroughfare. But I doubt whether to-day we have so much sense of locality left. One street is becoming so much like another, and Booksellers' Row is gone. I fancy that these actual changes in the aspect of the city must make a difference in our psychologies. You cannot be quite the same man if daily you joggle past St. Mary Abbott's Terrace upon the top of a horse 'bus: you cannot be the same man if you shoot past the terra-cotta plate-glass erections that have replaced those gracious, old houses with the triangle of unoccupied space in front of them—if you shoot, rattle and bang past them. Your thoughts must be different, and with each successive blow upon the observation your brain must change a little and a little more. And the change is all away from the

direction of leisure, of spacious thought, of ease.
Each acceleration of a means of access makes you
more able to get through more work in a given time,
but each such acceleration gives each of your rivals
exactly the same chance. With each, competition grows sterner and sterner, with each the mere
struggle for existence becomes more and more fierce.
And we leave things nowadays so irrevocably behind
us. It is a quaint thought, but a perfectly sound
one, to say that we are nearer to habits of barbarism,
that we could more easily revert to days of savagery
than we could pick up again the tone of thought, of
mind and habit, of the men of thirty years ago. The
terra-cotta and plate-glass will inevitably in the course
of ages be replaced by swamps, marsh and tidal
river-beds. That will return, but the old houses of
St. Mary Abbott's Terrace will never come back.
And as these things change, so, oddly, do our appreciations veer round. It was the custom of the
'eighties to talk of houses like those of Harley Street
as ugly, square, brick boxes, as the most contemptible
things in the world, as the last word of the art and
the architecture of a miserable bourgeoisie. They
seemed then permanent, hideous, unassailable. But
already we regard them with a certain tenderness,
and consider that they may soon be gone. We think
them quaint, Georgian and lovable, and it is with a
certain regret that we realize that before very long
they, too, will be swept away and another characteristic piece of London will be gone for ever. We
are unifying and unifying and unifying. We are
standardizing ourselves and we are doing away
with everything that is outstanding. And that,

I think, is the moral to it all, the moral of our day and of our age. We are making a great many little people more cheerful and more comfortable in their material circumstances. We are knocking for the select few the flavour of the finer things out of life. In the atmosphere of to-day the finer things cannot flourish. There is no air for them : there is no time for them. We are not rich enough : we do not care for anything, and we never can come to care for anything that we do not like at first. And the finer the flavour the longer we take to get used to it. So that that is going, and many, many, many little pleasures are coming. Whether you like it or whether you do not, depends solely upon yourself. There is no man living who can say for us all whether it is good or evil. An old shoeblack said to me the other day, " These are bad times we live in, sir. Now there ain't so many horse 'buses there ain't so much mud in the streets, and it's bitter hard to get a living."

XIV

AND AGAIN CHANGES

WHEN we look back upon the lives of our fathers the first thing that seems to strike us is their intolerable slowness, and then the gloom in which they lived —or perhaps the gloom would strike us first. Theirs seemed to be a land where it was always afternoon, with large gas-lamps flaring in white ground-glass globes, wasting an extraordinary amount of light. So that when I read in a novel of Miss Thrackeray's that the lovers stepped out into the sunlit park, and the gay breezes fluttered their voluminous trousers, or their flounced crinolines, I simply do not believe it. I do not believe they had sunlight, though they probably had a park, and indeed in those days there were more elms in Kensington Gardens than to-day the Gardens can show. They certainly must have had trousers then, and as for crinolines, will not your old family cook, if you coax her, produce from a cupboard somewhere near the ceiling of the kitchen, a structure like a bird-cage connected by strips of what looks like very dirty linen ? This, she will assure you with an almost reverential tone of voice, was the last crinoline she ever wore—and she says that she hears they are coming in again. They are always of course coming

271

in again, though for the moment skirts are so tight that, helping a lady to get into a cab yesterday, I was almost tempted to pick her up and drop her in. I thought she would never have managed it. But no doubt, by the time that I am correcting the proofs of what I have just written "they" will be "coming in," again. My own grandmother used to say that she was the only woman in London who never wore a crinoline. That of course was Pre-Raphaelism, but I feel certain that she did wear some sort of whalebone stiffening round the bottom of her skirt if she did not have a hoop half way up.

Yes, they certainly had crinolines but I do not believe they had any fresh breezes to blow them about. They could not have had. It was always brown, motionless fog in those days, and our mothers and grandmothers sat sewing with their eyes very close to the candles. I do not believe that they even ever went out. What did they have to go out in? There were, it is true, four-wheelers with clean straw in the bottom; but there was the danger that if you went out in a four-wheeler, a straw would stick in the bottom flounce of your crinoline and would show that you had come in a hired conveyance when you stepped out into the comparative brightness of your rout or conversazione. Of course if you were of the mistily extravagant class that kept its own carriage, you might drive somewhere, but I do not believe that John would take the horses out in the evening—John being either your tyrannous coachman or your somnolent husband, who was in the habit of reading his *Times* after a heavy dinner consisting of soup,

fish, an enormous joint and probably a milk pudding
which you took at seven. You had a great deal of
heavy mahogany furniture, so that it took the foot-
man an appreciable time to get the chairs from the
dining-room wall and arrange them round the solid
mahogany table. But time did not matter in those
days, you had all the time in the world on your
hands. Why, the table-cloth was even whisked off
the table after dinner, over the heads of the diners,
before the wine circulated. I know at least in some
families that was done, and I dare say that even
nowadays you could find some families still doing
it. In those days, too, when a telegram came the
lady of the house prepared to faint—the lady's maid
rushed for the smelling-salts, and a sort of awful
hush pervaded the house from the basement to the
garrets where in incredible discomfort the servants
slept. And perhaps some of this feeling as to the
ominousness of telegrams is returning. Nowadays
with the telephone everywhere it is a comparatively
rare thing to receive one of the yellow envelopes
—except when you happen to be away at the
seaside and your man goes off with your silver-
gilt shaving set. I think I have only received
one telegram this year, and that from a gentleman
living in Richmond, to which distant place modernity
has not yet spread. And this slowness of pace
caused, as I have elsewhere pointed out, all the
conditions of life to be very different. In those
days intimacies between man and man, and woman
and woman, were comparatively frequent, because
there was more home life. You would be accustomed
to have some one living round the corner who came

in every evening and smoked a cigar with you, or if you were a woman it would be a "lady friend" who brought her sewing. Nowadays I fancy that no one above the station of a house-maid or a green-grocer's assistant would have a "lady friend" at all, or would at least use those words to describe her. We are all men and women nowadays, and we have not got any friends.

A quarter of a century ago, say, there were practically no restaurants, though there were chop-houses for men; there was not a place where a woman could get a cup of tea in all London town. This I fancy led to a great deal of drinking amongst ladies. The respectable married woman went shopping; she felt tired, she entered a "confectioner's," and had a bath bun and a glass of sherry. So it began, and so it went on from sherry, through cherry brandy, to the consumption of strong drinks at home in secret. And again in those days there was an iniquitous institution peculiar to the male sex called a club. The erring husband returned home at night. Hanging up his umbrella on a gas-bracket, his boots upon the hat-rack, and, climbing upstairs in his stockinged feet to deposit his top hat on the ground outside his bedroom door, he would be met by an irate female in a yellow peignoir, carrying a flat candlestick with a candle dripping wax. To her he would explain that he had been spending his evening at the club, when really he had been at the Alhambra, which in those days was a very wicked place. I fancy, that London middle and upper class society in those days was a rather scanda-lous and horrid affair. Certainly the term "middle

274

class " as an epithet of reproach had its origin about
then. London was full of a lot of fat and overfed
men with not too much to do and with time hanging
heavily on their hands. Their social gifts were
entirely undeveloped. They had no conversational
powers and very little to talk about, and the sexes
were very much shut off one from another.

Flirtations in those days were almost impossible,
or they became secret affairs with all the attributes
of guilt. Nowadays, when you can meet anybody
anywhere, when there are teashops, picture galleries,
men's clubs, ladies' clubs, cock-and-hen clubs,
restaurants and the rest-rooms of the large shops,
flirtations take place comparatively in public and
you do not have to bolt to Boulogne in order to have
a ten minutes' *tête-à-tête*, which is all you might
require to bore you with a member of the opposite
sex. But in the 'seventies and 'eighties there was
nothing else in the world to do, just as in centuries before there had been nothing else to do. We
are supposed to be more frivolous and I dare say
we are, but I should say that on the whole we are
healthier and less vicious. We are, that is to say,
more natural. We can get a great deal more of
what we want without kicking our shoes over wind-
mills and we do not want so much more than we
can get. For the matter of that it is easy to get
much further than we ever want to.

There used to be a time when it was the height of
dissipation to dine on the terrace of the Star and
Garter at Richmond. One of Ouida's heroines, who
was, I believe, no better than she should be, is at
least represented as sitting on that terrace and

throwing oranges to the swans in the Thames. And since the Thames is perhaps three-quarters of a mile distant from the Star and Garter, we must consider the lady to have been as muscular as she was dangerous and dashing. Alas! yesterday I was at Richmond. It took me about as long to get there as to get to Brighton, and there was the Star and Garter closed. Enormous, abhorrent and dismal, it was like a stucco castle of vast dimensions from which no hero would ever again rescue a heroine.

It was very sad, the moon shone down, the river was misty in the distance. I should like to have sat upon the terrace amidst the buzz of voices, the popping of champagne corks. I should like even to have seen the Guardsmen with the Macassar oil dripping from their enormous moustaches—I should have liked even to throw oranges to the swans in the river, though I did not know what the swans would have done with them. But alas! all these things are ghosts, and the world of Ouida is vanished as far away as the lost islands of Atlantis.

If nowadays we want to dine rustically, we run thirty miles out of town, though it does not happen very often that we have an evening disengaged, so that we move about, not very hurriedly, but quite hurried enough in all conscience, from one electrically lit place to another. We get through three or four things at night; we manage a dinner, a theatre, an after-theatre supper and possibly the fag-end of a dance after that—and we turn up to breakfast at nine next morning, just as serenely as our fathers did. I fancy that we even turn up more fresh at the breakfast-table, for we are a great deal more abstemious in the matter of alcoholic liquors. What the preacher entirely failed in, the all tyrannous doctor has triumphantly achieved. The other day, a lady talking about the book of a woman novelist, remarked to me :

"I do not know how Miss —— gets to know things. How does she know so exactly the feeling of craving for drink that she describes ? I have never seen a drunken man in my life."

This last sentence seemed to me incredible, but when I come to think of it, I have not myself seen a drunken man for a very long time. Indeed, I think that the last intoxicated individual that I have seen was in a political club of the shade that most strongly advocates restrictions upon public-houses. But I may digress for a moment to report a couple of sentences that I heard at an exhibition the other night. They seemed to me to be so singular that I have felt inclined to build up a whole novel upon them. A woman was sitting by herself behind the bandstand, in an atmosphere of shade and aloofness, and a man came up to her and said "Your husband is very drunk now. We can go off." But upon the whole the doctor triumphs. You hardly ever see a drunken man in the western streets of London, you practically never see a drunken woman. And the bars of music halls, which not so very many years ago were places for alcoholic orgies, are now almost deserted, except in the interval, when the band plays a selection. In the case of music halls, this is partly due perhaps to the fact that nowadays you can take a woman to them, you can even take a clergyman to them. And the other day I saw a

Roman Catholic priest watching Russian dancers. And of course, if you take a woman, a clergyman, or a priest to a music hall, you do not desert your seat to sit in the bar. But for the better-class music halls, it is none the less mainly the doctor who has done the damage. The Church has told us for a century or so, that drunkenness was a sin and we went on sinning. Our wives and mothers have told us for many years, that to be drunk was to make a beast of oneself, and we went on getting by so much farther from the angels. But the doctor has gone abroad in the land and pronounced sternly that alcohol is bad for the liver, and now we drink barley-water at our clubs. And what the doctor has done for the audiences of the dearer music halls, the cheaper music halls have done for their own audiences. You will see, about eleven o'clock, an immense crowd streaming along the pavements, from any suburban Palace or Empire—all these people will be quite sober. Twenty-five years ago, more than half of them would have been spending their time and much more money in the public-houses. And this is a very pleasant thought, which gives me satisfaction every time it comes into my head, for I like to see people happy in this land where happiness is counted as sin—I like to see people happy and yet not demonstrably damaging their pockets, their healths, or their morals. So that what with one thing and another—what with the ease of getting about and the multiplicity of means of communication, we see a great deal more of the ways of the world. We may be becoming more shallow, but we are certainly less hypocritical. We may possibly be becoming more

timid, but we certainly grow much more polite—
London is lighter and London is more airy. It is
so, demonstrably at any rate, in its wealthier regions
and in its main thoroughfares. I do not mean to say
that you will not find what you might call pockets
of late Victorian gloom and squalor in the north and
in the north-west of London. There is no knowing
what you will not find in London and certainly there
are survivals of horrors as there are survivals of the
picturesque. One lives on one's own little modern
ring, one has fairly good times, one has the perpetual
arousing and distracting of one's interest. But two
years ago I was coming back on Saturday night
from a small town of a manufacturing type, not
very far outside the London radius. The little town
in itself was one of the ugliest places that it was
possible to imagine. There was not a building in
it of any approach to dignity. In every one of the
windows of the squalid cottages that made it up,
there was a pair of Nottingham curtains; the inhabitants were utterly uncivil if you asked them the way,
and they appeared to be all operative manufacturers,
drawing small wages from a slowly decaying trade.
It was as ugly, as dirty, as dusty and as modern a
town as you could find even in the eastern states of
America. The railway station was badly illuminated, and in the dim shadows of the platform great
crowds of the Saturday night inhabitants were
waiting for the last train to the next small town
on the line. It was a most disagreeable scene. Underfed and stunted men sang the coarsest popular songs
of the year before last of London; underfed and
stunted boys shouted obscene remarks in hoarse

voices. The elder women were all dressed in badly
fitting garments imitating, I should imagine, the
clothes that Queen Victoria wore. The young girls,
on the other hand, as long as you could not perceive
them closely in the gloom, wore a most distinguished
summer finery, but all their things were put on very
badly; the frilled hats raked over to one side; the
shoulders were one higher than the other. Petticoats
showed beneath the bottoms of skirts; the flesh of
faces was unhealthy and lacking in complexion; the
teeth were mostly very bad and the voices usually
harsh, cackling and disagreeable, the words being
uttered with that peculiar intonation which has
spread from West Essex all over the country, and
which is called the cockney dialect. It was in
short a sort of American effect. One might have
been on a Saturday evening at the steam-car dépôt
of the cotton-manufacturing town called Falls
River N. J.

And this crowd of unpresentable people uttering
disagreeable sounds, packed itself into an ill-lit
train; and we rumbled through an ugly night,
emitting from each compartment trails of nasty
sounds. We screeched popular songs, called out
foul epithets, occasionally we punched each other's
heads; we swayed from side to side of the compart-
ments, in solid struggling masses. And this type
of life seemed to continue all the way from the heart
of Bedfordshire to about the middle of the north-
west of London. Changing at the terminus, we
took an entirely unfamiliar London local line whose
termination was, I think, Hammersmith. And there
as it were in a long trail from the north-west to the

extreme west of London, was the same atmosphere of gloom, of yellow light, of disagreeable humanity and really hateful sounds. So that in our clean, white, spick-and-span London, with its orderly and well-behaved, pleasant crowds, there remains this—corners into which, as it were, the housemaid's broom has swept the dust and detritus of a dead age. It was like, that journey, going back a quarter of a century. We were Victorians once again, Victorians in our ugliness, in our coarseness, in our objectionable employment of the Saturday night, in our drunkenness and in our sham respectability. For amongst the crowd at the London terminus, I perceived a gentleman—a working-man of the most awe-inspiring respectability, who occasionally cleans my windows and reproves my frivolity with quotations from Ruskin, as if I were a worm and he a calvanistic Savonarola. This gentleman the day before had come to me with a piteous tale. He had founded a lecture hall in Lambeth, where he was accustomed to read extracts from William Morris's socialistic pamphlets, from the works of Henry George, Joseph McCabe, Upton Sinclair, Ruskin and Carlyle, Mr. Galsworthy, Mr. Wells, Mr. J. K. Jerome and other social reformers—he had founded this lecture hall where, every Sunday morning, he was accustomed to act the part of preacher. On the Friday night, he had come to me with the lamentable story that the landlord had seized the furniture, had seized his library and had closed the hall. My function was to head his subscription list and I suppose I headed it. I had always been taught to consider Mr. —— the most

respectable of men, though he cleans my windows
shockingly badly. But then the poor fellow had been
out of work for nearly eleven years, employers dis-
liking his free thinking and radical outspokenness.

And then on that Saturday night I perceived
Mr. —— upon the platform of the terminus. He had
a peacock's feather in his billycock hat, he was
dancing to the tune of " God save the people ! "
in a ring that the railway police vainly endeavoured
to move on—and there was not a trace of priggish-
ness about his face. He was in his shirt sleeves and
snapping his fingers over his head. I doubt for the
moment if he could have quoted Ruskin, but he
shouted " Down with the landlords ! " just before
the police reached him, and hustled him off into a
cloak room.

Filled with curiosity, I went next morning to his
lecture hall. It was open, and Mr. —— himself was
arranging pamphlets for sale upon the trestles.
He was very forbidding, in a decent suit of black
broadcloth with a turn-down collar, a prominent
Adam's apple and a red satin tie.

He said that the landlord had consented to let
him open the hall again, though he still wanted
thirty-two shillings for the rent, and had taken
Mr. ——'s typewriter in pawn until that sum should
be paid. Mr. —— once more quoted Carlyle and
Henry George. He proved that landlords were
unmitigated villains and that I—it was in his tone
of haughty seriousness and earnest moral effort—
that I was a frivolous puppy. Upon investigation
I discovered that I had paid the whole quarter's
rent of the hall. Mr. —— had misrepresented the

figure to me, a fact which he had forgotten upon the Sunday morning. Other friends had found still more money, which I presume had assisted to put Mr. —— in spirits on the night before. I did not mention these things to Mr. ——, who continued to overwhelm me with moral sneers as to the uselessness of my life. He, a poor working man, had worked his way so high, whereas I, with all the advantages of education and what he was pleased to declare was lavish wealth, had achieved no more than a few frivolous books. And mind you, so fully did Mr. —— believe in himself, that I retired apologetically as his audience began to file in. I was filled with a sense of my own unworthiness.

I should say that Mr. —— is just another Victorian survival; I remember so many of these figures in my extreme youth. There was W., a socialist cabinet-maker, with flashing eyes, who founded a free-labour association for the supply of blacklegs to firms whose employees had gone on strike. W., I remember, frightened me out of my young life, he was so vociferous, and his eyes flashed so. He was generally in my grandfather's kitchen eating excellent meals, and persuading my grandfather that he was wanted by the police for political reasons—a romantic lie which very much appealed to Madox Brown's simplicity. Then there was also a Mr. B., a usually intoxicated paper-hanger; he had, I think, no political aspirations, but he was largely supported by my family, because of his flow of Shakespearian quotations. These never stopped, and they seemed as romantic in those days as it was to be in hiding for political reasons. They never stopped. I remember once when Mr. B. was standing on the top of a ladder, putting up a picture rail and more than reasonably intoxicated, the ladder gave way beneath him. He grasped the picture rail by one hand, and hanging there recited the whole of the Balcony Scene from *Romeo and Juliet*, waving his other arm towards the ceiling and feeling for the top of the ladder with his stockinged feet, his slippers having fallen off. He was a nasty, dirty little man, but he too impressed me with the sense of my unworthiness. So they all did. I remember at the time of the great Dock Strike, being taken to dinner by a Manchester Labour leader who was anxious to improve my morals. There were present Prince Krapotkin, Mr. Ben Tillett, Mr. Tom Mann and I think Mr. John Burns. The dinner took place at the Holborn Restaurant, and the waiters were frightened out of their lives amidst the marble, the gilding and the strains of the band. For such a group in those days was considered a wildly dangerous gathering. Prince Krapotkin might have a bomb in the tail pockets of his black frock-coat, and as for Messrs. Tillett, Burns and Mann, there was no knowing whether they would not slay all the customers in the restaurant with single blows of their enormous fists.

" We must destroy ! We must destroy ! " Mr. Mann exclaimed.

" On the contrary," Prince Krapotkin replied in low tones, " we must take example of the rabbit and found communistic settlements."

So they thundered, and the waiters trembled more and more, and there were a great many emo-

tions going ; as for me, I felt the same emotion of
unworthiness. In those days I had written a fairy
tale which had met with an enormous, and I suppose
deserved, success; and I remember that, as we walked
away from under the shelter of the restaurant in
torrential rains, Prince Krapotkin told me that it
was a very bad, a very immoral book. It dealt
entirely with the fortunes of kings, princes, the
young, the idle or the merely beautiful. And I was
so overwhelmed with the same sense of unworthiness,
that, as I was about to sink into the wet pavements,
it occurred to me that I might find salvation by
writing a fairy tale all of whose heroes and heroines
should be Labour leaders. I did indeed write it—
that was exactly twenty years ago—and from that
day to this I have never been able to find a publisher
for it.

But do not let me be misunderstood. I am not by
any means attempting to condemn Mr. —— of the
lecture hall. He got money out of me so that he
might elevate his brother workmen, and so that he
might get drunk on the Saturday night. But I am
convinced that in the atmosphere in which he lived,
the one thing would have been impossible without
the other. I fancy that no man can be a really
moving preacher without committing sustaining sins.
I am quite certain that the trainloads of people from
these gloomy midland towns, contained hundreds of
excellent and respectable persons, all recruiting themselves by the orgies of the Saturday night for the
cramped formalities of Calvinistic worship on the
Sunday morning. They could not bear the monotony
of their lives without occasionally letting hell loose,

and that is really all that there is to it. But there
is this much more. The other day I went out to post
a letter about 12.30 a.m. Upon the pavement lay
a man bathed in blood, his pockets had been rifled,
his watch was gone, his tie-pin was no longer there.
I understand that since that date some seven months
ago, he has never recovered his reason, so effectually
had he been sand-bagged. And this happened at a
little past 12 at night, in one of the broadest, most
well-lit and most populous highways of London,
the man being not forty yards from the entrance
to the Tube Station, and not twenty-five from a
coffee stall. It had been done so quickly and so
silently that as Froissart says in his chronicles: "They
slew him so peaceably, that he uttered no word."
And the police never discovered a sign of the man's
assailants. The point is that behind my house for
a distance of nearly two miles there stretches towards
Wormwood Scrubbs Prison a long dreary neighbourhood containing all the criminals and outcasts of
London. This of course, is a sombre comment on
the brightness and gayness of which I have spoken
before. It means, that the breaking up of the slums
in western London has driven these unfortunate
populations in a body into this now dangerous
quarter, just as similar movements, commercial or
economical, drive other classes of the convention-
ally undesirable population into other considerable
portions of the western regions of London.

XV

WHERE WE STAND

UPON reconsidering these pages I find that I have written a jeremiad. Yet nothing could have been farther from my thoughts when I sat down to this book. I said to myself: I am going to try to compare the world as it appears to me to-day with the world as it appeared to me, and as I have gathered that it was, a quarter of a century ago. And the general impression in my mind was that I should make our life of to-day appear to be a constant succession of little, not very enduring, pleasures, a thing as it were of lights, bubbles and little joys —a gnat-dance into the final shadows. I want nothing better, and assuredly nothing better shall I get. I want nothing better than to be in Piccadilly five minutes after the clock has struck eleven at night. I shall be jammed to the shoulders in an immense mass of pleased mankind, all pouring out of the theatres and the music halls. We shall move slowly along the pavement between Leicester Square and the Circus. In that section it will be a little dark, but before us, with the shadowed houses making as it were a deep black cañon, there will be immense light. Perhaps it will be raining very slightly. All the better, for from the purple glow before us light will be reflected on a thousand, on half a million little points. The innumerable falling drops will gleam, born suddenly out of the black heavens. The wet sides of the house walls will gleam; the puddles in the roadway will throw up gleaming jets as carriage after carriage passes by, their sides, too, gleaming. The harness of the horses will gleam, the wet wind-shields of the innumerable automobiles with the innumerable little drops of rain caught upon them will gleam like the fairy cobwebs, the cloths of Mary, beset with drops of bright dew.

I will have upon my arm some one that I like very much; so will all the others there. In that short passage of darkness there will be innumerable sounds of happiness, innumerable laughs, the cries of paper boys, the voices of policemen regulating the massed traffic; the voices of coachmen calling to their horses. And then we shall come out into the great light of Piccadilly.

No, I ask nothing better of life. Then, indeed, amongst innumerable happy people I shall know that we are all going to Heaven and that Turgeniev will be of the company.

Such indeed was my frame of mind when I sat down to this book, and so it remains. But yet, my jeremiad! I have personally nothing to grumble at; I dislike no one in this wide world. If anybody ever did me an injury it was so slight a one that I have forgotten all about it. Yet, in this frame of mind of a perfect optimism—for my fellow-creatures are all too interesting to be disliked when once one can get the hang of them, and if some poor devil desires to steal my watch, forge a cheque upon my bank, or by telling lies about me get for himself a "job," an appointment or an honour that might well be mine, surely that man's need is greater than my own—yet in this frame of mind of a perfect optimism I seem to have written a jeremiad. I have praised the 'seventies, the 'eighties and the 'nineties, I have cast mud at our teens. I remain unrepentant. I take nothing back; what I have written is the exact truth. And yet . . .

To-day we have a comparative cleanliness, a comparative light, we have as it were reduced every-thing in scale, so that no longer are we little men forced to run up and down between the mighty legs of intolerable moralists like Ruskin or Carlyle or Tolstoi, to find ourselves dishonourable graves. We are the democracy, the stuff to fill grave-yards, and our day has dawned. For brick we have terra-cotta, for evil-smelling petroleum lamps we have bright and fumeless light; for the old Un-derground that smelled and was full of sulphur vapours we have bright, clean and white Tubes. And these things are there for the poorest of us. And yet—a jeremiad !

Is this only because one sees past times always in the glamour of romance which will gild for us even a begrimed and overcrowded third-class smoking carriage of the Underground ? No, I do not think that it is only because of this. I would give a great deal to have some of the things, some of the people, some of the atmosphere of those days—to have them now. But nothing in the world would make me go back to those days if I must sacrifice what now I have.

We are civilized; we are kindly, we have an immense deference for one another's feelings; we never tread upon each other's corns; we never shout our political opinions in public conveyances, we never say a word about religion because we are afraid of hurting some one else's feelings. We are civilized—used to living in a city; we are polite, fitted to live in a πόλις; we are polished by the constant rubbing up against each other, all we millions and millions who stream backwards and forwards all the day and half the night. We could not live if we had rough edges; we could not ever get so much as into a motor 'bus if we tried to push in out of our turn. We are Demos.

And how much this is for a rather timid man, who would never get into any 'bus if it were a matter of pushing—how much this is I realized some years ago when I spent some time in the close society of a number of very learned Germans. It was terrible to me. I felt like a white lamb—the most helpless of creatures, amongst a set of ferocious pirates. It was not so much that I could never remember any of their bristling titles; that did not matter. It would have mattered if I could ever have got a word into a conversation, but I never could. My voice was too low; I was used to the undertones of our London conversations, where we all speak in whispers for fear of being overheard and thus hurting somebody's feelings.

But these German savants were simply pirates. They were men who had issued savagely forth into unknown regions and had " cut out " terrific pieces of information. There did not appear to be one of them who did not know more than I did about my own subjects. They could put me right about the English language, the Pre-Raphaelite movement, the British constitution, the reign of Henry VIII. or the Elizabethan dramatists. They knew everything, but it was as if they had acquired, as if they held, their knowledge ferociously. I did not know that there were left in the world men so fierce.

Take German Philologists. These are formidable people. To set out upon the history of a word is an adventurous and romantic thing. You find it in London or in Göttingen to-day. You chase it back to the days of Chaucer when knights rode abroad in the land. You cross the Channel with it to the Court of Charlemagne at Aix. You go back to Rome and find it in the mouth of Seneca. Socrates utters it in your hearing, then it passes back into pre-historic times, landing you at last in a dim early age amongst unchronicled peoples, somewhere in the Pamirs, on the roof of the world, at the birth of humanity. Yes, a romantic occupation—but, in a sense, piratical. For why otherwise should a comfortable and agreeable gentleman over a large pot of beer become simply epileptic when one suggests that the word " sooth " may have some connection with the French *sus*, the perfect participle of *savoir*, which comes from the Latin *scire* ? Personally I care little about the matter. It is interesting in a mild way, but that is all. But my friend became enraged. He became more enraged than I have ever seen in the case of a learned gentleman. You see, some rival Captain Kidd, or some rival Francis Drake had enunciated the theory as to the word "sooth" which I had invented on the spur of the moment. Individualism in fact flourishes in Germany still in a way that died out of England when Ruskin died and Carlyle died. And being badgered, in my civilized timidity, by these formidable and learned persons, I feel very much as I used to feel when as a boy I was brow-beaten by the formidable great figures that flourished when Victoria was queen. Perhaps it is only that in England we have lost interest in great subjects, or perhaps it is that we know better how to live since it takes all sorts to make a world. In an English drawing-room I should never think of abusing a Protestant, a Nonconformist, a Jew or a Liberal. I should never think of airing my own opinions. There might—probably there would—be representatives of all shades in the room. In a mild way I should call myself a sentimental Tory and a Roman Catholic. Now in a German drawing room I have never been for more than ten minutes without hearing the most violent abuse of Roman Catholics, of Jews, of Protestants, of Liberals, or of Reactionaries, according to the tastes or ideas of my hosts. This makes society more entertaining, more coloured, but much more tiring. Good Friday before last I gave a lunch to four men at my London club. I passed the meat as a matter of habit, of good manners, of what you will. What was my astonishment to discover that each of my guests passed the meat. In short each of us five was actually a Roman Catholic of a greater or less degree of earnestness. Yet, although we were all five fairly

intimate, meeting frequently and talking of most of
the things that men talk about, we were not any one
of us aware of the other's religious belief. This,
I think, would be impossible anywhere but in London,
and it is just for that reason that London of to-day
is such a restful place to live in.

But no doubt it is just for that reason that this
book of mine has turned out to be a jeremiad. We
don't care. We don't care enough about anything
to risk hurting each other's feeling. As a man I
find this delightful, and it is the only position that,
in a democracy, mankind can take up if it is to live.
For the arts, the sciences, thought and all the deeper
things of this life are matters very agitating. We are
a practical people, but it is impossible to be practical
in the things both of Heaven and of earth. There is
no way to do it. We are materially practical when
we arrange our literature upon the scale of the
thousand words. But we cannot then be practical
when it comes to the machinery of the books we
produce. We cannot pay any attention to that
matter at all. A book has outlines, has ribs, has
architecture, has proportion. These things are
called in French technique. It is significant that
in English there is no word for this. It is significant
that in England a person talking about the technique
of a book is laughed to scorn. The English theory
is that a writer is a writer by the grace of God. He
must have a pen, some ink, a piece of paper and a
table. Then he must put some vine-leaves in his
hair and write. When he has written 75,000 words
he has a book.

Yes, we are an extraordinary nation. It seems

rather wonderful to me that, practical as we are, we cannot see that since every book has its machinery the best book will be produced by a man who has paid some attention to the machinery of books. But no, we roar with laughter at the very mention of the word technique. The idea of Flaubert spending hours, days or even weeks in finding the right word is sufficient to send us happy to bed, in a frame of mind beatifically lulled by superior knowledge. We know that a book consists of 75,000 words. It does not surely matter what those words are as long as in our mind we have had a great moral purpose and in our hair those vine-leaves. A practical people !

So, with our 75,000 words under our arm, we set forth in search of fame. And this we know we can only achieve if our book will forward some social purpose. For it is necessary for us to prove that we are earnest men. To be a good writer is nothing. No, it is worse than nothing, for it generally leads— in nine cases out of ten it leads—to the divorce courts. So that we must espouse some " cause " in our books. It does not much matter what it is. Personally I am an ardent, I am an enraged suffra- gette. So far I have not found that this fact has led to my books selling one copy more. But I hope that when Miss Pankhurst is Prime Minister of England she will nominate me to some humble post —say that of keeper of her official wardrobe. I shall be a gentleman by prescription, and my immense earnestness will be recognized at last, and publicly.

"For the thing to do"—I am taking the liberty now of addressing a supposititious and earnest

294

young writer—"the thing to do if you would succeed is to identify yourself prominently with some 'cause' or with some faith. I myself have had in literature a success which I am quite certain I do not deserve. My books cannot by any measure of means be called popular, and they are of all shapes and sizes. There will be thirty-seven of them by the time this reaches your young hands. In the first place, because I have a German name, I am usually taken for a Jew, and this has secured for me a solid body of Jewish support. In the second place, a great number of Roman Catholics know that I am a Roman Catholic—though a very poor one—and *they* support me too. I also get some support from Socialists who think me a Socialist, and some—but not as much as I deserve—from Suffragettes. All the support I get comes from these accidental labels. The quality of my writing is nothing. So that, oh, young writer, I implore you very earnestly to take some label. Become the champion of the Church of England; write a novel all of whose characters are curates, in which there is no love interest, and all the villains must be Nonconformist grocers who refuse to give credit to the curates so that they all die of starvation. Something like that."

But I am afraid I am letting something of the bitter scorn that I feel peep through. That would be a pity. The fact is, all the tendencies that I have described are inevitable in our time. No one is to blame; it can't be cured; it can't be helped. I can't blame the literary editor who turns his pages slowly into a vehicle for catching advertisements. There are some who do not, but they will go, and it is the same story all the world over. The newspapers cannot live without advertisements, so that I cannot blame the newspaper proprietor for sacking the editor who does not bring him advertisements. If not to-day then to-morrow there will not be a newspaper left of which any man might not be the editor if he could guarantee from some other firm in which he is interested £30,000 a year's worth of advertisements. It is sad, it is tragic, but there it is. Neither do I blame the publisher who has cut me down to my one set of proofs that must be marked here with red ink, here with blue. He must do it. At his throat, too, is the knife that is at all our throats.

Life is so good, life may be so pleasant; must I not taste of it, and my publisher, and my newspaper proprietor, and my literary editor, and my advertisement canvasser? All of us? Yes, assuredly, we are all of us going to the Alhambra, and the Prime Minister will be of the company.

Life is good nowadays; but art is very bitter. That is why, though the light whirls and blazes still over Piccadilly, this book has become a jeremiad. For upon the one side I love life. On the other hand, Hokusai in his later years was accustomed to subscribe himself: *The old man mad about Painting.* So I may humbly write myself down a man getting on for forty, a little mad about good letters. For the world is a good place, but the letters that I try to stand up for are about to die. Will any take their place? Who knows? But as for anything else, let me put down the words of the Ritter Olaf, who was also about to die. He had married the king's daughter and was to be beheaded for it when he came out of church. But he begged his life till midnight so that he might dance amidst the torches of his bridal banquet. Then he went to death saying :

"Ich segne die Sonne, ich segne den Mond
Und die Sterne, die am Himmel schweifen;
Ich segne auch die Vögelein
Die in den Lüften pfeifen.

"Ich segne das Meer, ich segne das Land,
Und die Blumen auf der Aue;
Ich segne die Veilchen, sie sind so sanft
Wie die Augen meiner Fraue.

"Ihr Veilchenaugen meiner Frau,
Durch euch verlier' ich mein Leben!
Ich segne auch den Holunderbaum,
Wo du dich mir ergeben."

Brave words !

INDEX

299

Index

Index

Index

Index

Lightning Source UK Ltd.
Milton Keynes UK
UKHW020627110722
405680UK00005B/432